The Rebirth of Russian Democracy

The Rebirth of

Russian Democracy

An Interpretation
of Political Culture

Nicolai N. Petro

Harvard University Press
Cambridge, Massachusetts
London, England

First Harvard University Press paperback edition, 1997

Library of Congress Cataloging-in-Publication Data

Petro, Nicolai N.
   The rebirth of Russian democracy : an interpretation
   of political culture / Nicolai N. Petro.
      p.   cm.
   Includes index.
   ISBN 0-674-75001-2 (cloth)
   ISBN 0-674-75002-0 (pbk.)
   1. Political culture—Soviet Union.
   2. Political culture—Russia—History.
   3. National characteristics, Russian—History.
   4. Civil society—Russia (Federation).
   I. Title.
   JN6581.P47   1995
   306.2—dc20   94-45431

Contents

Preface

C oming to this country as a young college student, I remember being surprised by the widespread portrayal of Russian history as somehow uniquely authoritarian, and by the equally common view that Russians saw the repressive communist regime as legitimate. Having been raised in Europe and exposed to several generations of Russians in exile, I had been brought up with a rather different view, and was frankly puzzled by the uniformity of American perceptions of Russia. My curiosity soon led me to take every course that I could on Russia and the Soviet Union at the University of Virginia, and finally to write an honors thesis on dissent under the firm but encouraging tutelage of the late Professor Thomas T. Hammond. In 1979, Professor Hammond even encouraged me to offer a seminar on the history of dissent.

Subsequently, I decided to learn more about my adopted country, the United States, and so in graduate school chose to concentrate on the workings of U.S. foreign policy, under the wise guidance of Professor Kenneth W. Thompson. The idea of attempting a thoroughgoing revision of the standard presentation of Russian society, however, never completely left me. If anything, it became stronger after a brief exposure to government service facilitated by the Council on Foreign Relations. Thanks to an International Affairs Fellowship, I was able to spend a year as special assistant for policy at the State Department's Office of Soviet Union Affairs, including a month in early 1990 as political attaché with the U.S. Embassy in Moscow. Those hectic weeks were spent reporting on political developments and meeting with Russian nationalist leaders around the country.

Government experience reinforced my conviction that the major stumbling block that remained to improving relations with a rapidly changing Russia was our inability to recognize the historical roots of Russian aspirations for democracy. The deeply ingrained assumption that Russians were really not prepared for democracy, or worse, actually preferred that an authoritarian leader tell them what to do, clearly conditioned our foreign policy thinking. As one senior U.S. official told me bluntly, "Gorbachev is the best Russian we're likely to get." Yet, few scholars ever get such an opportunity to test their ideas in practice, and I am ever grateful to the Council and to my supervisors at State, Alexander Vershbow and John Tefft, for the opportunity.

Returning to academe, however, I resolved to resist the temptation to pen yet another instantaneous commentary on the changes in Russia, and to try instead to explain the origins and the logic of the transformations we were witnessing. I wanted to go beyond merely reassessing Sovietology and produce something that might serve as a guide for understanding the future development of Russian politics. This book is the result of those efforts.

The ideas in this book are not entirely new; rather, they revive and bring up-to-date an old perspective on Russian politics, widely shared among scholars of the first generation of refugees from communism. The popularity of this perspective in Russia today makes Western reacquaintance with it especially timely.

Although I bear ultimate responsibility for the views expressed here, a book of this nature necessarily reflects the contributions of many people. Professors Robert F. Byrnes, Geoffrey Hosking, Eve Levin, Jerry Pankhurst, Bernice Rosenthal, Elisha Rountree, Richard Sakwa, Paul Shoup, Peter H. Solomon, Jr., James W. Warhola, and Charles Ziegler were kind enough to comment extensively on my original proposal and to suggest additional sources. Professors Lowell Dittmer, William Reisinger, and Howard J. Wiarda offered their keen insights on the role of political culture. Professor Abbott Gleason kindly hosted a talk I gave at Brown University, and casually suggested a theme that has since become central to the book: that an alternative Russian political tradition might be traceable to the Slavophile writings of the early nineteenth century. I also wish to express my deepest appreciation to Donald D. Barry, Carl A. Linden, Alvin Z. Rubinstein, and S. Frederick Starr for their unwavering confidence in my ability to complete such an ambitious project.

This book could never have been completed without the generosity of my colleagues at the University of Rhode Island, and the help of my students, who went over each chapter with me, challenging me to clarify ideas that I had foolishly assumed to be common knowledge. My principal assistant, Todd Anderson, was able to prepare this manuscript for publication in record time thanks to a generous grant from the University of Rhode Island Council for Research. I am also keenly grateful to Christine Thorsteinsson, my editor at Harvard University Press, for clarifying my meaning and improving my prose.

My wife, Allison, did much more than keep our children contented while their father disappeared for days on end. In addition to juggling paragraphs and moving commas, she was an indispensable sounding board, constantly challenging me to simplify my presentation so as to appeal to a broader audience. If this book is readable, it is in large measure due to her efforts.

Finally, this book also allows me to acknowledge, in a very inadequate way, the great gift given to me by my parents and godparents. Their sacrifices so that I and others like me born abroad could share in the wonderful richness that is Russian culture were not in vain. May God speed the intertwining of the diverse strands of Russian culture, abroad and at home, that is so essential to Russian democracy.

Note on Transliteration

The transliteration system used follows that of the Library of Congress, with some minor exceptions. Both hard and soft signs have been omitted. When a soft sign appears in the middle of a word, however, it has been replaced by a "y." In addition, the sounds *iu* and *ia* are transliterated as *yu* and *ya*. Otherwise, established English usage has taken precedence in the spelling of common Russian words and proper names. When citing translations and quoting from them, I have preserved the original transliteration.

The Rebirth of Russian Democracy

Political Culture and the Failure of Sovietology

The fatal attractiveness of the political culture approach is that it may be made to explain too much. —Dennis Kavanagh

Russia is today not a bad subject for long-term prognostication, and a very inappropriate subject for short-term analysis. —Former Russian Prime Minister Yegor Gaidar

This is a book about Russia's past and about Russia's future. It is about the survival, despite harsh repression, of democratic ideals in Russia. It is also about why, after having devoted such enormous resources to understanding the Soviet Union, Sovietologists came up so short in predicting the collapse of communism.

The reason analysts failed to predict the demise of communism, I believe, lies in the conventional wisdom about Russian political culture. Despite their political and methodological differences, nearly all students of Russian and Soviet politics agreed that Russian political culture could safely be characterized as more centralist, more interventionist, and more collectivist than its North American or European counterparts.

Perestroika, however, laid bare the inadequacy of this received wisdom. The astonishing upsurge in civic activism after 1987 (more than sixty thousand independent associations involving nearly fifteen million people emerged) was clearly inconsistent with the image of a politically passive population.[1] And when the first extensive opinion surveys in more than seventy years were conducted, the results were equally confounding. Indeed, on many key indicators of political awareness and desire for democracy the Russians seemed to differ little from their counterparts in France or Germany.[2]

The commonplace explanations that modernization had finally taken its toll on the Soviet system or that Mikhail Gorbachev had somehow single-handedly transformed the political landscape are both clearly unsatisfactory.

Not only do they fail to tell us anything about why a regime that had survived civil war, horrific domestic upheavals, and foreign invasion suddenly
collapsed like a house of cards, but they are powerless to explain the widespread popularity of democratic values commonly associated with developed
civic cultures. The truth is that Sovietology failed because it started from a
faulty premise. The desire to restore civil society, the rule of law, private
property, free enterprise, and political pluralism existed in Russia well before
the Soviet regime collapsed and even before perestroika began. By the end
of 1991 this desire had become so pervasive that, much as in February 1917,
no significant constituency willing to defend the dying regime or its values
was left. Sovietology had failed to notice what was, in essence, a congenital
weakness of the system, and a large part of the blame for this lies in the
field's approach to political culture.

Back in the 1960s, as a new generation of Sovietologists searched for alternatives to the totalitarian approach to communist politics, many saw the political culture approach as ideally suited to their needs. It promised fresh insights
into why some political systems were more stable than others. Its emphasis on
subjective behavior and survey data seemed to offer a way around the "biases"
inherent in a field heavily dominated by émigrés. Finally, it offered a ready-
made framework for linking Soviet studies with the mainstream of comparative politics. The absence of hard data from communist countries could be
overcome by more imaginative use of memoirs, interviews, and literary and
historical interpretation. The result, reinforced by the existing consensus
about Russia's autocratic political heritage, was a depiction of the Soviet
Union as "a dramatically successful case of a planned political culture."[3]

By assuming that official political expression reflected popular sentiment
most analysts failed to recognize that democracy, or *narodovlastie* in Russian,
has deep roots in Russian history. These roots become quite apparent if
the traditional focus of political culture is broadened to include the Russian
emigration, dissident groups inside the USSR, and contemporary postcommunist Russian politics. In each of these arenas the struggle for Russian
civil society can be traced from Muscovite times through to the collapse of
communism and beyond. The historical persistence of an alternative political culture is the key to understanding the survival of democratic ideals after
1917. The alternative political culture was transmitted from generation to
generation in the nonpublic arena described so well by dissidents such as
Aleksandr Solzhenitsyn and Vaclav Havel, until it could finally manifest itself publicly. Hence, the emergence of pluralism in the late 1980s was not a
new ideal for Russian political culture, but the first *public* manifestation of
an ideal centuries old.

This alternative political culture (or as Clifford Geertz might term it, Russia's "political imaginary"[4]) is reflected in the struggle to define the proper scope of the autocracy, the proper nature of church-state relations, and Russia's proper national identity. These three issues formed the political and cultural battleground between the official statist and the Slavophile political traditions during the late nineteenth century. In 1905, civil society, inspired by the alternative political culture, succeeded in forcing Tsar Nicholas II to recognize the principles of popular government and civil rights. Then, in February 1917, civil society replaced the monarchy with a republic committed to duly elected popular representation. Although this victory was snatched away just nine months later, the battle to restore it continued throughout the entire Soviet period.

The mainstream approach to political culture, however, does not allow for the simultaneous existence of two competing political cultures within a single nationality. Nor does it look far beyond the public expression of political views to ascertain deep-seated political values. Instead, it has concentrated on defining the components of a "civic culture" common to advanced industrial democracies.[5] As a result, political scientists were unequipped to recognize the alternative political culture in Russia and in other communist countries. By contrast, an interpretive approach to political culture allows us to trace the transmission of society's complex political-cultural symbols in the nonpublic arena, and to relate these to the restoration of civil society. By focusing on the underlying meaning of behavior, rather than just measuring aggregates of behavior, interpretive theory can offer insights not only on why communism collapsed, but on why alternative values emerged so quickly in its wake.

The importance of these political-cultural symbols can be seen on three levels. The first is the failure of the official concept of "the new Soviet man" to take root in Russian society. In nearly every arena of private life (as distinct from the coerced requirements of public life), be it religious worship or preference for the works of the "village prose" writers, the populace showed a stubborn rejection of communist values. The alternative political culture's ability to preserve private pockets of alternative religious, historical, and national identity thus mitigated the regime's efforts to unravel the past and replaced it with a new "Soviet" cultural fabric. This explains the spontaneous popularity of prerevolutionary symbols such as the tricolor flag, the blue-and-white flag of St. Andrew, the two-headed eagle, the emblem of St. George, the Church of Christ the Savior (blown up in 1931), and, of course, the rechristening of Leningrad as St. Petersburg after more than three generations of communist rule.[6]

The second is the transmission of information about taboo subjects across several generations. This includes items that question the infallibility of

Marxism-Leninism or the country's political leadership, any historical information about the costs of collectivization, of religious persecution, the purges, the scope and extent of the GULag, or popular opposition to the regime. The newly opened Russian archives may eventually reveal a great deal more about underground organizations that preserved this information inside Soviet Russia, but a significant portion of it was preserved for posterity by Russian émigrés and is already beginning to re-enter Russian life.

The third, most specifically political, level is substantive opposition to the regime. Efforts to forge an alternative political system did not end with the defeat of the Whites during the Russian civil war. During the Second World War such efforts were manifested in the Russian Liberation Army headed by General Andrei A. Vlasov. In the 1960s and 1970s they spawned the "human rights" and dissident movements. In the 1980s they assisted the transition to perestroika. By the early 1990s they were strong enough to overcome a weakening apparatus of repression and emerge from the private into the public arena as "informal" political associations, or *neformaly*. The survival of a highly consistent set of alternative political values does much to explain the unexpected resilience of Russian democratic values today.

The Quest for a "Scientific Theory of Democracy"

The failure of Sovietology is rooted in its infatuation with political culture. Indeed, by asserting that "the most distinctive aspects of the Soviet system are in fact based upon a deep and fairly widely distributed base of popular support," Sovietology led analysts to minimize the alternative social and intellectual movements that eventually led to the collapse of communism in Russia.[7]

The stability of the Soviet state was taken as proof of an affinity between the policies of the regime and Russian political culture. In the absence of public opinion surveys, the preferred method for measuring political attitudes, this affinity was proven through subjective historical analysis.[8]

Despite its misapplication, however, political culture remains a uniquely valuable tool for understanding the collapse of communism and the future of Russian politics. Scholars such as Howard Wiarda, Daniel Bell, and Clifford Geertz have all made the point that cultural factors are as important in shaping political development as technology, modernization, economic development, or institutional change. Others have argued that culture conditions the pace and style of economic development.[9] In order to fulfill its potential, however, political culture must move beyond its behavioral origins and embrace the more pluralistic analytical approaches used in history and anthropology.

Although the attempt to define the cultural attributes of political systems is as old as the study of politics itself, the modern usage of the term political culture is less than forty years old. It was first proposed by Gabriel Almond in a seminal article entitled "Comparative Political Systems."[10] In this article, Almond defines political culture as the "particular pattern of orientations to political action." Every political system, he suggests, is embedded within a particular pattern and hence constrained by it. By understanding these constraints analysts might eventually learn to predict the evolution of political systems.

A key objective of the modern approach to political culture was to increase the relevancy of political science to public policy. If the essence of a successful democratic polity could be distilled then it could probably be exported. Indeed, much of the subsequent work of Almond, and of his colleagues Sidney Verba and Lucian Pye, in the field of "democratic modernization" seeks to establish a formula by which Western democracies could assist democratic, political, and economic development in the Third World. The political turmoil engulfing the world no longer allowed the cognoscenti to view politics in Europe and Asia with "detached curiosity or . . . as interesting pathologies," says Almond. "We are called upon to extend our discipline and intensify it simultaneously."[11]

Both Almond and Pye borrowed from Talcott Parsons's and Edward Shils's studies of systems and roles among primary social institutions — the family and close friends. But whereas Parsons and Shils concluded that culture could not be identified with any concrete system of action ("it just 'is'"), Almond argued that political culture could indeed be linked to "empirically observable behavior."[12] Pye also acknowledged his debt to Harold Lasswell's work on the psychological dimensions of political behavior. But whereas Lasswell felt that political systems functioned independently of the psychological make-up of individuals, Pye argued that conclusions drawn from individual psychological values could be valid for the entire social group, even for the nation as a whole.[13] Thus, by essentially standing modern psychology and sociology on their heads, Almond and Pye suggested that it is possible to identify a set of specific attitudes, beliefs, or sentiments that give order and meaning to the political process.[14]

What this approach now needed was a set of tools appropriate to gathering and measuring subjective political information. Almond and his colleagues found these tools in the new survey techniques that were being developed to gauge the attitudes of the American electorate. Determining a nation's political culture could thus be reduced to an almost mechanical task, "in effect, filling in . . . a matrix for a valid sample of its population. The political culture becomes the frequency of different kinds of cognitive, affective, and evaluative orientations toward the political system in general, its input and output aspects, and the self as political actor."[15]

Almond's efforts to construct a matrix that would apply to various countries resulted in a pathbreaking study entitled *The Civic Culture*, in which Almond and his colleague Sidney Verba set out to define the political culture of democracy and "the social structures and processes that sustain it."[16] By matching the patterns of particular national political cultures against the patterns of Western democracies, they believed they could determine whether a country had the type of political culture necessary to support democracy — the "civic culture." The authors defined civic culture as "a pluralistic culture based on communication and persuasion, a culture of consensus and diversity, a culture that permitted change but moderated it."[17] The key to democratic stability lies in balancing competing impulses. Heavily influenced by his studies of British politics, Almond's definition of the civic culture resembles nothing so much as the Anglo-American political ideal of checks and balances internalized by each individual citizen.

Despite the fact that its findings were based on a rather select group of democratic societies, *The Civic Culture* quickly became the standard by which other approaches to political culture were measured. It was followed two years later by another highly influential study, this time by Sidney Verba and Lucian Pye, that applied political culture to a broader variety of political systems, including the Soviet Union.[18] And in 1973, the Harvard professors Samuel Beer and Adam Ulam, the latter a long-time director of the Russian Research Center at Harvard, adopted this approach in their popular college textbook *Patterns of Government*. Commenting on the extraordinary success of political culture in transforming comparative political research, Princeton's Robert Tucker quipped that "the political-cultural approach is by now rather deeply embedded in the culture of American political science."[19]

The very success of this approach, however, soon led to criticism. According to its critics, the dominant approach to political culture suffered from four conspicuous flaws.

Behavioralism. The civic culture study openly embraced the behavioral approach to political science. A loosely defined group at best, behavioralists generally felt that politics should be studied in much the same way hard sciences are studied. To accomplish this, the basic unit of political analysis must be reduced as closely as possible to empirically measurable behavior. This core may be surrounded by various normative constructs that seek to explain the reasons for such behavior, but to understand politics one must go directly to the core. Thus sampling, interviewing, scoring and scaling techniques, and statistical analysis were deemed crucial to comprehending political behavior. These were the social patterns that mold behavior irrespective of normative or cultural overlays. With political culture's reliance on survey research and its emphasis on deriving general insights from the study of individual behavior, it is not hard to see why Lucian Pye describes it as a "natural evolution" in the behavioral approach to politics.[20] When the counterreaction to behavioralism emerged in the mid–1970s, many critics took aim at the claims of political culture theorists that they were developing a "scientific theory of democracy."[21] If anything, they countered, the political culture approach was less scientific than most because it assumed that aggregated snapshots of individual attitudes translate into long-term political support. Heinz Eulau calls this "the fallacy of personification," treating small social units as if they were big ones.[22]

Another problem stemming from too strong an attachment to the behavioral method was institutional determinism. Judging political values strictly by publicly observable and quantifiable measures of support infers popular support from the mere existence of certain political institutions. Soviet political institutions, for instance, are thus presumed to express the political values of the populace, unless specifically proven otherwise. The idea that an individual might find it advantageous to hide his true political sentiments from officialdom does not seem to have occurred to the authors of *The Civic Culture*.

Definitional fuzziness. A second critique often leveled at political culture was that it failed to define the empirical values being analyzed. The definition of political culture might stress psychological, cultural, anthropological, or political aspects of society, depending on what suited a particular author's purposes. This failure to define political culture as an independent variable made it all but impossible to identify what role it plays in the political process. In more than a few studies of political culture a particular pattern of behavior is taken to demonstrate the existence of a particular political culture, and is then also explained *by* that political culture.

Faulty methodology. The civic culture approach tended to treat political culture as the repository for officially sanctioned values. Since a strong relationship is already presumed to exist between political institutions and political culture, emphasizing the merits of consensual politics results in a strong bias in favor of system stability. This in turn makes it very difficult for alternative political-cultural values to be recognized, since to be political values they must be expressed in public and "transmitted, learned and widely shared over a substantial period of time."[23] Communist societies therefore face a conundrum which seems to preclude the very existence of any cultural values at odds with the state.

Recognizing the implausibility of such a uniformity of views, proponents of the civic culture model have acknowledged that certain "fragmented" political cultures may contain strong "subcultures" at odds with the dominant political culture. It is important to note, however, that the civic culture literature identifies such subcultures as having political orientations "strongly deviant" from the predominant one in society, and sees groups in a subculture as "isolated from one another by contradictory and incompatible orientations toward political life."[24] Typical examples include regions with distinct, compact religious or ethnic minorities, such as Northern Ireland, Quebec, and the border regions of India and Pakistan. The term political subculture, as used by the mainstream civic culture approach, therefore clearly does not imply a historically continuous strand of alternative political-cultural values. This makes it inappropriate for describing Russia, where an alternative strand of political culture was able to unite different ethnicities, regions, and social strata in the common pursuit of civil society.

Misunderstanding culture. For some the fatal flaw in the subjective approach to political culture was that it misunderstood culture. The civic culture model, they argue, is based on the notion that bargaining is the most appropriate means of resolving political conflicts. From there it is but a short step to using characteristics that are unique to Western societies as developmental norms for the rest of the world. Robert Tucker has argued that the very assumption that political culture is an autonomous part of the general culture is a view not shared, for example, by Byzantium, Islam, or Medieval Christendom.[25]

Nor should culture be viewed as just an inventory of "manifestation[s] in aggregate form of the psychological and subjective dimensions of politics," for this leaves out many fundamental meanings that resist quantification.[26] For the anthropologists Anthony F. C. Wallace and Clifford Geertz, such meanings (including political meanings) are not likely to be revealed to itinerant Western pollsters. They can, however, be gleaned through intense study of the interaction of deeply rooted symbols. "All political order," William Adams writes, "rests on culture, that is, [it] embodies in symbol systems and reproduces in symbolic action a complex conception of the world."[27] The total ensemble of such symbols constitutes a "social imaginary" in which individuals can relate to one another and to their collective tradition through the use of symbols. Social action is thus best understood by interpreting the symbols of a particular cultural tradition. The role of the political scientist should be to interpret the political significance of key symbols, hence the name "interpretive theory." Because the civic culture approach sees culture as no more than "a problem of aggregates," interpretive critics claim that it cannot comprehend what Geertz calls "the underlying grammar" of politics.[28]

Sovietology Meets Political Culture

At first glance, political culture would seem to be of little use to Sovietologists. Its natural environment is clearly the Western democratic world, where empirical data can be gathered and hypotheses about political values tested. Indeed, the lack of reliable survey data was at first considered a severe limitation to applying the civic culture model to communist countries.

But as émigré scholars retired they were gradually replaced by "homegrown" Sovietologists who had no personal knowledge of prerevolutionary Russia. The Soviet expression of Russian reality was the only one familiar to them. Unlike their predecessors, they tended to view the Soviet political experience as a reflection of Russian culture rather than a deviation from it, and they tended to view a gradual tempering of the Soviet system as much more likely than a violent rejection of it.

In addition, Khrushchev's Russia was clearly different from Stalin's. During Khrushchev's rule there was a noticeable decrease in the use of state-sponsored terror and a dramatic change in the leadership style of top Party officials. After 1956 it became possible for a few Western scholars to visit the Soviet Union and to report back on these changes. The evidence they returned with further discredited the view that the Soviet regime was a static monolith whose stability rested solely on coercion. One had to at least consider the possibility that the regime had forged a popular base of support after nearly half a century of existence. To deny this smacked of ideologically motivated anticommunism.

Political culture theory offered a way to explain the unanticipated stability of the regime that accompanied a reduction in overt coercion. With its emphasis on the qualities needed to develop a civic culture, modern political culture theory seemed perfect for identifying this trend toward gradual reform, and perhaps even assisting it. With its comparative framework, it took more seriously the regional differences (and even animosities) that were beginning to emerge in the "communist camp." By looking at the ways in which national identity shaped the particular political expression of communist rule, political culture theory spawned a new field—the comparative study of communist systems. And since the civic culture approach was explicitly quantitative and behavioral, adopting it would also bring communist area studies quickly into the mainstream of political science. Lastly, political culture would once again allow students of Soviet politics to consider questions of political change. The totalitarian model, though not altogether excluding the possibility of political change, had posited that the most likely type of change after Stalin's death would be a system-wide collapse. Proponents of political culture, however, argued that expectations of revolutionary upheaval were mere wishful thinking. The Soviet regime could now rely on considerable public support as a result of "the high degree of compatibility between traditional Russian beliefs and practices and important Bolshevik goals."[29]

The interest in political culture among Sovietologists was welcomed by behavioralists. A science, after all, can consider itself a science only if its tenets can be applied universally; hence there was considerable interest among non-Sovietologists in finding ways to include Soviet studies in the newly emerging framework of political culture. It is not surprising, therefore, that Clyde Kluckhohn, an early proponent of applied sociology, spearheaded the drive to establish Harvard University's Russian Research Center, the model postwar area study program. Its first major project was to develop a "working model" of the Soviet Union which could then be used to understand other advanced industrial societies.[30] In this massive undertaking, known as the Harvard Project on the Soviet Social System, more than three thousand Soviet refugees in Europe and the United States were interviewed in 1950 and 1951.

The impact of the Harvard Project on the field of Soviet studies is hard to underestimate. Its vision of Soviet society shaped more than one generation of scholars. In just the first six years, six books and sixty scholarly articles relying on project data were published. The project's results were cited for decades as the most authoritative assessment of the attitudes of the majority of Soviet citizens toward the communist regime.[31] Despite its age, the Harvard Project remained the single most influential study of Soviet mass values until the collapse of communism in 1991.

The project directors Alex Inkeles and Raymond Bauer found that, despite specific grievances against the collective farm system and the arbitrary use of state terror, the vast majority of Soviet citizens supported the Soviet system and valued its achievements.[32] Moreover, since these specific grievances were now being rectified by Stalin's successors, they concluded that the regime was likely to become even more popular as time passed and the standard of living rose.[33]

While noting that a significant percentage of Soviet citizens said they would "change everything" or "keep nothing" about their political system, Inkeles and Bauer pointed out that these same people would typically cite with approval the universal availability of health care and education. They attributed this discrepancy to a failure on the part of the Soviet citizen to recognize that it was the Soviet *system* that was providing them with these benefits.[34] Inkeles and Bauer concluded that the typical Soviet citizen's attachment to the values of Soviet society was comparable to the attachment of a U.S. citizen to the values of American society, any differences being attributable to the distinctive cultural heritages of Russians and Americans.[35]

Although the Harvard Project preceded the heyday of the civic culture approach by nearly a decade, its findings laid the groundwork for the application of political culture to Soviet studies. The researchers found, for example, that specific political culture values can be deduced from the mere existence of political institutions. By comparing the popularity of American and Soviet political values, they clearly ascribed the stability of the Soviet political system to these distinctive cultural values.

The Harvard Project failed to consider other possible explanations for the seeming popularity of Soviet institutions, however. A split between the rejection of system values and the apparent acceptance of specific institutions might also occur if the Soviet citizen sharply distinguished between the private and the public realms. The approval of social benefits might then reflect private concern for the well-being of society, rather than approval of the political system. The social benefits of Soviet society would be viewed as having been attained despite, rather than because of, the regime. Indeed, in areas such as the preservation of educational traditions and improved living standards in rural areas after collectivization, the Harvard data point to just such a conclusion.[36]

One of the few studies to call the findings of the Harvard Project into question was conducted by Ivan D. London, director of the project's interviews in the United States. In a follow-up study of how Soviet émigrés perceived the questionnaire, he found that the respondents interpreted many questions quite differently from the researchers. He concluded that there were fundamental discrepancies between what the subjects had said and what the Harvard Project team thought they had heard.[37]

Professor London studied the responses of one hundred émigrés to the questions in Section II of the original survey. This section dealt with one's choice of occupation and was considered one of the least complicated and politically controversial. The original Harvard study had concluded that Soviet citizens enjoyed considerable freedom of choice in their occupation and derived considerable satisfaction from their careers. London's respondents, however, said that the questions themselves had made them uneasy, since accurate answers might serve to identify them to Soviet repatriation authorities or prevent their immigration to the United States. Most said that as a result they had not given entirely truthful or complete answers.[38] This impression is confirmed by Inkeles's and Bauer's own brief description of the sharply differing responses obtained to the question of membership in the Communist Youth League. None of the seven people who admitted to membership during a lengthier personal interview had done so on the questionnaire.[39] London also noted a number of examples of poor translation and phrasing that seemed to his respondents indicative of an underlying pro-Soviet bias in the questionnaire.[40]

Interestingly, when the original survey was being conducted the émigré press had criticized the project for many of the same reasons. In *The Soviet Citizen*, Inkeles and Bauer describe the difficulties this posed for their research, but they insist that this hostility was "based on a simple misunderstanding" of the purpose of the survey.[41] A careful reading of the articles that appeared at the time in the émigré press, however, shows that the criticism was usually directed at the research methodology. The émigrés questioned the value of the information that such a survey would derive, not the gathering of information per se, as Inkeles and Bauer suggest.[42]

Confirmation that the Harvard researchers had seriously erred in interpreting their data was not long in coming. Based on their findings, Inkeles and Bauer concluded that: (1) the group least hostile to the regime was the intelligentsia, and the groups most hostile were "ordinary workers" and "collective farmers"; (2) the younger generation was quite accepting of Soviet values, and this would be even more true of succeeding generations; and (3) there was little evidence of discontent among managers and representatives of the technical intelligentsia. Even as Inkeles and Bauer were writing, however, the "thaw" that followed Khrushchev's 1956 "secret speech" on the crimes of the Stalin era revealed that the intelligentsia and young people were among the *most* disaffected groups in Soviet society. It was from these two segments of the population that organized dissent evolved in the late 1960s and quickly spread to include representatives of the technical intelligentsia. By the early 1980s discontent with the system had emerged within the Party itself, thanks mostly to the technical and managerial elites.[43] Also, contrary to the findings of the Harvard Project, subsequent interviews of Soviet émigrés in the 1970s confirmed that it was precisely the younger, better-educated citizens who were least loyal to the regime.[44]

Inkeles and Bauer failed to appreciate the importance of social discontent because of two conceptual errors. First, they firmly believed that the Soviet economy was a modern industrial success; hence they concluded that Soviet society would increasingly come to resemble those of other advanced industrial nations — an early version of the theory of convergence popularized by Samuel Huntington and Zbigniew Brzezinski in *Political Power: USA/ USSR*.[45] They did not anticipate the collapse of the Soviet model of production. Second, they assumed *a priori* that Russians favored "a paternalistic state, with extremely wide powers which it vigorously exercised to guide and control the nation's destiny, but which yet served the interests of the citizen benignly . . ."[46] When this assumption clashed with the survey results they had no alternative concept of Russian political culture with which to reconcile this conflicting data. By minimizing the conflict, however, they exaggerated the degree of social consensus in Soviet society.

These assumptions coincided with the work of an interdisciplinary team of scholars at Columbia University that had been set up just one year earlier than the Harvard Project to study Soviet attitudes toward authority. Headed by the renowned anthropologist Margaret Mead, this team found that Soviet patterns of authority reflected long-standing psychological attitudes of the Russian people, whom Mead described as "prone to extreme swings in mood from exhilaration to depression, hating confinement and authority and yet feeling that a strong central authority was necessary to keep their own violent impulses in check."[47] Mead's group in turn relied heavily on the Russian character structure developed by Geoffrey Gorer of the Russian section of the Columbia University Research on Contemporary Cultures project. Along with John Rickman, Gorer had published several works suggesting that Russians were predisposed toward extremes of submissiveness and explosive violence, of privation and gratification, and they showed a marked willingness to submit to brutal authority.[48] They surmised that these Russian character traits derived from the practice of tightly swaddling infants at birth, a theory subsequently derided as "diaperology."

It is worth emphasizing that Mead and her colleagues at Columbia saw these psychological traits as distinctively Russian. Since repressive Soviet institutions were consistent with the psychological traits ascribed to the average Russian, it was assumed that they merely reflected a popular desire for greater external control.[49] Mead's work on the political significance of anthropology reportedly influenced both Gabriel Almond and Lucian Pye.[50]

The Harvard and Columbia studies thus seemed to explain the puzzling stability of such an oppressive regime. For Almond and Verba a key indicator of a system's political stability had been the congruence between its political institutions and its political culture. One of the first attempts to apply the civic culture model to Soviet Russia, in fact, concluded that the stability of the Soviet system could be explained by the congruence between traditional Russian beliefs and Bolshevik goals.[51] This approach was later incorporated into several textbooks on the USSR.

As decades passed, however, the findings of the Harvard study, though still widely accepted, were seen as less than conclusive. An alternative to survey data had to be found if Sovietology was ever to embrace fully the political culture approach. The breakthrough came in 1974, when Archie Brown of Oxford University published his study *Soviet Politics and Political Science,* identifying several additional sources for the study of Soviet (and

Russian) political culture. His study was justly heralded as a pathbreaking work, and his sources are worth discussing in some detail.[52]

Creative literature. Even in communist countries, fiction writers are given some leeway in expressing personal points of view, and a comparison of areas of agreement among different writers could prove revealing. Of course, says Brown, the selection of authors and literary interpretations would have to rely heavily on the researcher's judgment.

Memoirs. This category includes materials officially published in the USSR and disseminated through the underground press *(samizdat),* as well as those published by émigrés in the West. Again, the choice of the most relevant and insightful authors is a decisive and highly subjective factor.

Historiography. As an example of the sort of conclusion that can be drawn from historiography, Brown cites the differences between English and Russian attitudes toward the monarchy and nobility: "One need only contrast English attitudes to King John and the barons with the Russian view of Ivan the Terrible and the boyars. If Stalin, with his enormous influence over Russian historiography, put Peter the Great and even Ivan the Terrible back on a pedestal, there is good reason to believe that he was acting in harmony with a strong element in popular sentiment."[53] Curiously, though Brown accepts both official and prerevolutionary historians, he overlooks émigré historians who trained in Russia, wrote for Russian émigré journals, and saw themselves as continuing the Russian cultural tradition abroad.

Writings of the "new Soviet man." A study of official attempts to raise a new type of individual, shorn of the psychological limitations of capitalism, would not only help to clarify official values, says Brown, but also indicate the extent of deviation from what is expected. One particularly rich area that Brown does not mention is anecdotes, ballads, and proverbs, which might justly lay a particular claim to representing popular attitudes.

Soviet sociological research. Most published research, Brown notes, deals only obliquely with subjects of interest to political sociologists. Nevertheless, he maintains, it is worth sifting through.

Western sociological research on the USSR. Brown cites as especially valuable the findings of the Harvard Project on the Soviet System. The conclusions of the project, now nearly three decades old, however, should be corroborated by other sources.

Accounts by long-term residents and interpretations of Russian history. Again, Brown acknowledges the tremendous variety of sources and urges that they be used with discretion and only in conjunction with other sources.

Brown argues that combining such sources can yield results comparable to those obtained by survey research alone. Unlike the modicum of objectivity which accurate surveys of public opinion can offer, however, Brown's approach serves mainly to confirm the researcher's *a priori* assumptions regarding Russian political culture and too easily overlooks evidence that might lead to a different interpretation. A cursory review of his sources reveals that their most salient characteristic is subjectivity. He repeatedly stresses the need for "insight" and "discrimination" on the part of the researcher in selecting sources. To safeguard against bias Brown suggests giving weight only to those views of Russian culture and history that are corroborated by other sources. Since all choices can be made subjectively, however, this constraint is easy enough to get around. The "insightful" researcher should have little difficulty finding corroborative views from different sources that "prove" his or her opinions about Russian political culture.

Partly in response to this disturbing level of subjectivity, Stephen White takes the next logical step and attempts to use history as a benchmark for measuring the continuity of fundamental Russian political values and experiences. Beginning with the rather questionable premise that historical analysis can be viewed as an impartial foundation for approaching Russian political culture, he finds that Soviet political culture is really Russian political culture "rooted in the historical experience of centuries of absolutism."[54]

Unfortunately, White's selection of historical sources is no less subjective than Brown's. Mary McAuley goes to the heart of the matter when she writes, "The political culturalists want to argue that past culture is a crucial factor in forming today's culture. Fair enough. But then the relationship has to be spelt out. This has to be done by examining and rejecting explanations of today's culture which do not include past culture as a variable, and by tracing the process by which perceptions are transmitted over time. It is strange that the subjectivists do neither."[55]

Despite these flaws, however, the political culture approach rapidly gained acceptance in the field of communist studies during the 1970s and 1980s. The subjective approach to political culture gradually replaced the earlier psychological and nature-oriented studies of human behavior. No longer isolated, Soviet studies became a respectable component of mainstream political science. By the mid–1980s the view that the repressive institutions of the Soviet state coincided with the desires of Russian political culture had become so commonplace that Stephen White commented, "It seems if anything to reflect too faithfully the mainstream scholarly consensus."[56] White would eventually come to edit the leading journal in the field, *Soviet Studies* (now *Europe-Asia Studies*), while the father of the field, Gabriel Almond, acknowledged the validity of this approach to Soviet studies and pointed to the Soviet Union as an important test of the explanatory power of political culture theory.[57]

Political Culture and Gorbachev

It is not the explanatory power of political culture, however, that explains its rapid acceptance in communist studies, but rather the fact that it reinforced the conventional wisdom regarding the continuity of Russian and Soviet history, as well as the dominance of authoritarian strands in both. This consensus was strengthened and given an aura of scientific credibility by the application of the civic culture model to Soviet studies. As a result, Sovietology increasingly came to emphasize the stability and popularity of the communist regime. Among analysts of the Soviet Union, the proponents of the subjective approach to political culture were often the most tenacious defenders of the view that socialism was popular among the Russian people, and hence that a rejection of the system was highly unlikely. They failed to recognize the systematic nature of Russian discontent because they could not distinguish its sources. As a result, they saw the Soviet political landscape as calm and tranquil when it was rife with subterranean discontent.

Part of this response has to do with the fact that political culture theory allows only one dominant strand to define the political culture of a nationality and asserts that this identity is not susceptible to rapid or profound changes. Almond identifies these "primordial values and commitments" that determine a political culture as ethnicity, nationality, and religion. Basic values in these three areas, he says, are "almost indestructible."[58] Large-scale changes in any of these three aspects of political culture occur only in exceptional circumstances, as the result of traumatic upheavals.

This leads to an obvious paradox. On the one hand, if political culture is to serve as a reliable standard it must be stable and its contents clearly defined. On the other hand, an excessively static definition of political culture limits a society's ability to develop. The solution, says Almond, is to distinguish between "basic political beliefs and values" and mere political mood swings.[59] The civic culture approach claims that such distinctions can be made by looking at the degree of popular trust in the political leadership and the legitimacy of the political system. If a regime does not reflect popular political values, then it will surely be overthrown. Therefore, according to Brian Barry, a change of regime provides the best natural test of political culture as an explanatory tool:

> If the "political culture" alters afterwards (e.g. in Germany after 1945, toward a "civic culture" type), this strongly supports the view that it is a more or less accurate reflection of the current political reality. If, on the other hand, it does not change, then this interpretation of the basis of "political culture" collapses; and if, some time before the change in regime, a change in "political culture"

in the right direction were observed, this would provide good evidence for the view which attributed to it causal efficacy.[60]

Nearly all noted Sovietologists, regardless of how they define political culture, agreed with Barry. This makes it all the more surprising, therefore, that political culture was hardly ever applied to understanding Mikhail Gorbachev.[61] His rise to power should have provided an ideal test of the proposition that Soviet political culture represented a continuation of Russian political culture. One would have thought that political culture theory could have shed light on one of the key questions plaguing Sovietologists after 1985: How could Gorbachev, a figure so dramatically different from past Soviet leaders, rise to the top of the Soviet system? Was he a throwback to earlier values? Or was he merely the product of some previously overlooked cultural subgroup of society?

There are, of course, many studies that highlight Gorbachev's youth, his personality, his education, his upbringing, his place of birth, or his nationality as the key to understanding his policies, but none that utilizes political culture to understand how a leader with Gorbachev's cast of mind could emerge from Russia's authoritarian political culture. Most observers simply chose to regard him as a historical accident, a misfit in the general pattern of Russian political culture.[62]

The "Gorbymania" that possessed some of the most seasoned Sovietologists becomes easier to understand in this context. Here was the rarest of all creatures: a reform-minded, capable, westward-looking leader the likes of which Russia had not seen since Peter the Great. For the first time in years Soviet studies was exciting and unpredictable. As Gorbachev's policies strained against the limits of the political system, analysts waited with bated breath to see if, like Houdini, he would once again escape the snares of the political system and the popular culture that conspired against him. What an extraordinary opportunity this must have seemed after years of interminably dull Brezhnevs, Andropovs, and Chernenkos.

Of course, Sovietology has always focused on the top political leadership, but with Gorbachev the ardor to understand the personality and aspirations of one man began to overshadow completely what was happening in the rest of society. From 1985 to 1991 Soviet studies might just as well have been called "Gorbachev studies." In a few short years the field reverted from stressing the variety of official and semiofficial sources of "institutional pluralism" in the Soviet Union to the view that the sun of reform rose and set with this new Soviet leader. After the August 1991 coup attempt, when Gorbachev was shown to be a largely irrelevant figure in Russian politics, more than a few prominent analysts could scarcely conceal their shock.[63]

By linking reform personally to Gorbachev, these analysts totally missed the significance of popular demands for the restoration of civil society. Russian society was dismissed as a co-participant in the process of social change not because it was unknown, but because it was thought to be too well known. To the vast majority of Sovietologists it was obvious that aspirations for civil society were too weak in Russian political culture to mount an effective challenge to the regime. The result was the rather bizarre image of "a political system without a social one, a state floating over everything else, over history itself."[64] Gorbachev's remarkable career seemed the exception that confirmed the rule: in Russia, political change could be contemplated only by a personality who transcended the constraints of Russian political culture and history. From here it is but a short step to the view, common at the time, that change would occur only if Gorbachev was kept in power.[65]

In retrospect, the conventional wisdom that guided Western Sovietology has proved to be embarrassingly inadequate: it failed to identify Gorbachev's increasing irrelevance to the process of political transformation; it failed to explain the consistent popularity of Yeltsin and of the most radical democratic political movements; it failed to appreciate the political impact of the Russian national revival; and, finally, it failed to recognize the alternative Russian political traditions that had survived seventy years of communism and were fueling the restoration of civil society.

Looking for Russia's Alternative Political Culture

What if a different approach had been taken? What if Gorbachev, instead of being viewed as outside the traditional patterns of Russian political culture, had been viewed as a natural part of its evolution? In her trenchant critique of political culture theory as applied to Soviet studies, Mary McAuley shows how a different selection of sources can lead to an entirely different interpretation of Russian political culture. Rather than the unitary view of Russian political culture adopted by the civic culture approach, she suggests that a number of diverse images emerge from both official and unofficial sources, and a number of different explanations of the relationship between them are possible:

> There was peasant individualism as well as collectivism, strong anarchist notions against any "state," repeated demands for and attempts to introduce representative institutions, criticisms of censorship, religious sects practising autonomy, generals complaining bitterly of the lack of nationalist and religious feelings among the troops. Neither the demands of 1905 nor those of 1917 put to the Congress of Soviets bear many traces of White's "distinctive and deeply-rooted pattern of orientations." And the myth of the Just Tsar was collapsing by the turn of the century, despite the autocratic system. Why? "Samod-

erzhavie" [autocracy] may have represented the views of latter-day Tsarist circles, a political order under threat from society and struggling to maintain its slipping grasp—but, as such, it represented a notion of authority and political order that had little support in society. It seems, at the very least, that we should talk of a clash of political cultures in late nineteenth- and early twentieth-century Russia. The Bolsheviks did not inherit a "distinctive set of orientations;" they inherited (and let us remember that their ideas too were a product of the old society) a most extraordinarily rich, jumbled and contradictory set of political perceptions.[66]

Following McAuley's lead, one could take each of the criteria used by Brown to define Russian political culture and come up with vastly different definitions. For example, Theophile Gautier's *Voyage en Russie* could be used to counter the better-known study of the same name by his contemporary the marquis de Custine. Popular anecdotes and folk wisdom provide an image of Soviet daily reality quite different from the official literary image of the "new Soviet man." And it is not hard to find historians who challenge the notion that Russia's political tradition was uniformly autocratic. One need only look at the works of Sergei Pushkarev, Vladimir Leontovich, Sir Paul Vinogradoff, Jacob Walkin, or S. Frederick Starr.

The point here is that under the criteria applied by the proponents of the traditional approach to political culture, it is no more difficult to prove that Russian political culture prizes individualism and freedom than it is to prove the opposite. McAuley is right, Russian political culture cannot be defined within the narrow framework of a unitary tradition. To do so inevitably leads to political and historical determinism. Indeed, political cultures so defined cannot escape the conundrum that what is "traditional" is identified by present-day political reality. If the political system should change in the wake of some political crisis, however, this can lead to the absurdity of abandoning one interpretation of what constitutes the "traditional" political culture for a completely opposite one! This has happened once before, in writings on German political culture. Scholars once discerned in Germany's patriarchal, authoritarian family structure strong tendencies toward servile obedience, xenophobic nationalism, ethnocentrism, and anti-semitism. A generation later, however, analysts write that Germany is characterized by "democratic and regime legitimacy and a participant political culture."[67] Such cultural acrobatics sharply undermine the claim that basic political beliefs and values are highly resistant to change and can be used as a reliable benchmark for evaluating the stability of a political system.

Almond, however, suggests that such astounding transformations in political culture can result from "powerful historical experiences" such as military collapse, occupation, forced migration, "imaginative constitutional en-

gineering," and economic reconstruction.[68] Even so, the rapid transformation of truly *fundamental* values and beliefs seems implausible if they
did not already form some part of the existing political culture. This may
be likened to a drunkard declaring himself to be a confirmed teeto-
taler — for the past five minutes.

To survive as an analytical tool, political culture theory must come to terms
with the rapid and startling transformations taking place in Russia. Moreover,
it must somehow account for the fact that this transformation has taken place
without any of the traumatic criteria considered essential by Almond.

The rapid collapse of the Soviet regime and the sudden emergence of a
civic culture supportive of democratic values suggest that a fundamentally
different approach is required to understand political culture in totalitarian
countries. If one accepts that basic values cannot be formed overnight, one
must allow for the possibility that alternative values were somehow preserved in Russia despite the constraints imposed by the regime. A viable
political culture theory would also have to explain how unsanctioned political values were transmitted from one generation to the next. It must specify
which segments of the population were involved in the preservation and
transmission of these values, and it must measure them. It must show how
individual attitudes and behavior are linked to the aggregate political behavior of society. Finally, it must account for how alternative attitudes coexisted
and interacted with the official political system.[69]

I believe that, despite its failings, political culture still offers the best approach for understanding the collapse of communism and the prospects for
Russian democracy. The subjective approach is especially apropos when
studying the implosion of communism because it resulted not from any
single, clearly identifiable factor, but rather from a wide variety of factors
that served systematically to undermine the values of the Soviet political
system over a long period of time. Only a methodology that approaches
political change as a long-term social and cultural process will allow us to
truly understand what occurred in former communist countries. But in order for political culture to be revived as a tool for analyzing political trends
in Russian society, it must be able to provide convincing answers to two
questions: Why did communism collapse so abruptly and so completely as
a political *ideal*? And what political ideals are most likely to replace communism in post-Soviet Russia?

An Interpretive Approach to Political Culture

Although the dominant approach to political culture has been the "behavioral" or "subjectivist" civic culture model espoused by Almond, Verba, and

Pye, another approach has gradually been gaining ground. The "symbolist" or "interpretivist" approach has been advocated by scholars such as Aaron Wildavsky, Lowell Dittmer, Howard J. Wiarda, and Robert C. Tucker. At the root of this dichotomy lies a sharp disagreement over how broadly one can define culture and still have it be useful for political analysis.

The definition of culture given by the interpretivists is far more expansive than that adopted by behavioralists. According to Robert C. Tucker, it shifts the focus in political culture studies away from systems analysis (another aspect of the behavioral revolution which relates underlying psychological propensities in a political system to its actual performance over time) to a view of the political system as "a complex of real and ideal cultural patterns."[70] It assumes that patterns of action and state of mind mutually influence one another and that *both* must form part of the definition of political culture. As Clifford Geertz put it, "Believing with Max Weber that man is an animal suspended in webs of significance he himself has spun, I take culture to be those webs, and the analysis of it to be therefore not an experimental science in search of law but an interpretive one in search of meaning."[71]

The impetus for this postbehavioral redefinition of political culture comes from anthropology. Rather than limiting political culture to a subjective orientation to politics, anthropologists see all culture (including political culture) as a "learned and transmitted way of life."[72] This way of life has both "overt" aspects, such as the patterns of behavior observed in a society, and "covert" assets which reflect the knowledge, attitudes, and values shared and transmitted. Of special significance to understanding cultures are the patterns reflected in action over time, rather than those observed at any given moment.[73]

It is the search for the more durable underlying meaning of political action that drives the interpretive approach to political culture. Thus Lowell Dittmer, a political scientist at Berkeley, describes political culture as a "subfield of political science . . . concerned with the context of meaning of political action; it is not concerned with the action itself . . . except insofar as that action is influenced by or in some way affects the context of meaning."[74] Whereas the behavioral approach seeks to identify the proper parts of speech and their appropriate roles, the interpretive approach lays claim to understanding the underlying grammar of political discourse.[75]

The interpretive approach has been disparaged as "mere political ethnography" by scholars who view the explanation of particular behavior as an essential function of political culture. Its "explanatory power," according to Gabriel Almond, is a main reason for political culture's widespread acceptance says Archie Brown.[76] Even scholars partial to the interpretive approach, such as Stephen White, agree that political culture ought to "provide a framework within which patterns of political belief and behavior, historically considered, can be located . . . [It is] a factor which will influence and constrain — though not determine — future patterns of development in a political system."[77] Dittmer, however, suggests that if one applies the anthropological notion of "symbols" to the search for the meaning of political action and political structures, the analytical usefulness of political culture is not only preserved but enhanced.

The importance of symbols to understanding and transmitting values has long been recognized. The British historian Walter Bagehot refers to symbols as the "theatrical part of government," those common traditions and ideals that strengthen social bonds.[78] According to Dittmer, the symbolic framework in a society acts as a set of codes, imposing order and meaning on the information to be transmitted.[79] The transmission of political values through symbols is known as political communication and constitutes one of the fundamental functions of a political culture. Recasting the study of political culture as the study of systems of political communication allows the analyst to think about political culture in terms of both its contemporary substantive content and its enduring significance. Moreover, when symbols are used in political communication they provide the analyst with concrete, empirical variables and a coherent internal structure with a degree of autonomy from both social structure and psychology.[80] Geertz further suggests that symbols can be studied just like any other event, since they are "as public as marriage and as observable as agriculture."[81]

Political symbols not only reflect specific world views; careful study of their content over time can also show how political meanings change. Dittmer refers to this as the "metalinguistic" quality of political symbols — events that are discussed will often refer to broader categories of events which evoke other, connotative, emotions and perceptions.[82] In the Soviet Union, for example, support for the issue of historic preservation was recognized by Russians as a symbol for traditional, religious, rural values. Similarly, the nostalgia for rural life in the works of the "village prose" writers was clearly incompatible with the principles of the "new Soviet man" and offered moral encouragement to Russia's patriotic-political opposition during the 1970s and 1980s.[83]

The mere reference to historic events that are officially taboo, such as the massive participation of Soviet volunteers in the German army during World War II, may be an attempt to broaden the framework of discussion to include alternative political values. If persistent over time, such discussions form one of the mechanisms through which nonofficial attitudes and perceptions are transmitted despite official censorship. When political symbols come with a clear plot structure, serve a practical argument, and appeal to a perennially or historically recurring constituency, they become *political myths*.[84]

The concept of political myth is very helpful in understanding how Russia's alternative political culture functioned. As the antithesis of the statist tradition in Russian political thought, alternative political culture spawned a series of alternative political myths that directly contradicted those of the official ideology, both tsarist and Soviet.[85] Thus, to the regime's claims that absolutism represented Russia's ideal form of government, the alternative political culture opposed the notion of constrained autocracy. To the official subordination of the church to the state, the alternative political culture opposed the ideal of a symphonic harmony and division of labor between secular and religious authorities. To the official state-centered ideal of Soviet patriotism, the alternative political culture opposed a vision of Russian national identity that emphasized moderate Slavophile virtues.

The October 1917 Bolshevik coup itself helped forge the greatest political myth of all — the myth of the betrayal of Russian democracy that has inspired countless opponents of the Soviet regime. By distinguishing between the existing culture and the "goal culture" that embodies the ideals of political society, these opponents laid the foundation for what would eventually evolve into what Anthony Wallace terms "revitalization movements" — deliberate, organized, conscious efforts by members of a society to construct a more satisfying culture.[86]

Wallace's notion of a "goal culture" strikes me as helpful for understanding the persistence of political opposition inside Russia after 1917, and the relative ease with which communism was overthrown. A goal culture is not simply a "subculture" with aspirations distinct from those of the majority. Rather, it is a broader movement that transcends class, racial, ethnic, and other social divisions in order to reshape the entire political culture. The historical-political framework for this goal culture can be traced back to Muscovite times. It resurfaced in the Slavophile movement of the early nineteenth century and became a potent intellectual counterweight to Marxism at the turn of this century. After 1917 it was further elaborated by émigré intellectuals. Meanwhile, inside the Soviet Union, dissidents, writers, and even some members of the clergy were forging nearly identical intellectual, cultural, and eventually political alternatives to communism. The notions of political myth and goal culture help to explain the persistence and intellectual consistency of opposition thinking both inside Russia and abroad.

Many analysts, however, still seem to be looking for the "smoking gun" — established, autonomous institutions that prove the existence of civil society.[87] Obviously, such institutions could not exist in communist countries,

where the Party, by definition, monopolized public life. It seems only logical, therefore, to refine the concept somewhat when it is applied to communist societies, and to define a civil society as one in which social groups
persistently *seek* to define themselves as distinct from the state despite efforts
by the state to prevent them from doing so. As long as the Communist Party
holds a monopoly on public discourse this process can only occur outside
the public arena, hence it is there that political aspirations must be sought.

But does not politics, by definition, require public expression? It does, but
the most appropriate way to gauge this expression in communist countries is
to see how consistently the values and authority of the state were challenged,
not simply whether it was overthrown. Such a formulation takes into account the aspirations of individuals and groups to struggle for political
change, rather than simply the vicissitudes of history.

The traditional dichotomy, taken from Almond's description of the civic
culture, between "domestic" and "political" society should therefore be seen
as far less significant for communist societies.[88] Under communism the with-
drawal of the individual into the circle of close family and friends is never
simply a retreat from politics. It is, rather, a defensive mechanism of civil
society that "allows for the preservation of a given society's social culture
. . . when that becomes impossible in public institutional life."[89] This private
realm then becomes the seedbed within which the concepts of independent
thought and action can germinate. Havel aptly calls this "the invisible realm
of social consciousness."[90] As the individual strives to vest his life with true
meaning, Havel says he begins the process of recreating civil society to serve
those true meanings. This process will inevitably put him in conflict with
the regime.

Havel gives the example of an ordinary, completely apolitical greengrocer
who begins this journey by displaying a placard in his window that reads
"Workers of the World, Unite!" Of course, passersby understand that this is
a parody, and with this small gesture the grocer has already committed a
serious infraction:

> He has shattered the world of appearances, the fundamental pillar of the sys-
> tem. He has upset the power structure by tearing apart what holds it together.
> He has demonstrated that living a lie is living a lie . . . Living within the lie can
> constitute the system only if it is universal. The principle must embrace and
> permeate everything. There are no terms whatsoever on which it can coexist
> with living within the truth, and therefore everyone who steps out of line *denies
> it in principle and threatens it in its entirety.*[91]

Havel emphasizes that the grocer's choice has an unambiguous political di-
mension, not because of the nature of the demands, but because the commu-

nist system demands total compliance. Human nature itself therefore challenges the system, and so long as it is not fundamentally altered, it must rise to challenge the regime.

When the repressive mechanisms of the state finally weaken to the point where the first timid efforts at opposition manifest themselves, these individuals often find, much to their own astonishment, that they share a common language and common aspirations. What each perceived as an individual rebellion actually occurred in a "field of hidden influence" whose significance extended far beyond its numbers.[92] The most visible dissidents — the Sakharovs, the Solzhenitsyns, the Havels — relied on an "invisible network of small groups submerged in daily life."[93] The existence of such a network, bound together by shared values and aspirations, explains how the seemingly all-pervasive communist system could disintegrate so completely in a matter of months. It had, in fact, been under siege for decades.

One possible way to measure whether or not these aspirations are shared widely enough to constitute an alternative political culture is to see how often they arise to challenge the official political culture. This can occur in at least three arenas: first, in the arena of underground society, which Vaclav Benda appropriately terms the "parallel polis";[94] second, in the arena of émigré society, which, by virtue of being abroad, cannot be stifled by the regime; and third, in the arena of political developments in postcommunist Russia, which afford an additional "safety check" on the durability of the alternative political culture. If a consistent set of distinctive political symbols, linked to an alternative political myth of Russian political development, finds expression in several of these arenas simultaneously, this should be interpreted as strong evidence of the existence of a viable, alternative strand of Russian political culture.

An alternative political culture is now commonly acknowledged to have existed in Central Europe and the Baltic states, but not in Russia or other members of the CIS. In reality, however, just as in its better-known counterparts in Poland and Czechoslovakia, Russia's alternative political culture had values that were formed in binary opposition to the values of the regime.[95] It offered its own political myth based on the betrayal of Russian democracy in 1917. This myth persisted throughout the Soviet period. It had its distinctive political symbols, which included the restoration of the prerevolutionary flag, prerevolutionary place names, the restoration of churches, and many other changes we see occurring in Russia today. Finally, it persistently emerged to challenge the political system in the three arenas previously described (émigré, dissident, and post-Soviet), confirming the continuity and vitality of its central themes. It is high time, therefore, to discard the notion that Russian political culture is an obstacle to the emergence of civil society and to adopt an approach that examines how Russian society responded to the opportunities for reform throughout history, as well as how Russian political culture provides the foundation for a modern, distinctively Russian version of civil society.

The interpretive approach to political culture seems to offer the best prospects for revitalizing Russian studies because it corrects two major flaws of the mainstream political culture approach: first, the notion that political culture is a given, rather than a multifaceted and evolving identity; and second, the view that political culture is at best a haphazard collection of beliefs whose concrete expression can be measured only by the quantitative analysis of attitudes and behaviors. In the case of communist societies, political culture can more accurately be described as a set of widely held aspirations that purposefully set out to "reappropriate society, to recover community . . . [and to] sever the bonds with communism that were . . . corrupting society."[96] By failing to identify civil society's nonpublic political component, Western analysts severely foreshortened the process of reclaiming civil society in communist countries and underestimated the fragility of communist political systems. What distinguishes Russia from its Central European neighbors in this process is not the absence of similar impulses, but the depths to which the alternative political culture needed to submerge in order to survive the assault of the state.

After reviewing the basic assumptions of political culture applied to Soviet studies, we might well wonder whether an approach such as the one I have just described would have enabled analysts to forecast more accurately the collapse of communism in Eastern Europe and the Soviet Union. To be sure, absolute certainty in forecasting political change is impossible, but I believe that Sovietologists might have had a better sense of the impending collapse of communism if they had recognized the significance of Russia's recurring alternative political symbols. The traditional approach to political culture did not allow for this because it presumed that only one version of political culture could exist at a time. The interpretive approach, being more flexible in this regard, might have alerted analysts to the discrepancies manifested within Soviet political culture, and hence given them pause in concluding that they were dealing with a stable political system. Indeed, during the early 1980s a number of émigré observers did try to point out the importance of these dissonant phenomena, but, without an intellectual framework to explain the political significance of these events, their analyses usually fell upon deaf ears in the West.[97]

Although Russian pollsters will now be able to offer us relatively reliable snapshots of Russian society, and the revelations of Soviet archives will fill many important gaps in our knowledge of what led to the collapse of communism, neither will be sufficient for understanding the politics of the new Russia because, as Peter Rutland has correctly pointed out, the failure to appreciate the fragility of communist rule stemmed from a lack not of resources or information but of imagination.[98] Clearly, we need to be far more imaginative as we prepare to face the Russia of the twenty-first century.

2

Constrained Autocracy in Russian History

The supreme authority, in its deepest sense, rested not with the popular assembly [*veche*] but with all the people of the land. This concept of self-governing lands appears in the earliest histories. It survives many centuries, many setbacks and adversities, and re-emerges under the country's new system of government.　　—Nikolai Kostomarov

The Saratov Zemstvo Union considers itself the direct inheritor of the zemstvo ideal, an ideal of conciliarity [*sobornost*], of brotherhood among countrymen, of self-government and self-initiative . . . We see this ideal as an uninterrupted continuation of the traditions of the zemstvo councils of the sixteenth and seventeenth centuries and the zemstvos active in Russia from 1864 to 1918.　　—Program of the Saratov Zemstvo Union, 1994

If political culture is to have any value as an analytical tool it must have certain constants by which it can be measured. Gabriel Almond, for example, has sought to link political culture to the attitudes and values associated with ethnicity, nationality, and religion, which he considers the most resistant to change.[1]

Such continuity is also essential to establishing the lineage of Russia's alternative political culture. If an alternative tradition can be traced through one or more of these three categories, the case for the depth and durability of democratic aspirations in Russian society is strengthened. Later I shall discuss symphonia, the alternative ideal of church-state relations, and the alternative national identity inspired by Slavophile thinkers, but first I will address the Russian concept of constrained autocracy.

At first glance, autocracy seems to bear little resemblance to ethnicity. Almond's broad usage of the latter term to encompass the traits, customs, and beliefs common to a particular ethnic group, however, indicates that ethnicity can be manifested in a number of ways, including culture, literature, music, language, or even political heritage. Indeed, as we shall see, subjectivists will often portray Russia's political heritage as so distinctive that it becomes, for all intents and purposes, synonymous with its ethnic identity.

Among political scientists, Stephen White has offered the most consistent defense of this position, and it is worth discussing his views in some detail. White sees autocracy as the defining principle in Russia's political history. Traditionally, he says, Russians have viewed citizenship not as a legal expression of independent spheres but as submission to a patrimonial authority. Political institutions, especially those which might aggregate popular demands and constrain the exercise of monarchical power, were always weak and poorly articulated. The Russian government, by contrast, was highly centralized and extensive in scope. Hence the political attachments of the majority of the citizen body were predominantly to the tsar himself, rather than to institutions within which popular sovereignty might have reposed, or to parties which might have competed for representation within them.[2]

Beyond this, White argues that absolutism was supported by an extensive "social fabric" composed of the gentry, the bourgeoisie or merchant class, and the peasantry. He underscores the absence of attempts by any of these groups to institutionalize opposition to the intrusive role of the state, and he finds this quite distinctive from the rest of Europe. Although a few popular institutions, such as the peasant *mir* (self-regulating peasant communities, increasingly common after the sixteenth century, responsible for preserving public order, regulating land use, and collecting taxes), sought independence from the state, White contends that it was widespread ignorance, conservatism, and a respect for patriarchal authority and collective consensus that ultimately frustrated their autonomy.

As a result, the principle of autocratic rule became identified with legitimate government for most Russians. Because Russia's very survival as a nation often depended on a centralized, autocratic government, Russian national identity, unlike that of Western Europe, became firmly fixed in authoritarian moorings. According to White, the absence, weakness, or lateness of institutional constraints upon the monarch exemplifies a "distinctive and deeply-rooted pattern of orientation to government" that he terms the "traditional Russian political culture."[3] These values are encapsulated in Count Sergey Uvarov's celebrated formula *samoderzhavie, pravoslavie, narodnost* (autocracy, Orthodoxy, nationality), which White says provided "the most distinctive contribution of the old regime to the political culture of the Soviet regime which succeeded it."[4]

Among historians, perhaps the most influential exponent of the view that Russia has a "very peculiar history, distinct from the rest of the world," is the historian Richard Pipes.[5] Pipes also describes the Muscovite system of

government as "patrimonial." The tsar's absolute and unconstrained authority rested upon his ownership of the country's resources, down to his individual subjects. As a result of this concept of patrimonial ownership, a tsar
could demand unlimited service from his subjects, who, for their part, lacked
any collective or individual rights.[6]

According to Pipes, patrimonial institutions have survived for so long that
they are now accepted as legitimate by the Russian people. It is this legitimacy that explains the stability of the Soviet regime. Indeed, Pipes says:

> A seventeenth-century Russian resuscitated today in Moscow . . . would not
> find the system all that different or hard to understand. There is a tsar, only he
> is called the general secretary, there are his boyars — the Politburo, indeed the
> whole nomenklatura — and there is no private property, naturally; law is what
> the authorities state they want you to do and, if they can enforce it, you do it.
> Moreover, you can no more think of changing the government than you can
> of changing the climate.[7]

Yet like the revisionist historians whom he criticizes for overlooking the
historical links between the "popular" October Revolution and the repressive regime that emerged from it, Pipes is unable to see the links that tie the
demise of the communist regime to earlier indigenous traditions. As a result,
his patrimonial view of Russian politics fails to account for the relatively
smooth transition to democracy that has taken place since 1991.

No doubt, there is much in Russian history that supports Pipes's and
White's interpretation. Russian tsars, particularly after Peter the Great,
certainly *wanted* to be viewed as absolute monarchs.[8] Although Peter was
the first to define his powers as unrestricted, subsequent Russian rulers
followed his example and attempted to formalize this view into a doctrine
of monarchical absolutism that far exceeded anything in Russian life before Peter.

But exclusive attention to the powers claimed by the tsar gives us a rather
one-sided view of prerevolutionary Russian society, for it ignores the rich
array of community-based and religious welfare institutions that James
Billington and S. Frederick Starr have repeatedly called to our attention.[9]
Formal institutions, such as the ones White and Pipes emphasize, are not
the only possible form of constraint that society may exert upon a monarch.
The British system of government, for example, has few formal constraints
upon the power of the sovereign, and even fewer specific guarantees of
rights for subjects. What is essential in Britain is custom. Similarly, in its
day-to-day affairs the Russian monarchy frequently confronted, and succumbed to, traditional customs and constraints.[10] Russian literature, folk
history, and even foreign memoirs are replete with examples of the ineffec-
tiveness of the bureaucracy and the moderating influence of popular tradi-

tion and culture. Taken together, these yield an alternative definition of the proper role of the autocrat in Russian political culture.

The Petrine principle of autocratic absolutism never went unchallenged in Russia. Criticism of it was regularly accompanied by references to prior eras and to better rulers from the past who were more responsive to the public. Because the same criticisms and alternatives reappear over the course of centuries, it is plausible to suppose that their appeal is rooted in an alternative strand of political culture.

In this alternative view the autocrat's duty was to ensure domestic tranquility and good government. If he failed to do so, however, the right to establish a new governmental compact resided with the people. As the nineteenth-century Russian historian Nikolai Kostomarov writes, "The right of the land as a supreme authority unto itself is evident throughout pre-Mongol Russia. The land [*zemlya*] must have its prince, for otherwise existence as a land was unthinkable. Where a land existed so did a veche, and where a veche existed there would have to be a prince chosen by the veche. The land was an authority unto itself; the veche was the expression of that authority; and the prince was its administrator."[11] In contrast to the prevailing view that nationality and religion served only to prop up the autocracy, I suggest that they constrained the autocracy by emphasizing the monarch's accountability to the popular will and to the Church.

Since scholars generally acknowledge that Kievan Rus was democratic on a scale comparable to its Western European contemporaries, I shall begin tracing the ideal of constrained autocratic rule with the Muscovite period of Russian history. For the same reason, I will deal only cursorily with the initiatives of the State Duma created in 1905, which is commonly acknowledged as the high point of Russian constitutionalism. The key to understanding the continuity of Russia's alternative political culture, it seems to me, lies in showing what unites these two historically distant epochs.

"The Voice of the People Is the Voice of God"

The gathering of Russian lands under the princes of Muscovy, as Vasiliy Klyuchevskiy has noted, was accomplished by creating a perpetual military system. Almost constantly at war on south, east, and west, Muscovy sought to establish the closest thing it could to a standing army, a concept previously unknown in Europe. In turn, this required a reliable system of taxation and an ever growing role for the state. The obligation to defend the state originally fell upon the gentry and the peasantry in equal measure, but it led to peasant enserfment when the latter's customary right to leave the service of the gentry once a year was abolished in 1649. George Vernadsky sums up the consensus among Russian historians when he writes, "Autocracy and serfdom were the price the Russian people had to pay for their national self-preservation."[12]

This slow ascendancy of the autocrat did not go unchallenged, however. Early tsars felt morally bound by established customs and traditions to listen to and carry out the verdicts of the *Boyar duma* (a council of senior noblemen). In times of crisis the tsar was expected to convoke a "Council of All the Land" to advise him on policy. These councils, known as *zemskie sobory*, were to be the voice of the people offering the monarch essential guidance and ratifying his decisions. In the nineteenth century the same principle would reassert itself in the form of *zemskie sobraniya*, more commonly known in English as the zemstvo movement.

Unlike Western parliaments, the zemskie sobory (sometimes referred to in English as "popular councils") emerged not from grievances expressed by the gentry but from the tsar's well-established custom of consulting "good and sensible persons" chosen by the people to advise him on matters of domestic and foreign policy. The first recorded popular council coincides with Ivan IV's adoption of the new title "tsar" in 1547 and clearly reflects an attempt to re-establish for all of Muscovy the semidemocratic practices customary in Kievan Rus.[13] Although White views the popular council as nothing more than an "embryonic parliament" whose members saw themselves as performing a state function rather than exercising a right, those on the council were, nevertheless, elected popular representatives who met frequently during the sixteenth and seventeenth centuries to help determine national policy.[14]

It was the "Time of Troubles" (1598–1613), however, that formalized the function of these councils. This most dangerous period in Russian history began when the last tsar of the Ryurik dynasty died, leaving no heir and no will. Taking advantage of the prolonged domestic turmoil, Polish-Lithuanian forces invaded Russia and, in 1610, occupied Moscow. In 1611, the rich Baltic principality of Novgorod fell to the Swedes. To save the Russian nation, the hierarchs of the Orthodox Church, under the guidance of Patriarch Hermogen, began a nation-wide campaign to defend the Church and the nation. Cities and monasteries around the country began to collect funds for a national militia. After an initial failure, this militia gathered in the central Russian town of Yaroslavl in April 1612 and formed a provisional government consisting of noblemen and elected representatives from major cities and peasant communities.[15]

After liberating Moscow from the Poles in 1613, the provisional government took upon itself the task of electing a new tsar. The precedent for popular election of the sovereign had been well established during Kievan times, and just fifteen years earlier the nobleman Boris Godunov had been elected tsar by a popular council representing all social ranks and all cities in the Muscovite kingdom.[16] The electoral proclamation of that council, authored by its head, Patriarch Job, reaffirmed the principle of popular election of the sovereign with the famous phrase, "The voice of the people is the voice of God [*glas bo naroda — glas Bozhiy*]."[17]

The provisional government set up an elaborate electoral system to ensure that the newly established royal house met with popular approval. The historian Sergei Pushkarev writes:

> [In October] the elected representatives from every rank of the military, from the cities and the northern peasant communities, from the . . . Moscow region, and from the Don Cossacks in camp near Moscow were summoned to the Council. In December elected representatives began gathering in Moscow. In January and through the beginning of February they held lengthy and difficult discussions, and finally agreed on the candidacy of sixteen-year-old Mikhail Fedorovich Romanov, a member of a popular noble family. Then a sort of referendum was arranged: the Council sent emissaries around to the cities to find out how people in outlying areas felt about the candidacy of Mikhail. The emissaries brought back affirmative responses, and in February of 1613 Mikhail was proclaimed "tsar of all Rus."[18]

Some historians have called Michael Romanov's "marriage to the kingdom" a "constitutional contract" with his subjects.[19] Although this is perhaps too strongly stated, the election of the tsar certainly confirmed the principle that the legitimacy of the autocracy rested, as Paul Dukes observes, "on the foundation of an informal contract with the boyars and other members of the gentry."[20]

Having served its function in establishing the monarchy, however, the popular council did not disband but continued to serve as the deliberative body of government. Subsequent sessions generally consisted of two bodies. The first, a gathering of the Duma nobles and high-ranking clergy, included both hereditary and appointed members. The second, a body of elected representatives, consisted of the military, city people, representatives from the Moscow "Black Hundreds" (the term for the impoverished street people), and representatives from outlying regions of the country. Although the peasantry had no distinct representation, their views were heard through the all-district mirs of the northern regions of Russia, which elected representatives jointly with the townspeople.

The popular councils played a decisive role in the passage of decrees on such matters as the organization and consolidation of government (1550); the rejection of an unfavorable peace proposal made during the Livonian War (1566); a review of whether or not the country should go to war with

Poland (in 1632 and again in 1634); the rejection of the tsar's seizure of the fortress of Azov for fear that it would precipitate a war with the Crimean khanate (1643); and the convocation of a special assembly (the *Ulozhennyi sobor* of 1648–1649) to draw up a new legal code. The consent of a popular council, for example, was considered essential before replying to Bohdan Khmelnitksy's request in 1653 for assistance in freeing the Ukraine from Polish domination, for Russian participation would launch a long and costly war with the Polish-Lithuanian kingdom. Thus, though it is true that the councils had no formal charter or authority, Muscovite tsars relied on them to provide legitimacy for actions that might prove unpopular, particularly wars. What some scholars have characterized as an inadequacy of Russian political development compared with the West—the lack of institutional-ized antagonism between estates—actually reflects a conscious choice to es-chew confrontation between social classes and to favor a blending of inter-ests that might combine the advantages of both autocracy and democracy.

It was, however, the lack of a formal process requiring consultation that eventually led tsars to dispense with seeking the advice of the popular coun-cils. By the mid-seventeenth century only senior members of the military and urban merchants were summoned for such consultations. As its admin-istration grew more extensive, and the monarchy more stable and prosper-ous, the government had less and less reason to listen to its subjects. The right of the popular council to elect the tsar was finally revoked in 1722 by Peter the Great.

Opposition to Tsarist Absolutism after Peter

It was Peter I (the "Great") who introduced the principle of absolutism, as distinct from autocracy, into Russia. To break with the corrupting influence of the past and establish a more modern, Western-style state, Peter instituted a number of innovations designed to recast Russian society. By introducing a new oath of loyalty to "the king and the whole kingdom" *(na vernost gosu-daryu i vsemu gosudarstvu),* Peter tried to replace the traditional Russian no-tion that government should be based on personal obligations between the monarch and his subjects with a government based on rational, impersonal administrative practices.[21] In so doing he sought to unfetter the monarchy from the customary bonds of respect for tradition and custom that had al-ways limited its scope of action.

Peter took an important step in breaking with traditional constraints in 1722, when he abolished the feudal system that obligated the tsar to respect hereditary ranks when rewarding service to the state *(mestnichestvo).* By rid-ding himself of this constraint Peter eroded the cohesion and local attachments of the gentry, forcing them to be more dependent upon the crown. He then further diluted the distinctiveness of the gentry by allowing anyone in society the opportunity to achieve noble rank through government service. By the end of the nineteenth century the social standing of the hereditary gentry, the intelligentsia, and the professional classes of Russian society would be virtually indistinguishable.

The next great constraint Peter rejected was the customary tutelage of the Orthodox Church. In 1721 he abolished the patriarchate and replaced it with a Holy Synod chaired by a governmentally appointed lay person. Peter thus made the Church an arm of the state and obligated it to play an active role in support of the policies of the monarch. This "westernization" of church-state relations greatly eroded the Church's ability to carry out its traditional function of acting as a moral restraint upon the monarch. "In place of the most pious tsar," writes the noted Church historian Anton Kartashev, "we find the sovereign emperor, wearing a European-style military uniform, residing at the Western extremity of his empire, isolated from the spiritual and religious life of his people."[22]

The subjugation of the Church to the state was a necessary step in consolidating Peter's vision of an absolute and unconstrained monarchy. In his "Spiritual Regulation" abolishing the patriarchy, Peter specifically cites the need to reinforce the single authority of the autocrat and to counter the popular perception that the patriarch "is a second ruler equal to the Autocrat, and perhaps even more than he is, and that spiritual rank is another and better kingdom."[23]

In the absence of these two all-important customary constraints on the monarchy—the blessing of the Church and the confirmation of "all the land" (a common phrase used to designate the popular councils, along with other elected or designated community representatives)—the tsar's legitimacy came to rest exclusively on the protection he could offer his subjects. This shift in the basis of the tsar's authority was further elaborated by the tsar's chief adviser on ideological and theological matters, Feofan Prokopovich (1681–1736), who likened a monarch's authority over his subjects to the authority of a father over his children. Prokopovich, who had studied in Poland and Rome, played a key role in abolishing the patriarchate and also in changing the law of monarchical succession to allow the reigning monarch to appoint his own successor.[24]

Peter's efforts to unfetter the monarchy from the constraints of tradition, however, did not go unchallenged. The gentry and the common populace reacted with resentment and confusion. In response to Peter's efforts to force a more rapid pace of westernization, civic associations spontaneously formed in the larger urban centers and among the northern peasantry (the former Novgorod lands) to defend their traditional customs, way of life, and self-government against state intrusion.[25] The most stalwart champions of traditional Russian customs, as the German historian Hans-Joachim Torke notes, were the Old Believers: "The conscious, deliberate, and stead-fast determination of the Old Believers to keep popular culture separate from the new elite culture gave rise to 'two nations,' two cultural universes, between which there was little if any exchange, even though residents of both worlds met daily and maintained constant communication."[26] Among the best-educated and most entrepreneurial groups at this time, the Old Believers managed to preserve portions of this alternative cultural heritage well into the latter half of the nineteenth century.[27]

The rift that resulted between Russia's traditional political culture and Peter's new vision could not have been more damaging to society. For half a century after his death, until the reign of Catherine II (the "Great," 1762–1796), palace coups seeking to restore the customary right of the gentry were commonplace. Keenly aware of the possibility of insurrection, Catherine quickly realized that she would have to forge an alliance with the gentry if she wished to rule. A devoted disciple of Montesquieu, Voltaire, and the French *Encyclopedistes,* Catherine was hardly prepared to abandon Peter's project for a traditional conception of constrained autocracy that she had little understanding of and even less sympathy for. Nevertheless, for the sake of self-preservation she was willing to restore some of the gentry's traditional privileges, and invited them to share in the responsibility of governing.

In 1766, therefore, Catherine created an elected legislative commission to help her rule the country, restoring to the gentry, townspeople, and peasants living on state lands some sense of involvement in politics. Of the 565 elected commissioners, only 28 represented state institutions. The rest were elected representatives from various groups of the population. The gentry elected one deputy from each *uyezd,* or district, city-dwellers one from each city, state peasants one from each province. In addition, there were special provisions for the representation of ethnic minorities, Cossacks, and lower-level public servants. In all, 30 percent were representatives of the gentry, 39 percent urban-dwellers, 14 percent state peasants, 5 percent government institutions, and 12 percent others.[28] Interestingly, the petitions submitted by this "embryonic electorate," as the historian Marc Raeff calls it, sought first and foremost a precise definition of their legal rights and status.[29]

Catherine's next step was to decentralize the state apparatus by allowing police, social welfare, and local governance to be administered by the local gentry. This stimulated gentry concern for local politics and helped to foster a sense of group identity and common interests. It also gave a public voice to a constituency that clearly preferred a more restrained and passive government. As Raeff notes, "The newly acquired esprit de corps helped to check the arbitrariness and brutality of tyrannical local officials, at least when it came to dealing with titled luminaries and wealthy merchants. Psychologically more secure, members of the elite now felt freer to embark on new ventures. Above all, they were able to form their own judgments, develop their own attitudes, and live in a way that was not dictated by the sovereign or imposed by fiat."[30]

Representatives of the gentry soon became local judges and administrators. They stimulated the regional interests that would eventually lead to conflict with the central administration in St. Petersburg and to calls for even greater local self-government and decentralization. Catherine's final step was to grant the gentry a charter listing the rights and privileges that set it apart from other groups in society. This charter also made permanent the electoral assemblies that had been set up in 1767 to compose the legislative commission.

Given these opportunities, why did the gentry fail to develop an independent corporate stance vis-à-vis the monarchy? One reason certainly is that the intentions of the charter remained largely unfulfilled. At the same time that authority was nominally being transferred to local regions, Catherine and her successors were greatly expanding the size and role of the provincial civil service. The gentry soon came to view election to local government as simply another administrative burden imposed by the state, and it devoted its ingenuity to finding ways to avoid it.[31]

But this criticism also reflects a misunderstanding of the purpose of the Charter for the Gentry. What the gentry sought was not a perpetual struggle over rights and responsibilities with the monarchy, but a restoration of the *status quo ante* Peter. With the passage of the charters, in fact, the gentry succeeded in obtaining what it wanted most — de facto recognition by the monarch that the gentry should be co-responsible for ruling Russia. As the Soviet historian V. N. Bochkarev writes, "In this alliance . . . the actual power of many small autocrats aimed at replacing the power of the great autocrat and restricting the limits of his freedom . . . Servilely declaring itself a nonentity before the boundless power of the all-Russian autocracy, the *dvoryanstvo* [gentry] was convinced that it alone held on its shoulders both the state and even the very power of the monarch . . . It had to penetrate into all organs of administration and unremittingly watch over every step of government."[32]

Catherine's reign is generally regarded as the high point of absolutism in Russia, and yet it was an absolutism constrained by dependence upon the gentry. In some respects, as Helju Bennet argues, the Russian gentry's charter of rights even went beyond anything subsequently obtained by the nobility of Europe.[33] By restoring the traditional role of the gentry, Catherine had forged a contract that now made it mutually advantageous for the monarchy and the gentry to safeguard each other's interests.

The precise nature of this contract, however, would be variously interpreted by Russian society over the next century. Whereas the gentry interpreted it as requiring further institutional constraints upon the monarchy, the tsars claimed that service to the state should now be equated with service to the monarch. In the absence of an adequate legislative and institutional framework within which to resolve such disputes, these two sharply contrasting visions of the role of government could only lead to direct confrontation. Hence, Catherine's tacit recognition that she was *not* unconstrained sowed the seeds from which direct challenges to the autocracy would subsequently emerge.

The absence of effective institutional constraints upon the monarchy, however, does not mean that the gentry never tried to impose such constraints. Shortly after Peter's death, for example, Prince D. M. Golitsyn organized a supreme privy council composed of six to eight nobles, all holding the highest civil service ranks. Inspired by the Swedish Constitution of 1720, the privy council sought to curtail the legislative power of the monarch and to separate legislative authority from administrative authority.

The councilors seized the opportunity of Peter II's death in 1730 to install Empress Anne and impose formal conditions limiting her power. In the charter they drafted, the armed forces were placed under the control of the council and the empress was forbidden to conclude any military treaties, introduce new taxes or spend state revenue, make any senior civilian or military appointments, deprive any member of the nobility of life or property without trial, or enact land grants or villages without the consent of the council. Anne was to promise not to marry and not to nominate a successor. Failure to comply with these conditions would result in forfeiture of the crown.

Golitsyn hoped that these restrictions would be a first step in the direction of serious constitutional reform. Apart from the privy council, whose members would be expanded to twelve, there was to be a senate of some thirty–thirty-six members, a two-hundred-member chamber of the gentry, and a chamber of town representatives. Reflecting a rudimentary sense of checks and balances, the senate would offer preliminary consultation on legislative matters, while the other two chambers were to defend the rights of their estates and safeguard the interests of commercial groups and common people against the excesses of the privy council. Golitsyn's attempt to impose a new structure of government failed to gain the support of the nobility, however. Sergei Utechin speculates that Golitsyn's secrecy about his ultimate objectives contributed mightily to suspicion about his aims.[34]

One can derive a good sense of the gentry's attitude toward the monarchy from a fascinating contemporary document entitled "The Unrestrained and Concerted Discourse and Opinion of the Congregated Russian Gentry on State Government." Its principal author, V. N. Tatishchev, was a civil servant who had at one point risen as high as provincial governor. This document tells us a great deal about the Russian gentry's perception of the ultimate source of legitimate political authority.[35]

The essay begins by asking where political authority resides in the event that a monarch dies leaving no heirs. Tatishchev unequivocally answers, "in the people." Existing institutions retain power solely for the purpose of preserving public order until a new legitimate authority is established. Tatishchev then asks who has the authority to amend ancient law or custom. Again, the answer is "only the people as a whole." The new monarch must therefore be elected by consent of all subjects ("all the land"), either personally or through delegation. It is precisely because Golitsyn and the conspirators failed to consult the populace that Tatishchev condemns their actions while agreeing with their principles.

Although Tatishchev remained convinced that monarchy is the system best suited to large states with external enemies, he nevertheless proposes that the supreme council be replaced by two chambers that would assist the monarch in governing. The upper chamber should draft laws and present them for confirmation to the empress. The lower chamber would deal with the "internal economy." Both chambers should meet regularly, and in extraordinary session if war were declared or if the monarch died. Tatishchev also urged that all key civilian and military appointments be made by joint appointment of both chambers, and he ultimately envisioned a constitution that would codify and extend the privileges of the gentry to the clergy and to merchants.

The crisis that surrounded Empress Anne's ascension to the throne demonstrates that Peter's absolutist ideas had only the most superficial hold among the gentry. In times of governmental weakness, the nobility sought to restore the principles that had traditionally inspired Russian political culture—an autocracy constrained by popular will and by religious tradition. Caught between its own inflexible desire to identify the tsar with the state, and the de facto compromises foisted upon it by a radicalized gentry and emerging intelligentsia, the autocracy continued to lose power during the nineteenth century. As a result, future attempts to co-opt the gentry, as Catherine had done, served only to further isolate the monarchy.

The tone for the nineteenth century was set by the young officers who returned from the Napoleonic campaigns. Deeply impressed by French laws and administration, they formed independent officers clubs in many regional centers to emulate French institutions in Russia. The most important of these was the "Union for the Public Good" *(Soyuz Blagodenstviya)*, established in 1818, which sought both to bring "enlightenment" to Russia and to assist the government in "raising Russia to the level of greatness and goodness to which she has been destined by her Creator." The club reportedly had more than two hundred members in St. Petersburg alone.[36]

After the military uprisings against the monarchies in Italy and Spain in 1820 and the unrest in the Semyonov corp (the soldiers of this elite unit rebelled against the brutality of their commander, an incident Alexander attributed to political motives), Tsar Alexander I officially disbanded the Union. Secret societies, however, quickly replaced those that were banned. The two most important of these were the Northern Society in St. Petersburg and the Southern Society near Kiev. Although the character of the two organizations differed—the Northern Society favored a gradual transition to a constitutional monarchy, whereas members of the Southern Society tended to favor abolition of the monarchy and a popularly elected republic—both groups were strongly influenced by the American and French revolutions, down to the adoption of a thirteen-state federal system for the empire.[37]

The reluctance of the tsar's brother, Nicholas, to assume the throne after Alexander's death gave the conspirators the opportunity they were looking for. Their plan was to march on the senate and block the new tsar's coronation (designated for December 14, hence the name "Decembrists") until he signed a manifesto relinquishing much of his power. The manifesto specifically mentioned abolishing serfdom and censorship, equalizing all classes before the law, allowing freedom of religious worship for all faiths, a fair and open trial system, the introduction of elections at all levels of government, and the convention of a "Great Council" *(Velikiy sobor)* that would decide on the most appropriate form of government for Russia.[38] After some initial hesitation Nicholas I was able to rally his loyal troops and crush the rebellion.

For a discussion of political culture, it is noteworthy that within just two generations the Decembrists were lionized as pioneers in the struggle for freedom. A tremendous gap still remained between the aspirations of the populace for freedom and the strivings of the gentry, but the Decembrists showed that the tsar could no longer assume that the gentry implicitly supported the principle of autocracy. Nicholas I's (1825–1855) attempts to impose a narrow view of autocratic privilege, therefore, only exacerbated public discontent, and led to an explosion of semipublic journals and societies that openly challenged the very premises of the autocracy and asked what form of government best suited Russia's needs. The answer of the Russian intelligentsia came in one of two forms, generally designated as *Westernizer* and *Slavophile.*

Westernizers argued that modern civilization reflected a single path of development with Western Europe as its culmination. European civilization had led the world in freedom and progress over the last century. Russia, being at the margins of this development, had just begun to follow this path under Peter the Great. Only by wholeheartedly embracing the European model of development would Russia prosper. Social critics and scholars such as Vissarion Belinsky, Timofei Granovsky, and Konstantin Kavelin popularized these ideas in newspapers, journals, and lectures.

Slavophiles, by contrast, believed that each civilization offered something unique to humanity. They rejected the view that history and culture progressed in a linear fashion, believing that each civilization followed a "natural" path of historical development. Russia's path embraced the Eastern Orthodox faith and the principle of spiritual freedom within a common search for truth known as *sobornost.* A philosophy developed by early Slavophile writers such as Konstantin Aksakov, Aleksey Khomyakov, and Ivan Kireyevsky, sobornost asserted that individual freedom and diversity could thrive only through one's voluntary subordination to absolute values.

Despite the philosophical differences between the Westernizers and the Slavophiles, their political aspirations were never very far apart. To be sure, there were vulgarizers of each position. For some Westernizers, socialism and the revolutionary overthrow of the monarchy seemed the only way to cover the historical gap between Russia and Western Europe. At the other extreme, some Slavophiles embraced the simplistic formula advocated by Minister of Education Count Sergey Uvarov that Russian society should be based on the principles of "autocracy, Orthodoxy, and nationality." In the subsequent interpretation of reactionary ministers frightened by the rise of revolutionary terrorism, these principles became a caricature of what the early Slavophiles had meant. But, beyond the caricatures, leading spokesmen from each group often came to remarkably similar conclusions about what needed to be done. They agreed on the value of public accountability of the bureaucracy, on the importance of personal liberty, individual rights, freedom of the press, and the abolition of serfdom. As Michael Karpovich notes, early Slavophile doctrine was permeated by a profoundly liberal spirit:

> The autocracy they were thinking about was not like that of Nicholas I, with its suppression of public opinion and glorification of bureaucratic control. It was a patriarchal and in a way even a democratic monarchy, serving the cause of social justice and based upon freely-given popular support. Similarly, the Slavophile's conception of Orthodoxy was that of a free and independent

Church which would occupy a leading place in the country's spiritual life because of its inherent strength and not because of governmental protection. And finally, what they wanted was a spontaneous and untrammeled development of Russian nationalism and not a rigid formula of official nationalism forced upon the country from above.[39]

In practice, therefore, both groups recognized the need to constrain absolutism, though they disagreed on what forms that constraint should take. Slavophiles favored custom and tradition over what they considered "artificial" legal institutions, whereas Westernizers promoted the concept of the rule of law and institutionalized constraints upon the monarchy.

It was the Russian writer Fyodor Dostoyevsky who first pointed out the similarity between these two great strands of Russian sociopolitical thought. He attributed their affinity to the fact that both were being subtly guided by the spirit of the people.[40] Indeed, Dostoyevsky's description of this spirit and its role in shaping political discourse is remarkably similar to interpretive political culture's description of how underlying cultural patterns can affect political actions. It was left to the Westernizer Alexander Herzen, however, rather than the Slavophile Dostoyevsky, to capture the essence of the relationship between Westernizers and Slavophiles. Referring to Russia's imperial emblem, the two-headed eagle, Herzen remarked that though one head looked east and the other west, its heart beat as one.

The Zemstvos

The early years of Alexander II's reign (1855–1881) filled Westernizers and Slavophiles alike with hope and expectation. In his first year as tsar, Alexander established a governmental council to elaborate a plan for the abolition of serfdom. Recognizing that the liberation of the serfs would create millions of new electors, the council simultaneously proposed a dramatic expansion of local self-government.

The first step in this direction came in 1864, with the creation of local organs of government known as *zemskie sobraniya*, or, more simply, zemstvos. Russian citizens in zemstvo regions were divided into three electoral curias: local landowners, peasant societies, and city-dwellers, each of which elected its representatives to local zemstvos for a three-year term. The local zemstvo in turn elected an executive consisting of two to six electors and a chairman ratified by the provincial governor. Local zemstvos also elected representatives to the provincial-level zemstvos, which were chaired by a member of the gentry and which, in turn, elected a small executive committee whose chairman was confirmed by the minister of internal affairs in St. Petersburg.

The total number of assemblymen in the original thirty-four provinces where zemstvos were instituted was 13,000. This figure includes 6,200 landowners or representatives of the gentry (48 percent), 5,200 representatives of peasant assemblies (40 percent), and 1,600 urban representatives (12 percent).[41] The original statute permitted zemstvo institutions complete autonomy in the management of zemstvo land and capital; the installation and maintenance of local communications; providing the population with food; charity and church construction; property insurance; the development of local commerce and industry; the organization of public health and education; the issuing of warnings on plants and pests; local military and civilian administration; the appointment, collection, and expenditure of local taxes; and representing local petitioners before central authorities.

Once granted the authority to administer funds and raise taxes, the gentry took a keen interest in local politics. The zemstvos soon attracted the best and the brightest among Russia's newly forming middle class. The social and political mix within local zemstvos, however, varied widely from region to region. Some regions had relatively conservative zemstvos, while in other areas the new political leadership saw the zemstvos as a natural stepping stone to universal suffrage and a constitutional monarchy.

Thus, in 1879, the provincial zemstvos of Tver and Chernigov both presented the emperor with petitions urging him to grant popular representation to the Russian people, as he had just done for the Bulgarians. Their efforts were supported within the tsar's inner circle by Count Mikhail Loris-Melikov. Melikov eventually convinced the tsar to allow zemstvos at all levels to discuss formally how to move the country toward a representative national assembly. This project, known as the "Loris-Melikov Constitution," was terminated in the aftermath of Alexander II's assassination in 1881.

Wherever zemstvo institutions were introduced they quickly became the vehicle for organizing the private and corporate interests of the population — the framework of civil society. Indeed, the zemstvos could not help violating the government's injunction that they limit themselves to issues exclusively within their particular region since almost any project, from building roads to preventing the spread of disease, required joint effort. From their very inception, therefore, the zemstvos served as the vehicle for the sweeping social and political transformation of society.

Sensing what it had unleashed, the government began to curtail the autonomy of the zemstvos through decrees that increased the powers of zemstvo chairmen and the jurisdiction of appointed local governors. In 1890 Alexander III's minister of the interior, Count D. A. Tolstoy, recognizing that the zemstvos had adopted a stance of "systematic opposition to the government," changed the electoral statutes to give the gentry a disproportionate weight in the assemblies. But since it was primarily the gentry re-formers who dominated local politics, his strategy backfired. As soon as Tsar Nicholas II came to power in 1894, he was presented with numerous peti-tions by zemstvo assemblies to convene a popularly elected national as-sembly.[42]

Although Nicholas II did not realize it, any attempt to impose restrictions on the zemstvos was already a hopeless task. Whereas in 1895 the total zem-stvo budget stood at 66 million rubles, by 1914 it had grown to more than 347 million. It is largely because of the zemstvos that public education, med-ical care, and agricultural support became major government expenditures. The following figures for 1914 illustrate just how significant zemstvo expen-ditures (not including revenues from trade and insurance activities) had be-come in the forty-three provinces of European Russia:

Expenditure	Million rubles	Percentage of zemstvo budget
Education	107.0	30.8
Medical care	82.6	23.8
Agronomy and economic measures	28.9	8.2
Local administration	23.4	6.7
Roads	17.5	5.0
Veterinary services	10.5	3.0
Public welfare	5.1	1.5
Other (including service on debt and contributions to central government expenditures)	72.5	21.0
	347.5	100.0[43]

By 1914, the zemstvo institutions that Tsar Alexander II had established as a means of increasing administrative efficiency had introduced local self-government to 112 million people, more than 65 percent of the population. In the waning years of the empire, the budget of the zemstvo provinces would grow at nearly twice the rate of the state budget.[44] As the influence of the zemstvo in the political life of the country grew, so, inevitably, did its conflict with the autocracy.

Civil Society Demands a Constitution

There can be no better proof of Russia's ripeness for constitutional monar-chy at the turn of century than the fact that, when activists failed to convince Nicholas II to voluntarily adopt a constitution, they first used the zemstvos to apply pressure on the monarch. Although proposals for a constitution had abounded during the nineteenth century, they had come mostly from the gentry and senior government officials. What made these new appeals different (and ultimately irresistible) was the direct support of large segments of the population galvanized by the zemstvos.[45]

Boycotts and demonstrations became commonplace occurrences after 1901. The tactic began in 1899 when, following the government's restrictions on university autonomy, students at St. Petersburg University declared a strike which soon engulfed other Russian universities and institutions of higher learning.[46] In 1903, a general strike in southern Russia shut down most of the country's industry for weeks. By 1905 more workers had participated in strikes in Russia than in any other country up to that time.[47]

Such massive and nationally coordinated labor activity required the formation of unions. Although legally recognized only in 1906, professional associations had, in fact, begun to organize spontaneously more than a year earlier. This explains how the *Unionist Herald,* the official organ of the trade union movement, could write of the existence of 652 trade unions with nearly a quarter of a million members just months after the passage of legislation first allowing for the creation of unions. In short order a Union of Unions was formed, calling for elections to a constituent assembly by "universal, direct, equal and secret" ballot.[48]

By early 1904 any public gathering seemed a good excuse to adopt a political resolution. A typical example is the resolution passed by the Pirogov Congress of Physicians at their 1904 congress in St. Petersburg. In the section dealing with social medicine, internal medicine, and tuberculosis, the physicians noted that "the sound and proper fight against infant mortality, tuberculosis, syphilis, and other common diseases, representing in Russia social ills of great importance, is possible only under conditions guaranteeing the broad spread of information about their causes and prevention, and for this, full freedom of person, speech, and assembly are necessary prerequisites."[49]

Remarkably, all this civic activity among various groups remained tightly focused on the need to institutionalize representative government. Even two bulwarks of the autocracy, the Holy Synod and the bureaucracy, publicly declared themselves for self-government.[50] But what made the current social movement for constitutional reform successful was not the appeals of the intelligentsia and the gentry, nor even the haphazard and inept administration of censorship and police controls, but rather the engagement of Russia's civil society. As Terrence Emmons points out, "Administrative, educational, and economic development combined to produce a civil society of sufficient size and autonomy to challenge the regime's monopoly on political authority."[51]

The zemstvos thus served as the primary mechanism by which various segments of the population participated in local government, and by which various social classes carved out spheres of political influence distinct from, and often in opposition to, the government. The famous opposition lawyer and political activist Vasiliy Maklakov called them Russia's "school of constitutionalism . . . Constructed on the idea of popular sovereignty [narodopravstva], their natural evolution led to the Constitution. The very shape their activities took — collegial, public, responsible executive organs — made the zemstvos resemble a parliament. They became the prototype for the State Duma, just as the zemstvo activists became the forerunners of future deputies."[52] Only during Prime Minister Peter Stolypin's brief reign (1906–1911), however, did the government actually encourage the zemstvo, expanding it to nine more provinces and directing government ministries to be more receptive to requests from the local level. After Stolypin's assassination, the government returned to its short-sighted policy of regarding the zemstvo as its ideological enemy, all the while relying on it to organize relief supplies and munitions for the country's war effort against Japan.

Thanks to the lessons learned at the zemstvo level, by the turn of the century the aspirations of Russian civil society could no longer be derailed. In 1903 a radical group among the zemstvo technical staff, the "Zemstvo Constitutionalists," managed to push through resolutions in the majority of local zemstvos calling for some form of constitutional government. In November 1904 representatives from across the empire met illegally, but quite openly, for the First All Russian Zemstvo Congress, and adopted a resolution calling for constitutional government.[53] In May 1905 the tsar was forced to hear the petition of the Third Zemstvo Congress for transition to a constitutional form of government, and on October 5, 1905, the tsar promulgated the historic edict accepting a constitutional monarchy.

Most zemstvo leaders had hoped to work together with the government to smooth society's transition from absolutism to constitutionalism. They supported the monarchy and wished to see it survive as a source of continuity and stability for the nation. This emphasis on continuity, however, became both an asset and a liability to the zemstvo movement. It encouraged political leaders to seek a gradual transition to nonauthoritarian government, and encouraged popular involvement in accomplishing this transition. The bloodless revolution of October 1905, which replaced the autocracy with a constitutional monarchy, was, in no small measure, the result of the preparatory work of the zemstvos. Yet its very success highlighted Nicholas II's intransigence, shortsightedness, and weakness. It pointed out society's deep contradictions, later seized upon by revolutionaries and exacerbated by the monarch's efforts to rescind his concessions to Russian civil society. By delaying the institutionalization of popular aspirations for a constrained autocracy, Nicholas II did much to bring about the monarchy's demise.

"A Hundred Thousand Peasant Republics"

Special mention must be made of the political aspirations of the peasantry, who numbered more than ninety million, constituting a large percentage of the total population of the empire. To facilitate tax collection, local institutions of self-government had been established in rural areas at the end of the eighteenth century. In larger villages every ten households had a *desyatskiy,* or ward head, who acted as liaison to the local administration, whereas smaller villages simply elected a *starosta,* or elder. Regional administration was conducted by the *volost,* an administrative unit comprising no more than three thousand males. As the population grew, the volost came to be headed by a peasant assembly elected for three-year terms. Such assemblies in turn elected two trustees to the volost court, which was presided over by the head of the assembly.

This experience with self-government prepared the peasantry well for the time when they would take their place alongside the gentry in local zemstvos. The Slavophile writer and political activist Aleksandr Koshelev describes his astonishment at the opening session of the zemstvo assembly in Ryazan province in the summer of 1865: "The peasant assemblymen, who had been our serfs yesterday, took their seats among us simply and without ceremony, as if they had been sitting there forever. They listened to us attentively and asked us for explanations of what they did not understand, and came to sensible agreements with us."

Sir Donald Mackenzie Wallace, a British author and journalist who spent nearly six years in Russia, describes the zemstvo assembly in Novgorod province in similar terms:

> What especially surprised me at these assemblies was that, being composed partly of nobles and partly of peasants (the latter being a majority), there were no traces of antagonism between the classes. The masters and their former serfs, freed only ten years before, were at that moment meeting on an equal basis. It was primarily nobles who conducted the discussion of issues, but on many occasions representatives of the peasants spoke out; their remarks were always clear, practical and relevant, and were listened to with great attention.[54]

Like the gentry, the peasantry showed little interest in politics so long as the government restricted their electoral representation. The 1861 "Statute on Peasants Who Are No Longer Dependent Serfs" gave the peasantry complete jurisdiction over the election of all officials, all matters relating to membership in the mir, the apportionment of taxes, the fulfillment of military service, the raising and expenditure of local taxes, money lending and assistance to the needy, and the appointments of legal guardians for minors. Although the peasantry as a whole may have been less interested in politics than other segments of the population, they displayed a keen interest in matters that directly affected their well being, such as the abolition of class distinctions, access to educational facilities, freedom of speech, press, and association, and, of course, land reform.

According to Terrence Emmons, when it appeared that the Duma would indeed take up the issue of land reform, the "peasants took a lively interest in the elections . . . and sent to the provincial electoral assemblies, and thence to the Duma, a considerable number of alert representatives who were prepared to pursue peasant interests aggressively."[55] Conversely, when their ability to participate in the political process was curtailed during elections to the Third and Fourth Dumas, peasant interest in the electoral process waned and peasant radicalism increased.

This pattern of peasant voting shows that even among the least-educated portions of the Russian population the concept of political representation of corporate interests was well understood by the turn of the century. As Walkin points out, "The extraordinary activity in education and organization during the Duma period cannot, in fact, be explained without the great interest in both generated among the peasants by the hectic events of the [pre–1905] revolutionary period."[56] After the fall of the monarchy, the interests of the peasantry quickly expanded to embrace issues of more general concern to society. The historian Marc Ferro conducted a survey of the first hundred motions made by peasant councils in March and April 1917 which shows that, after the seizure of state lands and the lands of large propertyholders (with compensation), the most commonly mentioned issue was the establishment of a democratic republic, followed closely by motions for a quick and just peace with Germany.[57]

All these activities belie the common perception of an ignorant and apathetic peasantry unconcerned with politics. As Pitirim Sorokin once remarked, it would be more accurate to say that "under the iron roof of an autocratic monarchy there lived a hundred thousand peasant republics."[58]

The Strengths and Weaknesses of Russian Civil Society (1905–1917)

On October 17, 1905, Russia formally became a constitutional monarchy. Tsar Nicholas's proclamation marked the end of absolutism and established a representative, popularly elected assembly to constrain it—the State Duma. It also granted extensive civil liberties, including freedom of conscience, speech, assembly, and association, and established the principle that no law could take force without the approval of the State Duma.[59]

According to the Basic State Laws issued on April 23, 1906, to give substance to the October Manifesto, "supreme autocratic power" remained in the hands of the tsar. Over the objection of Nicholas II, however, the word "unlimited" in the draft had been removed in the final version. The Basic Laws go on to state that the authority to govern "in its totality" rests with the sovereign, but that the sovereign is required to exercise legislative power "in unison with the State Council and the State Duma." Any imperial decree had to be approved by the Duma within two months or it would automatically become invalid. In an effort to restrain the populist impulses of the Duma, the tsar also created a State Council and made it the de facto upper chamber. Members of the State Council were appointed by the tsar and given equal right to approve new legislation.

The October Manifesto was viewed by many segments of Russian society as restoring the balance between autocratic and popular sovereignty, rather than representing a revolutionary break with the past. Indeed, the newly created system was officially described as "a renewed system." The monarchical principle remained prominent but could no longer pretend to be absolute. Perhaps the best indication that this combination did in fact correspond to popular aspirations was the rapid waning of opposition activity after the promulgation of the October decree. The appeals by the more radical *soviets* (workers' and peasants' councils) to overthrow the monarchy had no resonance in Russian society until the tsar attempted to renege on his promises to the people.

The authority of the Duma extended into every aspect of life. It enacted important legislation granting peasants the right to leave the commune and further expanding local self-government. The Duma could also demand a formal justification of government policy from the appropriate minister. Although the Duma could not dismiss members of the government, the publicity the press gave to unsatisfactory answers exerted considerable pressure on the tsar's government.

Despite these powers, however, many scholars still view the Duma as weak and ineffective. Stephen White even goes so far as to suggest that representative institutions were actually losing power during this period.[60] Although there is some evidence to support this view, it must be measured against the impressive gains made by the vast majority of the population. The manifesto of October 17, 1905, and the Constitution of April 23, 1906, guaranteed the inviolability of the person, residence, and property, the right to assemble in public, to organize societies and unions, as well as freedom of religion and the right "to express one's thoughts orally, in writing and in the press."[61] Censorship was limited to those works that attacked the tsar personally (not the principle of monarchy, which was openly derided by the intelligentsia) or reviled the Orthodox faith and Church. As a result, the works of all revolutionary leaders of previous decades were commonly available. In 1912 Lenin began to publish *Pravda,* the organ of the Bolshevik Party, and all attempts to shut it down permanently proved unsuccessful. In addition, speeches in the Duma could not be subjected to censorship, and stenographic accounts were published in the official government newspapers and distributed throughout the country. The Duma's mere existence thus bolstered the public's understanding of both civil and political rights.

Travel abroad was also relatively easy. A passport was usually issued in a matter of days, and a visa consisted of a stamp at the German border crossing. In 1913 alone some nine million persons traveled by rail across the border into Prussia.[62] Finally, the phenomenal growth of industry, investments, and agricultural production during this period must also be attributed to the impact on public life of the Duma and the zemstvo institutions.[63] The most dramatic of these changes was the growth in private peasant land holdings. By 1915, 23 percent of the peasantry had left the communes to become private farmers, and another 20 percent had submitted the paperwork to do so.[64]

The Duma succeeded in shifting the focus of political life in Russia from the local to the national level, immediately and quite self-evidently eclipsing both the zemstvos and the newly organized soviets. The process of voting for national public office helped to develop a sense of political accountability to the populace, even though this sense was severely strained by changes to the electoral law after the Second Duma. If the government expected a compliant Duma after its change in electoral laws, however, it certainly did not get it. Even the progovernment Octobrist Party, thrust into the majority after the electoral law changed, increasingly came to see the need for an effective counterweight to the autocracy. In a famous speech on October 25, 1915, its leader, Alexander I. Guchkov, urged his party to adopt a stance of "direct conflict with the authorities" who were pushing the country toward revolution. To prevent such a revolutionary catastrophe and save the monarchy Guchkov privately hoped for a palace coup along the lines of the Decembrist uprising of 1825.[65]

Finally, the Duma helped to strengthen the public's sense of the rule of law and, most critically, the perception of the tsar as subject to the rule of law. The Basic Laws of April 1906 not only devoted the entire second section to the inviolability of personal rights (the equivalent of the American Bill of Rights), but specifically identified the Russian empire as a state ruled by law. Opposition deputies in the Duma subsequently asserted the view that the tsar was subordinate to the law, and open discussion of this issue had a noticeable impact on political activity. Even the tsar's change of the electoral laws after the Second Duma could not reverse this trend, a fact reflected in the debate that occurred at the very beginning of the Third Duma over how the tsar ought to be addressed. The traditional title, "Autocrat of All Russia," was rejected by the majority, a motion supported, interestingly, by the generally promonarchy Octobrists.[66]

The traditional view of Russian political culture thus clearly overemphasizes the success of the autocracy in shaping popular attitudes, and unrealistically downplays the impact of the alternative Russian political traditions. Despite the opposition of the monarchy, the traditional notion of a constrained monarchy resurfaced frequently in Russian society, promoted at various times by the gentry, the clergy, and the populace. The longevity of this view may be attributed to the existence of an alternative political culture that reinforced the notion of a constrained autocracy as the only legitimate form of rule.

For this alternative political culture, popular support for the tsar was never unconditional. If the monarch failed to live up to popular expectations, then the right to establish a new governmental compact resided with the people. As Hans Rogger reminds us, "Russian autocracy was not an ancient despotism in which neither law nor custom protected persons and property from a totally arbitrary authority."[67] The limits of Muscovite autocracy were quite apparent in the tsar's constant need to appeal for support from various factions of the gentry, who often viewed the tsar as simply *primus inter pares*. It was customary for the boyars to act as advisers to the tsar and to share their concerns on matters of state with him. Administration without the assent of the gentry, in whose hands rested the levers of local government, would have been impossible.

The proper function of autocratic government in Russia was therefore essentially passive. When an Ivan The Terrible or a Peter the Great exceeded his proper authority, Russian society was thrown into turmoil. It is worth noting that both rulers acknowledged that they had broken with tradition and paid a heavy price for it in the eyes of their contemporaries. Toward the end of his life Ivan was so ashamed of the *oprichnina* (his insane reign of terror against the boyars) that he deleted all mention of it from official documents, telling his foreign emissaries to deny it had ever existed. Peter died almost universally reviled by his contemporaries, his death celebrated in a popular woodcut of the time entitled "The mice bury the cat."[68] It is only much later, in the nineteenth century, that the value of Peter's efforts to modernize Russia were appreciated by segments of the intelligentsia.

The great tragedy of Peter's rapid westernization is that it excluded many invaluable groups, such as the Old Believers. By turning away from public life, however, these groups were able to preserve and transmit their own image of "proper" relations between the monarch and his subjects. This view later reasserted itself in the middle of the nineteenth century in Slavophile writings and historiography, and has led to a lasting ambivalence over Peter the Great's ultimate legacy.[69]

The gradual encroachment of the state into the arena of civil society, initiated by Peter, was continually challenged, however. The customary conceptions of governmental legitimacy resurface time and again. It is evident in the wording and tone of Catherine the Great's *Nakaz* (the instructions she composed for the commission set up to formulate a new code of laws; they were deemed so radical that French censors prohibited their distribution in France) and the charters for the gentry and the cities, as well as in the writings of senior advisers close to the throne, and in the political writings of both Slavophiles and Westernizers. Catherine the Great was able to placate the gentry only by granting it a charter of exclusive rights. After this charter, Russian absolutism took the shape of a collective contract between the gentry and the monarch that, in fact, restored the spirit of the *status quo ante* Peter.

After these charters the power of autocracy steadily declined. "The official ideology's poverty, its lack of self-confidence and resonance," Hans Rogger concludes, "stem in part from the regime's lack of a social basis, from its failure to identify itself with a vital social or historical force from which it could have drawn political and moral justification."[70]

By the end of the nineteenth century even stalwart defenders of absolutism, such as Oberprocurator of the Holy Synod Konstantin Pobedonostsev and the philosophy professor Mikhail N. Katkov, began to refer to themselves as "the last of the Mohicans," admitting privately that there was little hope for absolutism.

The image of a vibrant Russian civil society capable of bringing down the monarchy may seem difficult to imagine today, but it was certainly a familiar one to many contemporary observers, including Germany's ambassador to Russia, von Hintze, and President Woodrow Wilson. Most telling of all, though, was Lenin's own assessment of Prime Minister Peter Stolypin's reforms: "There have been occasions in history where such policies have succeeded. It would be empty and stupid democratic phraseology if we were to say that such policies cannot succeed in Russia."[71]

The events of October 1917 took everyone by surprise, not least of all the Bolsheviks. The inept handling of the war, of food distribution in the cities, the collapse of the monarchy, and the internecine fighting within the ranks of the Provisional Government are testimony not to the weakness of Russian democratic aspirations but to the weakness of the institutions established to express these aspirations.

By setting itself apart from and above the traditional political culture, the Russian monarchy heightened the rift between Russia's official political culture embodied in the zemstvo movement. And though the Slavophile reformers tried valiantly to re-establish an organic link with the pre-Petrine past that would preserve the best of both worlds — European modernity and the distinctiveness of Russian culture — ultimately, they failed. Russian civil society was too debilitated by the inflexible view of many Slavophiles that institutionalized constraints typical of the West were an unsatisfactory compromise of lofty principles. A few moderate zemstvo leaders, such as Dimitriy Shipov and A. N. Naumov, tried to promote a form of regionally based representative institutions that we would today call federalism.[72] In the end, however, their efforts seemed contrived and their influence waned. In the twentieth century this view began to change, but not before it was uprooted by the events of October 1917.

The peculiar inability of pre–1917 popular institutions to re-establish their legitimacy during Russia's civil war seems closely related to this rift. Had the reform process begun earlier, the zemstvo movement might have had more time to deepen the role of local government, and it might even have been able to institute a constitutional monarchy earlier. It would be wrong, however, to equate the victory of the Bolsheviks with the demise of Russia's alternative political culture. The traditional aspirations of Russian political culture quickly made themselves felt under Soviet rule.

National Bolshevism and the Search for Legitimacy

Given the disastrous conclusion to Nicholas II's reign and his obstinate refusal to acknowledge Russia's civil society, it may seem surprising that any monarchical ideal at all managed to survive the collapse of the empire. It survived, most obviously, in the Russian emigration, where many leading political thinkers continued to view the ideal of a constrained monarchy as preferable to the shaky and unstable democracies that surrounded them in the West. Typical in this regard is Ivan A. Ilyin, a leading political figure of the interwar period. Ilyin favored a monarchy because it embodied the Russian ideal of government as a spiritual rather than a coercive authority.

According to Ilyin, a Christian monarch assumes power out of a desire to serve, and therefore feels a responsibility in the exercise of power even when no one demands it of him. As such, he can rise above party factionalism, embody the ideals of national unity, and represent a synthesis of social concerns. For Ilyin, as for most émigrés, there is a crucial distinction between an absolute monarch and an autocratic monarch. The latter allows for the existence of civil society, whereas the former does not.

Western scholars were even more surprised, however, to learn that the monarchical ideal had survived inside the Soviet Union, and that it seemed to be especially popular among young people.[73] Sovietologists generally explain these findings as the result of a yearning for "patriarchal authority," overlooking the fact that this represents an astoundingly high reservoir of popular support for an ideal that has no viable pretender to the throne.

The persistence of this autocratic ideal can be explained by two factors. The first is the social chaos and vulnerability that engulfed Russia during the civil war and that plagues it today. Many hoped to bring an end to this second "Time of Troubles" by supporting a strong central authority, since the monarchy has always symbolized stability and continuity in times of crisis.

The second factor is the Bolshevik tactic of staging strategic retreats in order to shore up public support for unpopular policies. A classic example was Lenin's abandonment of war communism in favor of the New Economic Policy (NEP). This respite from utopianism encouraged the intelligentsia to view the new regime as merely a different form of autocracy, one that would eventually be constrained by its sense of obligation to the welfare of the nation. This attempt to wed the notion of autocracy to Soviet institutions is known in Russian as *smenovekhovstvo*, and in English as "National Bolshevism."

The term "National Bolshevism" was first used by Peter Struve to identify those who saw communism as the next, inevitable epoch in Russian history. Fearing that further civil war would only serve to weaken Russia, National Bolsheviks accepted the legitimacy of the communist regime, justified its historical victory, and tried to work within the new system to remove its more cosmopolitan, antinational characteristics. They hoped that the Bolshevik regime would eventually adopt the characteristics of a Russian national state.

National Bolshevism subtly replaced the monarchical principle with the notion of a "guiding" force represented by the Communist Party. This is an important substitution because it highlights both the extent and the limits of the regime's ability to tap into the alternative political culture to bolster its own legitimacy. We shall see this pattern of co-optation repeated in other key areas of Russia's alternative political culture. It explains the survival of many seemingly contradictory combinations of Russian and Soviet political rhetoric in postcommunist Russia.

The National Bolsheviks sought to parry the ideas of the influential *Vekhi* (Signposts) anthology that had appeared in 1909. The *Vekhi* group called on the intelligentsia to reaffirm its ties to nation and state, to reconcile with the Orthodox Church, and to accept the rule of law as the foundation of good government. The National Bolsheviks countered that Russian interests were now de facto being defended by the Soviet regime, and that the past could not be restored. Their "realism" appealed not only to industrialists and military leaders but to political figures weary of conflict on all points of the political spectrum. Even the monarchist leader Vasiliy Shulgin, for instance, wrote in 1920 that "under the cover of Soviet power a process is being completed which has nothing at all in common with Bolshevism . . . The standard of a united Russia has de facto been raised by the Bolsheviks."[74]

An important reason for the sympathy evinced by many who did not share the new regime's ideology was that, in their own way, the Bolsheviks had tapped into the desire of the intelligentsia to heal the rift between the populace and the intelligentsia that had resulted from Peter the Great's forced westernization. In his essay on the origins of Russian communism, Nikolai Berdyaev suggests that the Bolshevik struggle for total control coincided with the Russian intelligentsia's striving for wholeness. By bringing down the old "consecrated" Russian empire, he argues, the Bolsheviks created "an inverted theocracy" whose rhetoric resembled that of the Slavophiles.[75]

Berdyaev was severely criticized in the émigré community for appearing to justify the Bolshevik coup. Still, he is quite correct in pointing out that the measure of popular support the Soviet regime was able to maintain throughout its existence rested largely on Bolshevik efforts to restore a unitary, national, pseudo-religious social identity. Though the Bolsheviks disparaged traditional Russian values and considered them subversive to their ultimate purpose of creating a "new Soviet man," many both in the Soviet Union and abroad convinced themselves that the new regime's antinational fervor would dim after it had consolidated power. The new leadership would eventually have to see the benefits of relying on traditional mainstays of Russian national and cultural identity.

The most important National Bolshevik thinker, Nikolai Ustryalov, actually considered himself a Slavophile. He came from the same political environment as Struve and Bulgakov, namely, the right wing of the Constitutional Democratic Party. "Contemporary Slavophiles," he wrote in 1926, "are not at all concerned with Slavic identity, but insist on the distinctiveness of Russia's historical path and national mission . . . In the Russian Revolution they welcome the obvious signal of a radically new era in the history of humanity."[76]

Ustryalov parted company with contemporary neo-Slavophiles on the issue of religious beliefs. Like Danilevsky before him, he adopted a utilitarian distinction between political and personal morality. Whereas Peter Struve,

Sergey Bulgakov, Semyon Frank, and other leading twentieth-century intellectuals in the tradition of Russia's alternative political culture saw the Bolshevik destruction of the foundations of prerevolutionary society as an absolute evil, for Ustryalov it was only a relative evil because it would ultimately enhance Russia's national greatness.

Tellingly, Ustryalov also applauded Peter the Great's approach to the challenge of transforming society, and described the Bolsheviks as worthy successors of his strand of Russian history.[77] Ustryalov thus deftly replaced the Slavophile aspiration for a free society guided by a common spiritual purpose with a common purpose identified simply as "national greatness." This substitution remains the defining characteristic of National Bolshevik thought to the present day.

Tensions between these two strands of patriotism — that of the alternative political culture and that of the Soviet regime — have generally been minimized by analysts.[78] To many, both in Russia and abroad, Stalin's highly selective embrace of tsarist symbolism and emphasis on Russian leadership in the new Union seemed to confirm the National Bolshevik's view that the regime had finally succumbed to Russian nationalism. The notion that the communist regime now embraced the very same values that it had been trying so hard to eliminate did not seem in the least bit strange to most Sovietologists.

It is important to remember, however, that National Bolshevism originated as a grudging and purely utilitarian acceptance of Bolshevism. Its popular appeal lay in the assumption that communism was only a temporary phenomenon that would inevitably be replaced by another ideal that more accurately reflected the Russian character. For its most prominent advocates, the survival of Russia demanded only loyalty to the state, not to its ideology. This ideal of an autocracy of service, motivated by the welfare of the nation, resonates well with the tradition of a constrained autocracy. Simply put, National Bolshevism offered a way to combine traditional conceptions of legitimate autocratic authority with Soviet institutions.

The best-known modern manifestation of National Bolshevism is The National Patriotic Front "Memory," or *Pamyat*. Pamyat was originally conceived as a movement to preserve Russian cultural and historical inheritance and to raise historical self-awareness among the population.[79] Founded in the early 1980s as a literary-historical society attached to the USSR Ministry of the Aviation Industry, the society arranged meetings with writers, artists, and historians, and helped restore historical and cultural monuments. Being one of the first spontaneously organized groups to address these issues, it quickly won a receptive audience.[80] By late 1984, however, a core of activists within the group, led by the journalist and photographer Dimitriy D. Vasilyev, had developed the notion that a "Zionist-Freemason" conspiracy was leading the Russian people to physical destruction.

The first task Pamyat set for itself was to draw the attention of the public and the Party leadership to the decaying Russian national patrimony. Pamyat then identified the main culprits — Zionists and Freemasons — and called upon the Party to cleanse itself of their pernicious influence. It also offered a specific program aimed at improving the wretched state of Russian life and culture: each person should build a home during his lifetime; ownership of the land should be turned over to those who cultivate it; people should abandon today's mega-cities and "return to the land" en masse; religious believers should be granted complete freedom of conscience; and those responsible for the "criminal slaughter in Afghanistan" should be held accountable. To assist the Party in these tasks, Pamyat called for the establishment of "people's committees for perestroika" *(narodnye komitety perestroiki)* in local institutions, schools, factories, and collective farms. This appeal, penned in December 1987, is strikingly similar to Gorbachev's later call for the establishment of "Popular Fronts in Support of Perestroika."[81]

Pamyat's relations with officialdom have been the subject of considerable debate both inside and outside the Soviet Union. There is impressive circumstantial evidence to support the thesis that local Party officials, particularly in two regions of Leningrad, were not adverse to an alliance with Pamyat.[82] Several prominent Soviet journals have suggested that the frequency and prominence of Pamyat-sponsored events indicate support at high levels. They generally link the ideology of Pamyat to that of outright Stalinists such as Nina Andreyeva.[83]

But while there are similarities between the views of Andreyeva and Pamyat, there are also important differences. Andreyeva, for example, criticizes the advocates of "peasant socialism" who are fascinated by what she calls the "moral values accumulated by peasant communes in the misty fog of centuries." Andreyeva's solutions to the crisis of socialism are clearly not Pamyat's solutions. She has no sympathy at all for revisions of Marx or Lenin, and very little for any revision of Stalin. She denigrates "mystical religious Russian philosophy" and praises "the industrialization, collectivization, and cultural revolution which brought our country to the ranks of great world powers."[84]

It had become apparent by the early 1990s that the Party leadership was using Pamyat primarily to discourage the growth of more moderate patriotic organizations. On Moscow television a citizens' initiative to build a monument to St. Sergey of Radonezh was dismissed by city officials because Pamyat was peripherally involved.[85] An appeal to authorities by the "Russian patriotic public in Leningrad" containing proposals to open private secondary schools and Sunday schools at major churches was also linked to Pamyat and summarily dismissed.[86] At one time or another the Soviet press has accused the historical-cultural groups "Fatherland" (Sverdlovsk), "Salvation" (Leningrad), and "Young Russia" (Moscow) all of being Pamyat affiliates. Only much later were these allegations refuted. By portraying perestroika as the only alternative to either extreme Russian chauvinism or extreme Western (read "Zionist") influence, Gorbachev's approach emerges as the only sensible approach to reform.

Although Pamyat managed to piggyback on the broad public support for the preservation of historical-cultural monuments for a few years, it has clearly failed to elicit any broad constituency for its political agenda. The largest Pamyat demonstration on record, in May 1987 in Moscow, drew no more than four hundred participants, and since 1991 Pamyat has all but disappeared from Russia's political landscape.[87] The failure of Pamyat and similar groups to attract any significant popular following confirms that national extremism, in its National Bolshevik guise, is only a marginal element in Russian political culture. Frederick Barghoorn has aptly termed this group the "pseudo-Slavophiles" as distinct from the true inheritors of the Slavophile tradition.[88]

Yet one should also note the striking similarity between the writings of many contemporary "Russian nationalists" and earlier National Bolshevik authors. Before the collapse of the USSR, prominent writers such as Peter Proskurin, Vadim Kozhinov, Vasiliy Belov, Yuri Bondarev, and Aleksandr Prokhanov all referred to the Soviet regime as the de facto defender of Russian national interests. More recently, the political analyst Sergey Kurginyan and a group of influential National Bolsheviks issued a modern, postcommunist version of this argument in the book *Post-Perestroika*. Summarizing their views, Kurginyan writes, "Yes, the communists are culpable before our culture . . . They are to blame for communist barbarism and for the fact that their assault was the equivalent of the destruction of the values of ancient paganism by the early Christians. We insist, however, that this was a fruitful barbarism, a barbarism of renewal."[89] With the collapse of the economy and the disintegration of the USSR this view seems, if anything, to have gained popularity.

The distance between this attempt to co-opt Russian political culture and the values of the alternative political culture, however, becomes clear when examined in historical perspective. National Bolshevism had virtually no adherents in the political or literary underground after Khrushchev's secret speech. With a few notable exceptions, it found almost no resonance among politically active émigrés, or within the dissident movement.

One can only conclude that National Bolshevism is not, as commonly suggested, deeply rooted in Russian political culture, but is rather a particular ideology whose popularity was directly tied to the fortunes of the Communist Party (CPSU). As a historical phenomenon of the Soviet period, it represented a fragment of Soviet official political culture quite distinct from the alternative tied to the tradition of constrained autocracy. The latter views Marxism-Leninism as the cause of Russia's travails. It rejects Marxism-Leninism for its hostility to religion, and blames the Communist Party for trying to impose a bloody dictatorship against the will of the people. Mainstream Russian nationalists prefer to be called "patriots," a term they feel completely distinguishes them from those who support the official ideology.[90] Whereas National Bolshevism wishes to redefine the role of the official ideology and curtail its deleterious influence, Russian patriots wish to abandon the ideology entirely.

Perestroika itself is perhaps best understood as the last official attempt to resurrect National Bolshevism. In both domestic and foreign policy, Gorbachev's efforts are classic examples of the regime's attempts to popularize socialism by making it seem more attentive to Russian national interests. This explains the overlap between two seemingly distinct political phenomena — Gorbachev's perplexing commitment to the ideals of socialism, and the initial enthusiasm shown by many Russian nationalists for glasnost.

Viewing perestroika as the Party's last attempt to nationalize the Bolshevik ideal goes a long way toward explaining popular ambivalence toward it. On the one hand it fulfilled certain aspirations of civil society by ending overt religious and political persecution. On the other hand, however, it sought to predetermine the outcome of society's search for political alternatives and moved much too erratically and uncertainly to tap into the broad base of popular support for radical reforms.

Despite decades of trying, the Soviet regime ultimately failed in its effort to legitimize the rule of the Communist Party. Although the principle of constrained autocracy could find no practical manifestation under totalitarian conditions, it nevertheless found outlets in underground and émigré circles. Meanwhile, the struggle to constrain the Soviet autocracy and restore Russian civil society continued in two other aspects of the alternative political culture — religion and nationalism.

3

Orthodoxy's Symphonic Ideal:
The Russian Church in Search of Tradition

Everything that had spiritual significance in the history of Russian thought and Russian creativity in the nineteenth century was not with you [socialists], but against you.
— Nikolai Berdyaev

Help us revive all the good things that were lost, all that which made Russia, Russia . . . the Russian spiritual heritage ravaged by a senseless and pitiless ideological struggle.
— Boris Yeltsin

Traditionally, students of political culture have tended to view religion as a purely private matter rather than as a common good, vital to the public welfare. While acknowledging its crucial importance to core identity, analysts paid scant attention to the distinctive role that religious consciousness plays in shaping a political culture. Despite recent criticism of this secular paradigm by sociologists of religion, most political scientists followed the lead of Gabriel Almond and Samuel Huntington in considering secular societies more progressive than religious societies. A secular self-identity was deemed an essential attribute of modern social development — indeed, one of the crowning achievements of Western civilization.[1]

But to understand the perspective on church-state relations that pervades Russia's alternative political culture we must place ourselves in the mind set of our premodern ancestors, for whom religion guided all personal and political choices. For them, as Emile Durkheim reminds us, religion was "the system of symbols by means of which a society becomes conscious of itself . . . the characteristic way of thinking of collective existence."[2]

Perhaps nowhere in Europe was religious identity so closely linked to national and ethnic identity as in Russia. As Robert C. Tucker has noted, "*Rus* developed in history as a community of right believers, meaning those of the Russian Orthodox faith. In its sustaining myth, Russian society was a political community of the faithful, an Orthodox Tsardom. So persistent was this pattern that as late as the early twentieth century a peasant—and the vast majority of Russians were peasants then—would speak of himself not as a 'Russian' but as 'Orthodox' *(pravoslavnyi)*. Russian was his language; Orthodoxy his identity."[3]

The ideal of church-state relations in Kievan times was the symphonic harmony of two equal sovereigns. This ideal quickly reasserted itself after the Mongol invasion (1236–1240), as the noted traveler Adam Olearius aptly commented after visiting Moscow in 1654: "The Patriarch's authority is so great that he in a manner divides the sovereignty with the Grand Duke."[4] Under Peter the Great, however, the Church lost its sovereignty and became a handmaiden to the state. The ideal of dyarchy, however, survived and became an essential component of Russia's alternative political culture. After Peter, the Church sought to restrain absolutism and actively supported the emergence of Russian civil society at the opening of this century. Forced underground after the October Revolution, it is resurfacing again today.

The "Liturgical State"

In Kievan times the Orthodox Church was considerably more influential than the state. Standing high above secular politics, the Church was both the supreme moral judge and the critic of the government. This was possible because the Russian Church had not yet become autocephalous and its head, the patriarch, lived in Constantinople, well beyond the reach of any Russian prince. Moreover, the political authority of Kievan princes was severely constrained. They shared authority with the *veche* (the early Russian town assemblies), with the *boyars* (noblemen who served as the prince's councilors and military officers), and even with the prince's own military contingent, the *druzhina*. Princes who exceeded their authority were "shown the road," that is to say, they were dismissed by the populace.[5]

Another reason for the Church's pre-eminence was that it had no single counterpart, but dealt with a number of regional princes. These princes shared with the clergy a sense of responsibility for the Russian land and transferred many administrative functions to the Church hierarchy, including jurisdiction over criminal cases and family law. The Church thus played a key role in developing early Russian jurisprudence by introducing concepts of Roman law common in the Byzantine Empire. Among its more notable successes were the elimination of blood feuds and torture, the abolition of the death penalty, the tempering of slavery, and enhancing the legal status of women.[6]

The ideal that emerged was one of church-state partnership in which each side bore responsibility for the welfare of the nation. This doctrine, known in Eastern Christian theology as *symphonia,* strives for a harmonious interaction of the realm of Caesar and the realm of God. The sixth novella of Justinian's *Codex* provides the classical statement on symphonia:

> There are two greatest gifts which God, in his love of man, has granted from on high: the priesthood and the imperial dignity. The first serves divine things, the second directs and administers human affairs; both, however, proceed from the same origin and adorn the life of mankind. Hence, nothing should be such a source of care to the emperors as the dignity of the priests, since it is for the [imperial] welfare that they constantly implore God. For if the priesthood is in every way free from blame and possesses access to God, and if the emperors administer equitably and judiciously the state entrusted to their care, general harmony will result, and whatever is beneficial will be bestowed upon the human race.[7]

Because the Church and the state were both established by God, it must be His will that they act in harmony with each other, the Church being responsible for heavenly affairs and the state for earthly matters. At the same time, each side maintains certain responsibilities toward the other. The state preserves Church dogmas and the honor of the clergy, while the clergy directs the functions of public life in a manner pleasing to God. The state per se has no purpose; it is merely an empty shell until filled with the spirit of God.[8]

This ideal of a society guided by a Christian sociopolitical agenda survived in the Eastern Roman Empire long after the sack of Rome, and was eventually adopted officially by the Eastern Orthodox Church. The *Epanagogue,* the ninth-century Byzantine imperial law book, asserts that "just as is man, the state [*politea*] is composed of parts, the most important and essential of which are the emperor and the patriarch. Unity and concord in all things among the government and the clergy, therefore, means peace and happiness for their subjects in spirit and in body."[9] This presupposes, of course, that the emperor is obliged to serve the best interests of his subjects; the *Epanagogue* continues, "He is called benefactor, and when he fails in this obligation to do good, he forsakes his imperial dignity."[10] The Russian Orthodox Church wholeheartedly embraced this Byzantine ideal and thus saw its proper role as one of moral suasion and influence upon the secular ruler. It emphasized that the monarch was not unlimited but appointed by a higher authority to serve and protect his subjects.

In contrast to Byzantium, however, where the emperor embodied the civil authority, in Kievan Rus the head of the Church had no political equivalent because political authority was fragmented. The main problem for church-state relations during the Kievan period, therefore, was not the intrusiveness but the weakness of government. This led to extensive involvement of the Church in civil, legal, and administrative affairs. Bishops and abbots commonly advised princes on governmental affairs, and clergy often tried to persuade members of the prince's druzhina and local elders to end the internecine struggles of princely clans.

Such direct involvement in politics also served the cause of Russian unity. Thus, in 1097, when Princes Vladimir, David, and Oleg were preparing to attack Prince Svyatopolk in Kiev, the people of Kiev appealed to their metropolitan, Nikolai, to act as a mediator. Nikolai passionately admonished the warlike princes, "We pray that you and your brothers will not destroy Russian lands. For if you begin fighting among yourselves, the pagans will rejoice and conquer our land, which your fathers and grandfathers earned with much labor and valor."[11] When Prince Vladimir ("Monomakh," 1113–1125) heard these words, Kievan chroniclers say that he abandoned his aggressive plans because "he loved the metropolitans, his bishops, his abbots, and especially the monks." Chronicles of the time are replete with examples of clergy urging the princes to think of Russia "with one heart."[12]

The Mongol invasion might have very well have marked the end of Russia as a nation, just as it had marked the end of the Khazars, the Polovetsians, and many other peoples. During this critical period it was the Russian Orthodox Church that led the struggle against pagan overlordship and became the symbolic repository of national identity.[13] The Church became the glue binding together the interstices of society, molding its different parts to a Christian vision of national responsibility. Metropolitans Peter (1308–1326), Aleksey (1353–1378), and Iona (1448–1461) carefully pursued policies designed to ensure that eventually one strong prince would emerge who could overthrow Mongol rule. Metropolitan Peter thus befriended Prince Ivan Kalita of Moscow (which was then a minor trading post) and assisted him in managing state affairs. His successor, Metropolitan Theognost, settled in Moscow permanently, raising the principality to national stature and significance. Theognost's successor, Metropolitan Aleksey, became the guardian of the prince's young son Dimitriy, helping him to ascend to the throne in 1362. It was Prince Dimitriy ("Donskoy") who commanded the Russian host at Kulikovo in 1380 that gave the Mongols their first serious military defeat. Aleksey's successor, Metropolitan Iona, encouraged the principle of patrilineal succession, first instituted by Prince Dimitriy under the inspiration of St. Sergey of Radonezh (n.d. 1392). The saint also served as the first witness to Dimitriy's will.[14]

St. Sergey himself occupies an unrivaled place in the pantheon of Russian saints for his efforts on behalf of Russia's political unity and independence. Legend has it that he blessed Prince Dimitriy before the battle of Kulikovo and sent two of his monks, Oslab and Peresvet, to fight alongside him. St. Sergey is also renowned as the father of Russian monasticism. During the fourteenth and fifteenth centuries, his followers opened up new territories as far north as the White Sea and east beyond the Ural Mountains, establishing more than 250 monasteries.[15] These monks cleared away the forests, built churches and libraries, converted the land to cultivation, and created islands of peace and tranquility in the wilderness that attracted peasants and pilgrims to settle there. Such settlers were given special tax exemptions, and serfdom in these regions was prohibited. Later, rich monasteries such as Solovetsk on the White Sea, the St. Sergey Trinity Monastery, the Kirillov Monastery in Belozersk, and the Tikhvinsky Monastery formed the first line of national defense against the Poles and Lithuanians. The wealthiest would occasionally lend funds to the princes of Moscow to cover the costs of national defense.[16]

The Church thus emerged from the period of Mongol overlordship with its prestige and influence heightened, and with the moral authority to guide the actions of the tsar on matters of both domestic and foreign policy. The symphonic ideal of dyarchy was reaffirmed in the daily rituals and practices of Muscovite political life, from the coronation conducted by the patriarch who strictly admonished the tsar on his responsibility to the people and to his faith, to the Church's participation in the "consecrated council," an integral part of the zemskiy sobor. The patriarch also had the right of *pechalovaniye,* or intercession before the tsar on behalf of anyone unjustly persecuted.[17]

Although actual relations between the Church hierarchy and the tsars were often far from harmonious, particularly during the reign of Ivan IV (the "Terrible"), the principle of dyarchy was never seriously challenged. During the oprichnina (1565–1582 c.), Ivan's insane reign of terror, several heads of the Church chastised the tsar for spilling innocent blood and demanded that he end his reign of terror or face the wrath of God.[18] When Metropolitan Philip did so publicly the tsar had him deposed through a mock trial and later strangled. The contest between the two did not end there, however. In 1652 the Church canonized Philip as a martyr. The new tsar, Aleksey Romanov, then transferred the saint's remains to the Kremlin, and, in a scene reminiscent of Henry IV at Canossa, he led a penitentiary procession to the shrine to beg for the saint's forgiveness. The tsar's prayer during this public exculpation is a noteworthy affirmation of the basic principles of symphonia: "I beg and hope that you will forgive the sin committed against you by my great-grandfather, tsar and grand prince Ivan . . . I bow before your holy relics and subject all my power to you, in the hope that you will forgive us because you were offended in vain . . . Oh holy father, holy bishop Philip, our shepherd! We pray that you will heed our sinful prayer and will come to us in peace."[19]

The breakdown of symphonia that occurred during the oprichnina can thus hardly be considered characteristic. Ivan recognized that he had over-stepped the boundaries that delimited his secular authority, and toward the end of his reign he tried to undo some of the damage that had resulted from his oprichnina. Moreover, even Ivan never seriously consider secularizing monastic lands throughout the country as his contemporary Henry VIII did in England.

The significance of the Church as a symbol of national unity again became apparent during the "Time of Troubles" (1598–1613), when civil war en-gulfed the land and Moscow was occupied by the Poles. It was Patriarch Ghermogen who kindled the spirit of national resistance by refusing to sur-render the monastery fortress of Smolensk to the Poles. Meanwhile, the stewards of St. Sergey Trinity Monastery, and the Kirillov and Beloe Ozero Monasteries, initiated a letter-writing campaign to Russian cities, calling upon all citizens to take up arms and march for country and faith. The first volunteer militia disintegrated because of rivalries between the nobility and the Cossacks. The second attempt, however, succeeded after Avrahm Palit-syn, steward of the St. Sergey Trinity Monastery, mediated a truce between the parties.

The epitome of church-state relations in Muscovite times was Patriarch Filaret's co-rulership of the state with his son Michael, the founder of the Romanov dynasty. This dyarchy, which lasted fourteen years, was vital to restoring the prestige of state institutions after the "Time of Troubles." Inter-estingly, it also coincides with the most democratic period in Muscovite po-litical history, when the tsar regularly consulted the popular councils.

Symphonia meant that in times of crisis for one partner of the dyarchy, the other would step in to help. Thus, monasteries provided economic and even military assistance when the state was beset by external foes; conversely, the tsar recognized the moral authority of the Church and delegated many essential political and administrative functions to it. Although symphonia did not work perfectly, it worked well enough that Russia was able to thwart the odds against its survival and maintain both its national identity and its Byzantine religious heritage. George Fedotov, a religious scholar who was passionately critical of Muscovite traditions, astutely captures the reason be-hind Muscovy's persistence as a political-cultural icon in Russian society:

> The Muscovite type is historically the strongest among the many changing im-ages of the Russian national personality . . . What is most astonishing, particu-larly in comparison with Russians of the nineteenth century, is his strength, his endurance, his uncommon will to resist . . . Even by the standards of the Middle Ages the Muscovite is primitive. He does not reflect, he accepts a few dogmas on faith and allows his whole moral and social life to rest on these. But even in religion there is something for him more important than dogma—

ritual. The periodic repetition of legalized gestures, obeisances, phrases and formulas bind his life and prevent it from dissolving into chaos, and even gives it that certain grace of a consummate existence . . .

From the Tsar's palace to the smallest chicken coop, Muscovite Russia lived with one and the same cultural content, one and the same ideals . . . This cultural unity is what gave the Muscovite type its remarkable endurance. For many it is the very symbol of Russianness. In any case, it survived not only Peter, but even the flowering of Russia's europeanism, and in the depths of the popular masses it lived on until the Revolution.[20]

Church Sovereignty Shattered and Restored

It was Peter the Great who shattered Russia's political-cultural unity. In Muscovite times the tsar's sovereignty in the political realm was balanced by the patriarch's sovereignty in religious affairs, and although the boundary between the two was never clearly defined, the tone was set by the Church's absolute internal autonomy and by the fact that the tsar remained, first and foremost, a "child of the Church" (chado Tserkvi).[21] In the eyes of one leading Church historian, Peter's attempt to reorder church-state relations along Swedish lines amounted to nothing less than "spiritual sterilization."[22]

Peter rejected the traditional view that the Russian Orthodox Church had a mission distinct from that of the state. For him it was only a "body of beliefs shared by the emperor's subjects requiring state-sponsored social and educational services." The Most Holy Synod, established by Peter in 1721, replaced the patriarchate with what amounted to a Lutheran consistory — an administrative body of clerical and lay officials appointed by civil authority.[23] It was supervised by a lay overprocurator, who transformed it into an extension of the government. In 1817 the overprocurator became the sole intermediary between the synod and the emperor. In 1835 he obtained cabinet status. By 1842 he was allowed to dispense with convening regular sessions of the synod. Not surprisingly, the authority of the Church weakened steadily over the course of the eighteenth and nineteenth centuries. The clergy was forced to relinquish most of its civil and judicial administration to local courts. Even the practice of local parishes' choosing their own priests was replaced by a system of administrative appointments resembling the Soviet nomenklatura system.

Peter replaced the symphonic ideal with a view of the Church as merely another branch of the modern, bureaucratic state. As a result the Church no longer had anyone to "symphonize" with — the government had become something alien to it. The triumph of the sovereign state over all other "sovereigns" in traditional Russian society (the people in the veche, the Church, the nobles in the zemstvo assemblies) introduced a new concept into Rus-

sian politics — that of the *unlimited* autocratic tsar whose personal will epitomized the public good. In such a state neither the Church nor any other
institution could assert a claim to spiritual guidance or moral authority. It
could only submit.

Peter and his successors, however, never succeeded in fully eradicating the
symbols of symphonia. Throughout the imperial era the Church continued
to "wed" each new tsar to the throne, thus symbolically establishing a symphonic context for his rule. Articles 62 and 63 of the Fundamental Laws of
the Empire even reiterated the customary religious basis of all political authority by stating that the Church perceived itself as subject not to lay
authority but only to divine authority manifested in the tsar. By stressing
that the monarch is ultimately accountable to God, and that only the Church
reliably interprets God's will, this doctrine implicitly limited the tsar's authority. Interestingly, this interpretation was upheld by Russian constitutional scholars of the nineteenth century.[24] Additionally, unlike the Church
of England, which recognized the English sovereign as "the only supreme
governor of [the] realm . . . as well in all spiritual and ecclesiastical things or
causes as temporal," the Russian Orthodox Church always retained complete
theological autonomy. No tsar could establish principles of Christian or ethical doctrine. His function was purely custodial. Indeed, the tsar was techni-
cally only the administrator of Church affairs; its actual head was the overprocurator.[25]

Still, this was meager consolation to a Church that had traditionally seen
itself as a sovereign power in society, and the clergy and the populace natu-
rally chafed under these restrictions. Already during Peter's lifetime St. Mi-
trofan, the bishop of Voronezh, publicly condemned him for usurping Russian tradition. In 1858, a parish priest, Ioann Stepanovich Bellyustin,
published an exposé of the life of village clergy that contemporaries compared with Radishchev's famous *Journey from St. Petersburg to Moscow.* But the
most dramatic evidence of the survival of the pre-Petrine ideal of symphonia
came at the turn of the twentieth century, when Russian civil society actively
helped to restore the autonomy of the Church.

The many individual appeals for Church autonomy coalesced into a national movement after the National Zemstvo Congress of November 1904.
Under mounting public pressure, the government enacted a decree abolishing many restrictions on non-Orthodox faiths. At the same time the metropolitan of St. Petersburg, Antoniy, addressed a memo to the tsar asking that
a special conference be convened to examine the enactment of guarantees of
"freedom from any direct state or political mission" in the Church's internal
affairs. Shortly thereafter, at a conference on ecclesiastical affairs sponsored
by the government, Sergey Witte, the progressive head of the tsar's cabinet,

publicly supported a statement that called the Church's dependent status "unlawful."

In 1905 the semiofficial religious journal *Tserkovny vestnik* added its voice by publishing a document signed by thirty-two parish priests of St. Petersburg. The priests called for a Church council to discuss, among other things, the election of bishops by their respective dioceses. The authors of this extraordinary document clearly placed the blame for Orthodoxy's low public esteem on its subordination to the state:

> The forthcoming liberation of the religious conscience from external restraint is welcomed with great spiritual joy by all true members of the Orthodox Church. The Church will at last be cleared of the heavy charge of violating and suppressing religious freedom. This was formerly done in her name under the pretense of defending her, but it was done against her will and against her spirit. The time has come for the Church to regain her proper influence in all spheres of national life, and this can only be achieved by a return to the ancient canonical order based on self-government and independence . . . [from] the state.[26]

In July 1905, to stem the growing ferment, the aging overprocurator of the Holy Synod, Konstantin Pobedonostsev, turned to the presiding bishops for advice. Pobedonostsev expected the bishops to support the status quo and intended to use this as an argument for ignoring all pleas to grant independence to the Church. To his consternation, however, the bishops were nearly unanimous in urging a comprehensive reform of both provincial and central Church administration. They urged a greater voice for the clergy in social and public affairs, and the convocation of a Church council to re-examine the basis of church-state relations. The majority favored the restoration of the patriarchy, abolished nearly two hundred years earlier, and hoped the patriarch would play an independent and socially meaningful role.

Their replies, collected and published in 1906, have been called "the most representative and comprehensive document on the Russian church's condition in the Old Regime's last years."[27] They show a clergy united on the need to re-establish Church autonomy and to restore a symphonic dyarchy with the state. These replies are all the more important because they provide a representative cross section of Church opinion: responses came from clergy in the capital and in the provinces, from theologians as well as parish priests. In the face of such evidence the stereotype of a hierarchy oblivious to its social responsibilities and content with its status under the old regime hardly seems credible. Moreover, the movement to restore Church sovereignty was part and parcel of the political and social reform movement to establish a constitutional monarchy, belying the common impression that the Church was "an intellectually and spiritually weak institution, incapable of acting as a counterweight, morally or politically, to the autocracy."[28]

Following the October Manifesto of 1905, the clergy expected a Church council to be held imminently. In January 1906 a precouncil commission began to meet to prepare for the formal separation of the church from the state. Tsar Nicholas II, however, interpreted this as a further erosion of his autocratic power and opposed it. As a result, the council did not convene until the fall of 1917. Meeting in the shadow of the Bolshevik coup, that council, the *Pomestnyi sobor,* nevertheless managed to introduce a number of important reforms and elect the first Russian patriarch, Tikhon, in nearly two centuries.

Although the Church was undoubtedly subordinate to the state after the early eighteenth century, it is clear from the astounding consensus that crystallized as soon as the autocracy's grip weakened that the Church never accepted its subordination. When the power of the autocracy declined, the Church also deliberately chose to reassert a symphonic model of relations with the state, rather than a more modern Protestant model which would have gained it more favor with the intelligentsia. Before 1905 it could not act unilaterally on this agenda (nor did it want to since, by definition, symphonia presumes a willing partnership with the state), but within a very short time it was able to define its distinctive political concerns, just as other social groups were doing at the time. Finally, at the Pomestnyi sobor in 1917, it simply asserted these independently of the state.

The year 1917 thus saw the crumbling of one part of the traditional order (the autocracy) and the restoration of another part (Church sovereignty). When viewed in the context of Russia's alternative political culture this is less of a paradox than it might seem. Whereas the monarchy was trying to prevent the restoration of a constrained autocracy, the Church was trying to restore the traditional symphonic order. Both these ideals still resonated with large portions of the populace. Nor is there any doubt that the delegates to the Pomestnyi sobor intended to re-establish the Church as a constraint upon the tsar. As Catherine Evtukhov points out, "Many of its members believed that the Petrine system of church government departed from the fundamental Orthodox tenet of symphonia (first promulgated in Justinian's sixth novella), which holds that sacred and secular power are inextricably connected and interdependent. Assuming the standpoint of the Orthodox believer in society, delegates worried that the Petrine autocracy violated the wholeness and integrity of individual existence."[29]

Public support for the Church was on the rise after 1905, thanks to the dramatic increase in educational and social welfare activities sponsored by the Church and to the freedom of action created for it by the Duma and the zemstvo. Even more dramatic was the Church's impact upon leading intellectuals, a number of whom publicly repudiated Marxism and urged a broad-based social reconciliation with Orthodoxy.[30] It is one of the tragedies of modern Russian history that, just when the Church was poised to reassert its moral leadership in society, the country's political leaders took Peter's ideas to extremes no one would have dreamed possible.

The Assault of the Soviet State

The Bolshevik attitude toward religion exacerbated the tendencies already inherent in church-state relations after Peter the Great, with one important difference. Whereas Peter wished to preserve the Church as an instrument of state authority, the Bolsheviks wished to completely eradicate the Church, whose very existence they viewed as an obstacle to human progress. Lenin's personal animosity is revealed by an order, brought to light after 1991, that one hundred priests be summarily hanged and left to rot in public because one local church refused to hand over its holy relics to the state.[31]

Despite the efforts of Patriarch Tikhon to remain aloof from politics by ordering the clergy to abstain from any political activity (Tikhon reportedly rebuffed Prince George Trubetskoy's request to send a blessing, under a seal of secrecy, to one of the White leaders), he was soon arrested along with nearly all the senior clergy of the Church.[32] He was released only after publicly acknowledging his "crimes" against Soviet authorities and "resolutely condemning" any attempt to overthrow the new regime, of which he declared himself "not an enemy."[33] Despite such atrocities, Bolshevik leaders believed that the "new Soviet man" would somehow emerge supremely conscious of the collective good, noble in spirit, hard working, and, of course, an atheist. In Stalin's first Five-Year Plan (1929–1934) nearly as much attention is devoted to the spread of atheism as to industrialization and collectivization.[34]

In accordance with the directives of the Church council, Patriarch Tikhon had named several caretakers in the event of his death. After the first designate died in Siberia in 1925, his successor, Metropolitan Sergey, became the *locum tenens,* or temporary administrator, of the Church. On July 29, 1927, Metropolitan Sergey issued a fateful statement which he said would give the Church "the possibility of existing in conditions of absolute peace and law" under Soviet rule. The Church's opposition to desecration, he wrote, had "provoked a justified anger on the part of the Government." The clergy and the faithful must prove to the government that they "are not with the enemies of our Soviet State, nor with the mad, insensate instruments of their intrigues." He therefore urged that "every blow directed against the Soviet Union [be] felt by us as though it were directed against us" and demanded that the Russian Orthodox clergy abroad sign "a written commandment of absolute loyalty to the Soviet authorities in all public activity."[35]

His missive inflicted a deep wound in the Russian Orthodox Church that festers to this day. Sergey apparently believed that Stalin would cease persecuting the Church if it swore allegiance to the new regime. Unfortunately, this assumption proved false. A detailed account of the Soviet persecution of the Church is beyond the scope of this study; therefore, a few statistics will have to suffice. During the first four years of the new regime (1918–1922) more than 20,000 churches were either closed or destroyed. In 1922 alone approximately 8,000 priests, monks, and nuns were sentenced to death for "counterrevolutionary activity." By the end of the first Five-Year plan nearly 95 percent of Orthodox churches had been closed. In Leningrad, Russia's second largest city, there were only 15 active priests on the eve of World War II. Several cities with more than a million inhabitants had no churches or priests at all.[36]

The total number of priests murdered during the first two decades of Soviet rule is difficult to determine. Vladimir Rusak, a former editor at the official *Journal of the Moscow Patriarchate,* notes laconically that "there were so many priests shot that it is impossible to gather the endless number of cases." He suggests that out of approximately 100,000 priests active before 1917, only 40,000 were still alive twenty years later.[37] A rare document published by the press department of the Soviet embassy in London on the eve of the Second World War claims that the Russian Orthodox Church had 4,225 churches, 5,665 priests, and 28 bishops and metropolitans.[38] Rusak, however, places the number of functioning Orthodox churches at this time as low as 100.[39] It is only slightly easier to determine the fate of the Church hierarchy. During this same period, 205 Russian bishops disappeared without a trace, 59 of them in 1937 alone.[40] When Stalin allowed Sergey to ascend to the position of patriarch in 1943, only 20 surviving bishops and metropolitans could be located to elect him.

Yet when Soviet power receded ever so briefly during World War II, the popularity of the Church quickly reasserted itself. Thousands of churches reopened in the territories under German occupation. The following data are from the single diocese of Kiev:

	1917	1941	1942
Parishes	—	2	410
Churches	1710	2	318
Monasteries	23	0	8
Priests	1435	3	434
Deacons	277	1	21
Cantors	1400	2	86
Monks and nuns	5193	0	387[41]

Impressed with the Church's patriotic effort during World War II, Stalin curtailed antireligious activity after the war and even permitted a few churches to reopen. Two spiritual academies, one in Moscow and one in Leningrad, were even established to train new clergy. Stalin's successors, however, renewed the campaign for atheism, closing nearly two-thirds of all Orthodox places of worship. This left approximately 7,500 Orthodox churches open for an estimated 50 to 115 million regular Orthodox worshipers, a number that remained constant through the late 1980s.[42] By comparison Greece, another predominantly Orthodox country, had twice as many churches for a population of less than 9 million.

The reasons for the vehement Soviet assault upon the Church can only be understood in the context of Russia's alternative political culture. Bolshevik leaders recognized that the symphonic ideal, which the Pomestnyi sobor had reasserted in 1917, meant that the Church intended to reassert its moral authority in the public arena and constrain the abuse of political power. Although the Church avoided challenging the regime directly, as long as an independent voice of moral criticism existed the regime would be held accountable for its actions. The objective of the state's massive antireligious campaign, therefore, was to thoroughly discredit the Church or, failing that, to terrorize and isolate the population and the clergy.

The determination of the regime to eradicate any vestige of religious identity from the populace cannot be doubted, but how well did it succeed? It appears that the regime was most successful in disrupting the overt practice of religious rituals. With each passing generation the total number of regular churchgoers, baptisms, and public observance of religious holidays declined. At the same time, however, the regime clearly failed in its attempt to sever the links between Russian national and religious identity. Although the Church hierarchy submitted to the regime under duress, many individual Orthodox clergy and laymen rebelled. According to one contemporary, Metropolitan John (Snychev), in some dioceses up to 90 percent of parishes sent Metropolitan Sergey's declaration back to its author.[43] The list of Church hierarchs who publicly condemned the declaration includes four metropolitans, four archbishops, nineteen bishops, and the cream of Russia's theological academies.[44] The Russian Orthodox Church Abroad, in words that evoked the memory of past struggles between church and state, also vehemently rejected Sergey's declaration:

> "You must only keep silent," Metropolitan Sergey tells us, "and not expose Soviet power because this would be a political act."
>
> "Silence, only this I tell you, silence," an enraged [Ivan the] Terrible once said to Saint Philip when he continued to condemn his cruelty and defend the truth he had trampled. Neither can we, the bishops abroad, heed Metropolitan

Sergey's appeal . . . since here, in the words of Gregory the Theologian, "silence betrays God."[45]

Meanwhile, inside the Soviet Union, thousands flocked to the underground, or "Catacombal Church," while others worked with dissidents to rewrite the legislation governing Church affairs. Each of these three arenas—émigré, catacombal, and dissident—clung steadfastly to the symphonic ideal of separate realms for church and state.

Vekhi and the Russian Religious Renaissance

Before the revolution the Russian intelligentsia had been overwhelmingly hostile to religion and to the Church. Infatuated with the positivist social theories of the age, it embraced religious indifference and sometimes even militant atheism.[46] It came as a clap of thunder on a calm summer day, therefore, when in 1909 a group of distinguished Russian intellectuals published *Vekhi* (Signposts), a powerful appeal to the intelligentsia to abandon revolution and embrace traditional religious and patriotic values.

Many would-be reformers simply dismissed the publication as a betrayal. The leader of the Constitutional Democrats, Pavel Milyukov, called it "pernicious and repulsive."[47] Nearly two hundred articles attacked it during its first year of publication, and still the book went through five printings in just six months.[48] What did these thinkers propose to arouse such interest and ire? Deeming Marxism and all other forms of positivist thought to be dead ends, the *Vekhi* authors called for a return to Christianity, and specifically to Eastern Orthodoxy with its strongly defined sense of the Church. They embraced a brand of patriotism and political activism redolent with Christian consciousness. They sought to inspire in the intelligentsia a sense of public duty that might heal the rift between the political cultures of Muscovite and Petrine Russia. Theirs was a modern manifestation of the values of Russia's alternative political culture. Having survived absolutism, the alternative political culture had been reinvigorated by the early Slavophiles and the zemstvo movement, and now called upon Russian intellectuals to abandon their infatuation with revolution and to work instead toward gradual social change.

Although *Vekhi* marked a definite turning point in the attitudes of the Russian intelligentsia, the healing process it initiated was interrupted after 1917. To consolidate the Bolsheviks' monopoly on social thought, Lenin in 1922 banished more than two hundred leading social theorists and philosophers.[49] By decapitating intellectual opposition to the new order, he hoped to clear the way for a new breed of intellectual dedicated to the humanist ideals of the October Revolution. But even though the search for an alternative path of political development was broken off inside Russia, it survived in the West, where a number of prominent intellectuals managed to continue their work.

Amid the turmoil and uprootedness of the interwar period it was again the Church that provided guidance and unity to the Russian diaspora, which, by the end of the civil war, numbered more than two million. It provided a context in which the leading luminaries of that generation were able to ask why this tragedy had befallen Russia, and to address the young who had lost their homeland. It gave the émigré community an audience, a mission, and a hope for the future revival of Russia.

A major vehicle of the Church abroad was the Russian Student Christian Movement. This movement brought the previously scattered intellectual elite back into the folds of the Church and began the process of educating a new generation of émigré Russians for the future. The spirit of the movement was summed up by the *Vekhi* contributor (later Father) Sergey Bulgakov:

> The epoch of Church history which began in the fourth century and which is associated with Emperor Constantine ended for us with the abdication of Nicholas II in 1917. We have all experienced the dark ending of that great period, but now we also see the new light in front of us. We are called to be creative. We must endeavor to apply Christianity in the spirit of Sobornost to all spheres of life, personal, social, national. Orthodoxy represents the universal truth, and its chief interpreter at present is the Church of Russia, but we can lose this position of leadership if we become unworthy of our calling.[50]

With the help of YMCA head John Mott, the Theological Institute of St. Sergey was established in Paris.[51] The leading intellectual gathering place of the Russian diaspora, the Institute supported the work of countless émigrés attempting to synthesize the political, cultural, and spiritual meaning of the October Revolution and to preserve the heritage of Russia's alternative political culture. The list of names composing this "Russian religious renaissance," as Nicholas Zernov aptly calls it, is too long to list here, but many had an especially keen interest in politics, law, and history.[52]

These thinkers left Russia with three objectives: first, to continue their personal search for a Christian life combined with social activism; second, to give meaning and purpose to the Russian diaspora and to Russian history after October 1917; and third, to leave a legacy that could be reintroduced into Russia after communism had run its course. Their writings span the gamut of social and political issues, but all are rooted in wholehearted acceptance of Orthodox Christianity. Within this context they defended the dignity of individual freedom and the importance of social justice.

Two outstanding examples of this tradition were Anton V. Kartashev (1875–1967), the son of a serf factory worker who became high procurator of the synod under the Provisional Government and oversaw the end of government tutelage over the Church, and George P. Fedotov (1886–1951), an active social democrat before 1905 who eventually turned to Christianity. The importance of religion as a restraint upon the government is a persistent theme in the writings of both — the former a lifelong monarchist, the latter a staunch defender of democracy.

Kartashev sets the tone for his classic essay "The Recreation of Holy Russia" with its very first words: "The Russia of St. Vladimir — christened, orthodox, Holy Russia — is our banner. Immersion into this heart of hearts of our Russianness will never cease to be the task of our national self-awareness."[53] In these two sentences he affirms the inseparability of religious consciousness and national self-awareness. Both are essential to the well-being of Russia, and establishing this vital tie is the most urgent task of "Holy Russia." The term "Holy Russia," Kartashev acknowledges, might seem pretentious, but it is an expression that has existed in Russian popular lore since before written annals. For Kartashev the phrase is evidence of the extremely close connection between Christian identity and national self-awareness in Russia.

The past order, he states, is irretrievably lost. The current task is therefore one of creating a new social and political ideal that is rooted in Russian historical traditions. Holy Russia is to be a state "lit up from within by the Orthodox spirit, christianized; or, more directly, a Christian state."[54]

For Kartashev, the basic principles of symphonia are still relevant today. The Church must work toward christianizing all spheres of society, even government itself, but it must do so independently of the government. This requires that a new and broader symphonia take the place of the traditional one between the Church and the government: a symphonia between the Church and society. Such a relationship, which he terms the "new theocracy," must recognize the trade-off between separation of church and state and subjection to the Church's spiritual authority. Countering the criticism that a formal separation of church and state will lead to a diminution of the Church's tutelary role in social life, Kartashev asserts that placing the Church on an equal footing with other social groups will actually free it from the ties with government that "distort the [Church's] image and weaken its prophetic strength."[55]

Kartashev stresses the enormous variety of Christian solutions to the social problem which, nonetheless, should always be guided by the transcendent purpose of salvation. The particular expression of Christian politics will differ given historical circumstances, but it will always, for Kartashev, maintain a sense of organized purposefulness. His contemporary George Fedotov, by contrast, was far more secular in orientation.

According to Fedotov, politics is more than just the struggle for personal rights, privileges, and interests. It is also the struggle for social ideals; it is the sphere that unifies spiritual culture, economics, and technology. Far too often, however, this ideal becomes a mere caricature of true democracy as election campaigns turn into "grandiose epics of lies and hypnotic befuddlement of the masses." The result, not surprisingly, is that "the populace does not recognize itself in its rulers."[56]

The scourge of revolution, in Fedotov's view, stems from the inadequate social guidance given by contemporary democracies. Most revolutions are inspired not by the desire for freedom but by the pursuit of some "new order" that will more rationally organize all aspects of life under government sponsorship. Such secular revolutions not only aim at changing the government and its political structures, but attack the very purpose of life itself. By seeking to create a society like that of "the first people on earth," without original sin, today's revolutions begin in the name of freedom and end in slavery.[57]

Like his compatriots in exile, Fedotov turns to Christianity for a different solution to the dilemmas of social existence. Early on, he says, the Christian Church had to choose between two paths: remaining a small community of saved souls awaiting the second coming of the Lord, or saving the world and conveying what it could of the Christian ideal. By choosing the latter path, the Church forces Christians to be at the forefront of social renewal.

The Christian social ideal is sobornost, "the organic equilibrium of personality and society."[58] Sobornost is inimical to totalitarian collectivism and to formalized democracy, both of which are based on "the number and equality of social atoms." "The ideal of sobornost," writes Fedotov, is "similar to the ideal of family or friendship, where subjects subject themselves freely and where the rulers do not rule but serve."[59] These qualities of solidarity and brotherhood are exemplified in the following passage by St. John Chrysostom, which Fedotov loved to cite: "Let us not be satisfied with the search for personal salvation; this would mean destroying it. In war and in the ranks, if a soldier thinks only of how to save himself by flight he will wind up destroying himself and his comrades. A dedicated soldier who fights for others and with others saves himself as well."[60]

But Christianity is called to do more than merely advocate social reform, according to Fedotov. It rejects secular social relations and offers instead a new social concept that asserts the equality of part and whole, of the Church and man's spirit. Since such lofty ideals do not fit neatly into a parliamentary framework, the Christian political ideal is to shape an "organic democracy" characterized by three elements: first, participation in government should be seen as a common obligation and a common sacrifice, rather than as an individual right; second, popular representation should be seen as the selection of the wisest and the most just, who will determine and create, rather than simply express, the will of the people; and third, government should be an expression of leadership, not the service of a slave to his master (here Fedotov approvingly cites the examples of American presidents and Roman consuls). In an organic democracy, Fedotov would say, the only truly binding mandate is the government's conscience and its understanding of the common good.

Fedotov's recommendations seem more appropriate to a society with a high degree of social and religious homogeneity than to the fractious world we know. But, though acknowledging that his ideal is probably unachievable, he feels it is worth striving for because it raises mankind's sights to the Kingdom of God. A fitting description of his social philosophy might well be, as he wrote in *The Christian in Revolution:* "We are not for the old or the new, we are for the eternal."[61]

In the West the study of this rich strand of Russian political-religious thought has been largely overshadowed by the victory of the Bolsheviks in 1917. Even specialists in the study of Russian religion can be totally unaware of the crucial role these writers played in shaping a political-cultural alternative to communism.[62] In the late 1980s, however, Gorbachev began to realize the extent to which the process of perestroika was being hindered by ignorance of the country's own political traditions. He hoped that greater political awareness would lead to broader public support for a reconstructed, more "humane" socialism. Hence, after 1986, the third and final task of reintroducing these ideals to their native soil began.

Contrary to official expectations, this exposure to Russian religious philosophy shattered the myth that any more humane form of socialism was possible. In one of the first reviews introducing these lost luminaries to Soviet readers, the literary critic Igor Vinogradov comments that, "were they alive now, V. Solovyov or N. Berdyaev, S. Bulgakov or S. Frank, they would likely ask . . . what of your level-headed, clever idea of erecting a happy social paradise on earth without God, without absolute moral principles rooted in Christian commandments, without belief in the unconditional meaning of good and of moral norms? Where has it brought us over the last seventy years in the life of our unfortunate country, [but] to the brink of catastrophe?"[63]

The eagerness with which these thinkers were welcomed back into Russian culture after 1988 is most easily explained by the fact that they offer a clearly defined historical and philosophical alternative to socialism. Assessing the significance of *Vekhi* some thirty-five years later, Simeon Frank wrote that, although it had come too late to influence the course of political events, "the ideas it expressed . . . helped to promote the initial unanimous rejection and energetic resistance of the intelligentsia to the Bolsheviks and to stimulate the spiritual revival and penitence which accompanied this movement."[64] The vexing issues of democratization, modernization, and the shattered ideals of the October Revolution were the subject of soul-searching debate in post-communist Russia. Russian religious philosophy was so attractive now because it had grappled with precisely the same issues half a century ago. Moreover, it identified a path of personal and social action that would bring Russia to peaceful and prosperous historical development — a tangible expression of a distinctively Russian national approach to politics.

Survival, Resistance, and Resurrection

Meanwhile, within the Soviet Union, the Church came to epitomize the struggle to preserve the alternative political culture. "As thinking people in the Soviet Union attempt to rediscover and resurrect the culture in their past (in its pure, as opposed to its ideologically distorted form)," Jane Ellis notes, "they encounter Orthodoxy at every turn — in art, architecture, music, literature, poetry."[65] After decades of communist indoctrination, the sociologist David Lane remarks, Orthodoxy still "epitomizes the Russian tradition . . . that enshrined the traditional against the modern: Russian as opposed to Soviet."[66] This distinction has obvious implications for political culture. Despite the fact that opposition to official policies governing church-state relations carried severe penalties, it was manifested in two forms in the Soviet Union: first, in the Catacombal Church; and second, after Stalin's death, in the rise of religious dissent.

The first major split within the Russian Orthodox Church came in 1927 when the metropolitan of Leningrad, Joseph, and eight dioceses disassociated themselves from Patriarch Sergey, claiming that he had exceeded the limits of his authority by declaring his allegiance to the Soviet government. Initially encouraged by the Soviet leaders, who saw the schism as a means of weakening the Church, the Josephine, or "right opposition," took on an increasingly anti-Soviet character and was eventually suppressed. It subsequently formed the core of the "Catacombal Church," a generic term used to denote several organizations and sects that continued their religious life underground. Some of these groups withdrew entirely from Soviet life, removing their children from kindergarten no later than the age of four and destroying all the children's official documents. The Soviet press has even reported cases of groups living, quite literally, underground, and infants who had never seen the sun, though this may just as likely be a ploy to dissuade parents from becoming involved with religious sects. Writing in the 1960s, Nikita Struve estimated that more than forty Orthodox sects existed illegally in the Soviet Union, some with hundreds of thousands of members. The total membership of the Catacombal Church, he says, may number up to five million.[67]

Such sects generally had a marked anti-Soviet character like that of the Red Dragon *(Krasnodrakonovtsy)*, an appellation referring to several antigovernment sects that identified the Soviet regime with the dragon of the Apocalypse and called upon members to resist actively the sovietization of life. The Krasnodrakonovtsy included the *Cherdachniki,* who wished to replace the current regime with one based on evangelical precepts; the *Chernokhristovtsy,* particularly numerous in the Ukraine, who wished to have absolutely no contact with Soviet reality to the point of disdaining contact with Soviet money; and *Lyudi ne znayuschie chisla,* whose hatred of planification caused them to ban all notion of numbers from their lives.[68]

Especially strong during the late 1920s and 1930s, many of these sects after World War II merged into the True Orthodox Church (TOC), which had its own clergy, including bishops, monks, and nuns. In underground documents circulated through samizdat, the TOC argued that the patriarchate's policy of appeasement had saved virtually nothing of the Orthodox Church, whereas the ties linking the official Church hierarchy to the Soviet regime "are such that there is no hope for an internal rebirth. Upheld by the Soviet regime, she [the official Church] will thus share its destiny to the very end."[69]

Metropolitan Sergey's declaration of 1927, according to the TOC, ignored the central role played by the Party and its ideology in the new system. As a result, his declaration transformed all those opposed to the ideology into political enemies of the Soviet regime. The Bolsheviks chained Sergey and his successors hand and foot not only to the government, but specifically to the communist ideology. A church so completely subordinated to the state, members of the TOC concluded, is "not the Russian Church of the Soviet period, but the Church of the Soviet State, the Soviet Church."[70]

The persistence of sects like the TOC is a direct result of the patriarchy's submission to the Soviet regime. Other clergymen and lay faithful shared the same anxieties as their brothers and sisters in the Catacombal Church but, having sworn allegiance to a "single, holy, catholic, and apostolic Church," chose to fight for reforms within the folds of the Russian Orthodox Church. The post-Stalin "thaw" that encouraged intellectuals and young people to believe in the possibility of reform within the system had a similar effect on the clergy and the faithful. When Khrushchev began to close down churches in the late 1950s, hundreds of people filled the chancelleries of bishops or sought the protection of the patriarch. During this period, the first open letters of protest appeared, predating political samizdat by nearly a decade. One of the first such letters, from three thousand inhabitants of the village of Pochaev, was addressed to the Ecumenical Council of Churches and to the leaders of the USSR. The letter, given to Western tourists in September of 1962, claimed that authorities had tortured local nuns, some of whom had died from the beatings they had received. In a second letter the townspeople protested the regime's attempt to close the abbey at Pochaev and demanded that the Party stop meddling in Church affairs.[71]

The most famous appeal of the early 1960s, however, was the forty-page letter to Patriarch Aleksey from two parish priests, Gleb Yakunin and Nikolai Yeshliman. They criticized the Council for the Affairs of the Russian Orthodox Church (the Soviet government agency that supervised "cult observance") for blatant violations of the separation of church and state, and they cited numerous instances of illegal registrations of baptisms, closure of churches, monasteries, and religious schools by civil authorities, intervention in funeral rites and other religious ceremonies by civil authorities, as well as the forcible removal of children from churches.[72]

The two priests called upon the patriarch to petition the government of the USSR to: 1) eradicate the effects of "subjectivism and administrativism" that afflicted church-state relations; 2) clearly define the legal jurisdiction of the Council for the Affairs of the Russian Orthodox Church; 3) discontinue all activities that contravened both Lenin's decree on separation of church and state and Article 124 of the Constitution. Like the Church reformers of 1905, the priests also called upon the patriarch to convene an All-Union Church Synod (Pomestnyi sobor) to review the activities of the Church hierarchy and all other aspects of Church life.

It is significant that this early appeal cited not only canonical reasons for restoring Church autonomy but also existing Soviet legislation, for the rallying cry "respect your own Constitution" would later became a central theme of the human rights movement. The more immediate result of this letter, however, was that both priests were suspended from office and sentenced to several years in prison. Whereas Father Yeshliman died in 1985, before any significant changes had occurred in the status of the Church, Father Yakunin was elected to a seat in the Russian parliament in 1989 and helped to draft the legislation that abolished the State Committee on Religious Affairs. Today he is a leading figure in the Russia's Choice movement that supports democratic reforms.

Fathers Yakunin and Yeshliman's letter broke the dam of silence that had engulfed Metropolitan Sergey's 1927 decision to submit to state authority.

In the ensuing decades Orthodox clergy and laymen became active in establishing the budding human rights movement. Anatoliy Krasnov (Levitin), a noted samizdat writer since 1958, helped found the Action Group for the Defense of Human Rights, the first formal human rights group. In 1968 a young parish priest from Pskov, Father Sergey Zheludkov, wrote an open letter of support to Pavel Litvinov, the grandson of Stalin's prewar commissar of foreign affairs and one of the seven who demonstrated against the invasion of Czechoslovakia on Red Square.[73] Other outstanding examples of noted human rights participants who specifically cited their Orthodox faith as the inspiration for their political activities include Tatyana Khodorovich, Mikhail Bernshtam, Sergey Soldatov, Tatyana Velikanova, Yuri Galanskov, Aleksandr Solzhenitsyn, Andrey Tverdokhlebov, Igor Shafarevich, Valeriy Senderov, and Rostislav Evdokimov.[74]

Although political and human rights appeals became far better known in the West, by the mid–1970s it was religious samizdat alone that accounted for more than half of all underground publications. By the end of the 1970s, religious dissidents of all faiths numbered roughly fifty thousand as compared with ten thousand human rights and civil rights dissidents.[75] For most of these people the struggle for a free society coincided with the struggle for a free Church.

In 1976 Father Yakunin, Deacon Varsonofiy (Khaybulin), Viktor Kapitanchuk, and Vadim Shcheglov formed the Christian Committee for the Defense of the Rights of Believers in the USSR, modeled, quite obviously, on the Helsinki groups. Its initial declaration stated that the committee would collect, study, and disseminate information on the condition of the faithful in the USSR; advise believers in cases of violation of their civil rights; appeal to the government on behalf of the rights of believers; conduct research on the actual state of religion in the USSR; and help to redefine Soviet laws on religion. Between 1976 and 1980, when most of its members were in jail, the Christian Committee distributed more than four hundred documents on violations of civil rights of the faithful of all religions.[76] Again, the Christian Committee did not see its activities as anti-Soviet-government, or even outside the fold of the Church, but as a natural extension of their Orthodoxy.

Father Yakunin's own decision to become a priest was the result of an encounter with another noted dissident priest, Father Alexander Men. This chance encounter illustrates one of the myriad patterns through which the alternative political culture was transmitted from generation to generation. Father Men, who became the spiritual father to hundreds of Christian activists, had himself been baptized and spiritually educated by priests of the Catacombal Church, a covert priesthood that provided the religious instruction suppressed by the state. Later, when the young writer Aleksandr Solzhenitsyn first read about Yeshliman and Yakunin's letter to the patriarch, their courage made a profound impression upon him. When a new patriarch came to office in 1972, Solzhenitsyn composed his own "Lenten Letter" in which he suggested that, if Metropolitan Sergey had refused to submit to the state in 1927, Russian history might have been "incomparably more humane," and he challenged the Church to reassert its autonomy and to lead through sacrifice.[77]

Solzhenitsyn's letter aroused great controversy among reformers. Father Sergey Zheludkov and Archpriest Vsevolod Shpiller criticized him for suggesting that the Church could have continued its pastoral mission in defiance of the state. Given the regime's militant atheism, they contended, the only alternative to Sergey's loyalty oath would have been for the entire Church to go underground, depriving millions of any pastoral services. Instead, Zheludkov argued, the Church hierarchy decided to accept the system "for the present and use those opportunities that are permitted" to change it.[78]

Zheludkov and Shpiller highlight the importance to the Orthodox within the Soviet Union of a theme vital to the religious philosophers of the diaspora, namely, the "churchification" of all society. In historical circumstances where the aspirations of church and state are incompatible, such as occurred during both the Imperial period of Russian history and the Soviet period, Orthodoxy holds that the church should not seek to overthrow the government, but rather should rise above it, judging it, and serving as a beacon of proper moral conduct. Such was the policy pursued by Patriarch Tikhon, reaffirmed after his death in a remarkable collective letter to the Soviet leadership from the bishops incarcerated at the Solovetsk Islands concentration camp. In their letter they specifically condemned Metropolitan Sergey for interweaving the realms of church and state. Now more than ever, they insisted, the Church needed laws strictly separating church and state.[79]

Apologists for the Moscow patriarchate, however, argue that the Church had an obligation to fulfill at least some of its mission, even in hostile circumstances. This is not the same as subservience to the state, they claim, but is rather a compromise that allows Christians to derive some good from oppressive circumstances. This reasoning is captured in the following conversation between the Canadian historian Dimitry Pospielovsky and Metropolitan Nikodim:

> To my remark that it is a bad temptation for a Christian to witness a bishop not telling the truth, [Metropolitan Nikodim] retorted: "It is you people in the West that react this way. We're used to this sort of thing in the Soviet Union, and we don't react."
>
> "But it is terrible," I said, "that lies are accepted in such a way."
>
> "I didn't say this was good or bad. I'm just stating a fact," said the Metropoli-

tan with a sad smile. And then he went on to describe his own strategy as that of a man who in dense traffic prefers to select small side roads, and thus a longer distance, while still going towards his aim, rather than get stuck in a traffic jam or end up in an accident on the main road. He hoped that in this way he would achieve more for the Church in the long run.[80]

It is important to note that the disagreement between advocates of a strict church-state separation and those who argue that it is doing the best that it can under hostile circumstances is not about the propriety of the symphonic ideal. Both sides agree that the Church must once again become an autonomous force in society. They disagree, however, over timing, strategy, and the price the Church should pay (has it already paid too much?) to achieve a modicum of good. To this day the Moscow patriarchate maintains that the benefits of obtaining legal recognition from Stalin outweighed the costs, and that the situation for Christians would have been even worse had the Church refused to compromise. Others, however, vehemently disagree, and during the 1970s they went over the heads of the hierarchy to appeal for support to the ultimate seat of authority in the Orthodox Church—the community of the faithful.

Krushchev's antireligious campaign of 1960–1964 thus had the unintended effect of increasing the social and political stature of Orthodoxy by involving Christians in samizdat and the human rights movement. The 1970s saw a sharp increase in the quantity of religious samizdat, as well as the appearance of underground journals devoted entirely to religion, and regular sections devoted to religion and to the religious thinker of the early twentieth century in many underground political and cultural journals. A typical example is *Obshchina,* the journal of the "Christian Seminar on the Problems of Religious Re-Birth" organized by Aleksandr Ogorodnikov. As a third-year university student, Ogorodnikov encountered fellow students interested in religious issues. The group began to meet regularly in 1974, and saw itself as continuing the tradition of the religious and philosophical discussion societies of Moscow and Petrograd dispersed in the 1920s.[81]

Interest in these seminars grew so rapidly, however, that by 1978 meetings were being held in ten cities, with up to forty persons attending individual sessions. The participants were mainly young students and teachers who "had come to Orthodoxy after rejecting the official ideology and having gone through a period of infatuation with westernism [*zapadnichestvo*]."[82] According to the founding declaration of the seminar, its objectives included service to the task of the spiritual rebirth of Russia; the building of communities as a means of overcoming the crisis of contemporary religious life and the "despicable division of the world"; fostering fraternal *(sobornoe)* unity with all those who suffered from repression and felt the division of the world as a Russian tragedy; and dialogue with other faiths in order to search for a means to overcome the world's spiritual crisis. Although these seminars ended after Ogorodnikov's arrest and the psychiatric detention of other seminar participants, in 1989 Ogorodnikov co-founded the Russian Christian Democratic Party, one of the two most visible political parties inspired by Christian ideals in postcommunist Russia.

The Church during Perestroika

A small minority of Christian activists actually did hope that the regime could be convinced to abandon atheism. In 1976 two of them, Hierodeacon Varsonofiy (Khaybulin) and the Orthodox layman Gleb Mileshkin, issued an appeal to the Twenty-fifth Congress of the CPSU. The Communist Party's efforts to eradicate religious beliefs had clearly failed, and although the episcopate had been reduced to telling half-truths, this had only strengthened the resolve of the populace to uncover the whole truth. Would it not be more advisable, the authors suggested, to enlist the Church as an ally? "If there were firm juridical guarantees that the State would not interfere in the internal life of the Church, Christians would be joyful comrades-in-arms of Communists in achieving their social and economic ideals."[83]

This appeal made no impression whatsoever upon the communist leadership in 1976, but it aptly characterizes the regime's policy toward religion after 1985. Believing that an easing of religious persecution might help to restore the popularity of socialism, Gorbachev relaxed certain restrictions on religion.[84] The further evolution of perestroika, however, illustrates how the persistent demands of Russia's alternative political culture pushed the reforms far beyond anything the Soviet elite had intended.

The regime's willingness to allow the Church greater public visibility led to a remarkable upsurge in lay activism during perestroika. The millennial celebration of the baptism of Rus in 1988 was frequently used to press the state for concessions, as when the Church asked for and received the Tolgsk Monastery, the Danilov Monastery, and sections of the Kiev Monastery of the Caves. Clerics, publicists, and scholars seized upon this historical event to publicize Christianity's importance to Russian national consciousness and to its formation as a nation. Thus, the editorial board of *Ogonyok,* one of the country's most widely read journals at the time, published an interview with Dmitriy S. Likhachev on the significance of one thousand years of Christianity, in which the noted medievalist pointed out:

> Sergey of Radonezh was a conduit for specific ideas and traditions: the unity of Rus was linked with the church . . . Dimitriy Donskoy began not with an

attempt at territorial unity, but with national and moral unification. In this respect the prince of Moscow, who stood at the head of the Russian troops [at the battle of Kulikovo Field], was remarkable. Because of this Moscow gained prestige in the eyes of all of Russia. She won not because, as some have tried to prove, she was located on very advantageous trade routes, but because in this most difficult situation, she led the unification of the Russian land; i.e., Moscow won spiritually.[85]

The Church soon pushed the regime even further, asking for and receiving permission to minister to the sick, visit penal colonies, and conduct charitable activities. Lay Orthodox, too, increasingly confronted the regime over church closings and publicly demanded an end to discrimination against religious believers. Religious dissenters, limited in the past to petitioning the authorities, now took advantage of glasnost and asserted their rights to publish their own journals, such as *Vybor* and *Bulleten Khristyanskoi obshchestvennosti*.

These semiofficial journals of the late 1980s were quite different from the religious samizdat of the 1970s.[86] They subscribed to an openly patriotic and religious orientation, and they regularly published the writings of Russian religious philosophers, not shying away even from pieces openly critical of socialism and the October Revolution. While these journals introduced readers to an entirely new interpretation of Russian history, philosophy, and politics rooted in Orthodoxy, "mainstream" journalists such as Aleksandr Nezhnyi depicted the Church and religion as forces vital to the country.[87] By 1990, more than a dozen major publications had inaugurated sections devoted to the legacy of Russian religious thinkers, including *Literaturnaya gazeta, Teatralnaya zhizn, Sever, Moskovskie novosti, Nash sovremennik,* and *Nashe nasledie.*

Prominent writers and academics openly indicated Russia's long-suppressed religious philosophical heritage as the place to search for remedies to Soviet social problems. Some even called on the Soviet Cultural Fund to establish a religious-philosophical society that would examine the contemporary application of Russian religious philosophy because "the more seriously and appreciatively it is assimilated, the healthier and more confident our intellectual and spiritual foundation will be."[88] In 1990 the Fund did organize a series of lectures entitled "Returning Forgotten Names."

For others, the struggle to restore the Church's moral voice led directly into politics. Father Gleb Yakunin became the chief spokesman for a democratic and politically assertive Church presence. He appeared frequently beside such key figures as Sergey Zalygin, the editor of the influential literary journal *Novyi mir,* Gorbachev adviser Tatyana Zaslavskaya, Boris Yeltsin, and Andrei Sakharov.

Yakunin was not alone, however. Liberating the Church so that it could play an active social and educational role was close to the hearts of a number of lay deputies. When first elected to the Congress of Peoples' Deputies in 1989, the actor Mark Zakharov, who made international headlines with his proposal to bury Lenin, described his agenda as follows:

> We must re-evaluate our relationship to universal values and to the moral sources of great Christian culture. We must look around us to see where and in what things we are still pagans, heretics who have forsaken the teaching of our forefathers . . . I will go even further and add that the great cathedrals of the Moscow Kremlin must sooner or later be resurrected, regaining their tattered magnificence and the natural life which cathedrals in Rome, Paris, Madrid, and other civilized cities have. I intend to assist in every way [the process of] distancing ourselves from pre-Christian barbarism and thoughtfully nurturing the seedlings of spiritual rebirth.[89]

In granting the Church greater opportunity to enter into the public dialog over the country's future, the regime thus got far more than it bargained for. An emboldened civil society took advantage of perestroika to argue that the Church was indispensable to the spiritual well-being of the country. It bolstered this claim by repeatedly bringing to public attention the role that the Church played during critical times in Russian history. The Church's greater involvement in social and political affairs during the years of perestroika gradually radicalized that segment of the Russian intelligentsia that was uncomfortable with communist rule but had not yet developed any alternative to it. For many of these individuals, Russian religious philosophy offered a road map on how to reach such alternatives.[90]

The ability of religion to anchor the rejection of Soviet culture in a concrete alternative historical and political context was demonstrated by a 1989 report in *Sovetskaya molodezh* of a liturgy celebrated for the deceased tsar and his family. The fact that this event was favorably reported in the leading young people's newspaper vividly illustrates how key political and religious symbols reinforce each other in the alternative political culture:

> Under the sounds of the national hymn of the Russian [*Rossiyskiy*] empire, "God Save the Tsar!," those gathered for the liturgy lit candles. Shortly thereafter a hymn was sung to the All-Russian new martyrs and confessors, and icons with the image of Nicholas II were carried out. Through their megaphones, the representatives of the militia demanded that the crowd immediately cease singing. At his arrival the second secretary of the October regional executive committee announced to all that the organizers of the gathering would be severely punished. Despite these threats the singing continued . . .
>
> After the liturgy, the Orthodox priest Father Vadim addressed the gathering with a sermon. He said that the terrible sin of regicide . . . lay upon the entire

nation and on the peoples of Russia. This sin had led to Stalin's GULag, the Brezhnev camps and psychiatric hospitals, and to the numerous persecutions of the faithful in Russia . . . He expressed the hope that the liturgy would open the eyes of the Church to the desire of many of the faithful to recognize the members of the tsar's family as martyrs . . .

Father Dionisiy, who heads a commission for the disclosure of the burial place and examination of the presumed remains of the members of the imperial family, seeks to obtain official permission to exhume the grave of the emperor's family, identify the remains, and bury them according to Christian rite in the necropolis of the Petropavlovsk fortress in Leningrad. During the three-week period preceding the liturgy service, its representatives gathered more than ten thousand signatures on their petition to the Supreme Soviet . . .

After the liturgy ended the militia attempted to arrest the priests who had conducted the service, but the crowd surrounded them in a tight circle and led them out of the monastery.[91]

Judging from this piece, in which the tsar and his family become the symbols of all patriots martyred for their faith, the Church and Russian national identity remain as closely intertwined in alternative political culture today as in centuries past. By allowing the Church a stronger social voice, therefore, glasnost and perestroika served only to magnify the public impact of Russian patriotic concerns. As in earlier times of trouble, each drew upon the other for strength and inspiration. Conversely, the persecution of one affected the other. The rediscovery, thanks to glasnost, of a well-developed Russian alternative to socialism in Russian religious philosophy spelled the practical end of Soviet legitimacy. Paradoxically, by granting the Church greater prominence, perestroika undermined any prospect for the rebirth of socialist humanism.

In postcommunist Russia, the Church will continue to play an important role in the reassertion of Russia's alternative political culture. For now it is primarily the politically conservative forces who have recognized this and tried to associate their agenda with the Church, but it is only a matter of time before these values will be espoused by a much broader political spectrum. Certainly Boris Yeltsin has made a point of appearing with Church leaders at every important public occasion. Without a proper appreciation of this religious context, it will surely be impossible to understand postcommunist Russian politics.

4

The "Russian Idea": Forging an Alternative National Identity

Russia cares not whether you believe in socialism, or in a republic, or in a commune. What matters to her is that you respect the greatness of her past and that you hope for and demand greatness in her future . . . Russia's past, and only her past, can be the guarantor of her future. From these ashes, into which the fanaticism of the socialist leaders and the debauchery of the masses they have deceived have thrown our great country, resurrection will come only from a national idea wedded to national passion.
— Peter Struve

A patriotism without sycophantic servility could become the force that unites the Russian people. But it must be very self-critical — a patriotism that is neither irrational nor overbearing, but which understands its limits.   — Aleksandr Solzhenitsyn

According to Sidney Verba, "The first and most crucial problem that must be solved in the formation of a political culture, if it is to be capable of supporting a stable yet adaptable political system, is that of national identity."[1] Following this reasoning, most Sovietologists assumed that a stable political culture like that of the Soviet Union must be an active expression of Russian national identity and Russian national ideals; or, as Adam Ulam succinctly put it, "'Soviet patriotism' today is an ideological veneer over good, old-fashioned Russian nationalism."[2] Reports of continued opposition to state-sponsored policies beyond the 1940s were seen as isolated instances, limited to marginal groups in society. After Stalin's death, however, these occurrences not only persisted, but mushroomed into a full-blown Russian nationalist movement. Despite the confident predictions of one leading Sovietologist that the Soviet regime was now "moored in familiarity, past successes, and Russian nationalism," the divergence between Russian and Soviet concepts of national identity persisted, becoming, if anything, more acute with the passage of time.[3]

Mainstream Sovietology failed to appreciate this crucial distinction because it saw Russian nationalism as an extension of the state, both before and after the October Revolution. This fit the assumptions of both mainstream historians ("continuity theorists"), who minimized the differences between the tsarist and the Soviet regimes, and the proponents of the mainstream approach to the study of political culture, who believed that only one political culture could be dominant. In reality, these assumptions masked fundamental differences between the official and the alternative political culture on how to define Russia's national ideals. The official ideology (both tsarist and Soviet) held to an instrumental view of nationalism, one that served the needs of the state and its ruling elite. The alternative political culture, by contrast, offered a far less coercive vision of Russia's national ideal. The quest to give concrete expression to this "Russian Idea," which, according to Nikolai Berdyaev, "corresponds to the character and vocation of the Russian people," miraculously survived the October Revolution and in the 1980s became the foundation for a comprehensive Russian nationalist opposition to the regime.[4]

The Slavophile National Ideal

Nationality consciously delimits social groups, generally along lines of common ancestry, language, territory, geography, customs, or religion. Political culture theory tells us that political institutions then evolve as a reflection of the particular history, national habits, and ideals of a people.[5] "Nationalism," as Hans Kohn put it, "breathes life into the form built by preceding centuries."[6] Yet as both Leonard Schapiro and Hans Kohn have pointed out, the term "nationalism" is a rather imprecise translation of the Russian term *samobytnost,* which Schapiro prefers to translate as "one's own way of being."[7] In Russian political culture this desire to preserve the distinctive character of Russian history and development was the specific concern of the early-nineteenth-century thinkers known as Slavophiles.

According to the early Slavophiles, Russian historical evolution stressed three qualities: first, the virtue of samobytnost as opposed to imitation of the West; second, the belief that only within the folds of the Orthodox Church could Russians find a "completely sincere sense of brotherhood"; and third, a rejection of Peter the Great's attempt to impose foreign standards on Russia. In contrast to Petrine *absolutism,* Slavophiles advocated the Muscovite notion of limited *autocracy.* Under absolutism, they argued, individuals lose the capacity for personal judgment and accountability that is so vital to civic responsibility. In Peter's system of government the emperor ruled *over* his subjects, rather than by their consent. By contrast, Muscovite autocrats felt constrained by custom. As to how to restrain the monarchy,

Slavophiles preferred the constraints of custom to those of constitutions and legal rules. "Law is something external," says Aleksey Khomyakov, "something which has accidentally become mixed up with life, while custom is an inner force which penetrates the whole life of a people, and enters into the conscience and thought of all its members."[8]

Slavophiles thus abhorred both the absolutist aspirations of the monarchy and Uvarov's doctrine of official nationality. They saw both as caricatures of Russian political culture. Above all else, they valued individual freedom and the public expression of criticism. Such freedoms were, indeed, an essential aspect of their belief in the monarchy, for they allowed the tsar to know the thought and desires of his people; without them, he could not achieve the unity of purpose with his subjects that Slavophiles saw as the only justification for the monarchy. The ideal political order, as Konstantin Aksakov wrote in a memorandum to Tsar Nicholas I, leaves to the government "the unrestricted ability to govern, for that is its exclusive concern," but it must also allow the people to retain "complete freedom both in [their] external and in their internal life. That is the Russian form of social order."[9]

The philosophical and political differences between early Slavophiles and Westernizers were initially not very great, but they became more pronounced when the monarchy forced its critics to choose sides. Whereas Slavophiles generally viewed the monarchy as a desirable form of government needing reform, Westernizers increasingly came to view it as the root cause of Russia's evils. The latter viewed traditional Russian political culture as an impediment to reform, and sought first and foremost to overthrow the established social order. For them it was better for Russia's historical traditions to be discarded on the way to a brighter future for mankind. By contrast, the Slavophiles would rather discard the brighter future than trade it for Russia's soul. By the early twentieth century, the Slavophile attachments to the peasant mir and a self-restrained monarch seemed like curious relics of the past to many Russian intellectuals, enthralled with fervor for social revolution.

Despite the rejection of Russian traditions by the intellectual elite, however, the Slavophile movement had touched a chord in Russian society that would resonate well into the twentieth century. The reason for its popularity lay not in the accuracy of its historical analysis or its political prescriptions, but in the powerful attraction of its vision of good government. Even as the momentum toward revolution gathered speed, latter-day Slavophiles such as Dimitriy Shipov and Boris Chicherin worked tirelessly to establish the zemstvos as a constitutional counterweight to the monarchy. Shipov hoped that the Russian monarchy would gradually move toward a system "analogous to the government structure of England," but in memoirs written just a year after the October Revolution he sadly concludes that "the path of political struggle along which the transformation of our state system developed — namely the opposing of the interests of government power to those of the population and the realization of the idea of popular sovereignty — led with astonishing rapidity to the disintegration of the national spirit and of the traditional attitude to life of the population. It . . . shattered and destroyed [the country's] economic, political and moral foundations."[10]

Despite the Slavophiles' failure to prevent this erosion, the movement's enduring historical significance lies in having drawn public attention to the ideals of the alternative political culture at the turn of this century. Leonard Schapiro writes, "As thought of revolution and of its alternative, reform, came to dominate the mind of the intellectual, the heritage of the Slavophiles or, more accurately, the permanence of the problems with which they were preoccupied, became increasingly apparent."[11] Political stability, however, required more than just an awareness of the country's problems: it required social reconciliation. The neo-Slavophiles understood that before a stable civil society could emerge in Russia, a new national consensus would have to be forged. In the wake of the October Revolution the burden of forging this consensus fell upon the Russian emigration.

The National Ideal of the Russian Diaspora

The desire to provide a healing national synthesis is a common theme of post–1917 émigré writings. In exile, Russian thinkers examined why the October Revolution had succeeded, and sought to identify a path of both personal and collective action that could put Russia back onto the road of peaceful historical development. The foundation for such a renewal, they felt, lay in restoring a holistic sense of national identity rooted in a close identification with the Russian Orthodox Church. Some also tackled the question of which political ideals were best suited to Russia's traditional national-religious identity, whereas others merely gave advice to various émigré political groups on strategy and ideology. Confident that communism was only a passing phase, they wrote for some future generation of Russians seeking to recover their heritage after the demise of communism.

Although Russian religious-philosophical thought showed a remarkable unity of theme, it was far from offering any single solution to Russia's problems. There were significant differences among diaspora thinkers, for example, on attitudes toward fascism, on the appropriateness of armed resistance to the Bolsheviks, and even on how to evaluate Muscovy's political heritage. Evident throughout, however, is a common philosophical approach and a common understanding that a religious and national reconciliation would have to take place before Russia could recover from communism. As Leonard Schapiro notes, these were "first and foremost nationalists and patriots [who] accepted the Slavophile veneration of Russian national tradition, while rejecting their romantic idealization of innate Russian virtues as a substitute for the more usual civic virtues."[12]

Perhaps the most famous harbinger of this intellectual evolution within the Russian intelligentsia was Peter B. Struve. The grandson of the founder of Russia's first astronomical observatory, and the son of the governor of Perm province, Struve was raised in an atmosphere of elite learning and culture. After studying law at St. Petersburg University he joined a Marxist circle, like many young intellectuals. At the age of twenty-four he published his first book, a Marxist analysis of Russian economic development. After several run-ins with the police, he left for Germany, where he edited the influential antigovernment weekly *Osvobozhdenie* (Liberation). Following the establishment of a constitutional monarchy in 1905, he returned to Russia and was elected to the Second Duma, but continued editing one of the country's best-known political monthlies, *Russkaya mysl* (Russian Thought). After finishing his doctorate, he was appointed professor of economics in Moscow and made a member of the Academy of Sciences. His scholarly writings garnered him many honors, including, in 1916, an honorary doctorate from Cambridge University.

Because Struve was considered an archetypal *intelligent,* his participation in the *Vekhi* anthology caused consternation among his peers. The scandal that resulted from his embrace of religious and national ideals was exacerbated by the fact that he did not retire from public life, but rather sought to realize his vision of a "Third Russia" that was patriotic, liberal, Christian, and progressive.[13] In 1917 Struve opposed the Bolshevik coup and eventually became minister of foreign affairs for General Wrangel's short-lived anticommunist government in southern Russia. In exile, he continued to struggle against the Bolshevik regime until his death in Paris in 1944.

Struve and his *Vekhi* colleagues got one final chance to reflect on the meaning of the revolution while still inside Russia, in a volume entitled *Iz glubiny* (From the Depths), published in 1918. Whereas *Vekhi* had been a warning to embrace Russian traditions or risk losing all in a moral and political catastrophe, this new compendium, of which only two original copies survived the revolution, was the beginning of an affirmative political and social agenda for Russia. The late Nikolai Poltoratzky wrote that "in sociopolitical terms it moved from the remnants of Marxist legalism, through liberalism, to a national-state world view, which subsequently came to be formulated as 'conservative liberalism' or 'liberal conservatism.'"[14]

Forced to flee Russia, the neo-Slavophile *Vekhi* authors forged a popular myth about Russian political authority that would help to sustain the values of the alternative political culture. This myth held that the best form of government for Russia was a monarchy, constrained by popular will, yet sufficiently strong to see the country through any crisis. Russia's present turmoil stemmed from the fact that the separation of the monarchy from these popular constraints had weakened rather than strengthened it.

This myth further posited that a synthesis of religious and national identity would be needed, to create a new type of Russian *intelligent* who could overcome the antinomies between Russian and Western cultures. In short, during the interwar years, these Russian neo-Slavophiles worked to craft a new concept of Russian nationalism, rooted in its Christian heritage and reflecting the traditional concepts of constrained autocracy, yet modernized to take into account the experiences of the West. Only by embedding Russian political culture in such an alternative concept of national identity could they hope to preserve and transmit the "social imaginary" of a democratic Russia to their offspring born and raised abroad, and thus allow these values to survive long enough to be restored to a postcommunist Russia.

Among émigré thinkers Ivan A. Ilyin most consistently saw Russia's political-cultural renewal in terms of forging a new national identity. One of the most popular émigré thinkers in today's postcommunist Russia, he is still virtually unknown in the West. After graduating from Moscow University's Faculty of Jurisprudence with honors, Ilyin spent two years studying philosophy in France and Germany. When he returned to Russia, he wrote on a wide variety of subjects, from the nature of the ideal state in Plato to the idea of the General Will in Rousseau. Exiled by Lenin in 1922, he moved to Germany and became a corresponding member of the School of Slavonic Studies at the University of London. A vocal opponent of national socialism, he fled Nazi Germany for Switzerland in 1938, where he resided until his death in 1954. His later writings reflect his abiding interest in shoring up Russian national and religious identity against the threat of totalitarianism.

Ilyin stresses that government begins where common principles abide. Without such principles there can be no consensus in government. Moreover, says Ilyin, in any system it is always a minority that govern. Even in a democracy the majority merely selects its elite and gives it general guidelines for how to rule. The fortunes of the nation thus depend on the quality of its elite. What Russia desperately needs, argues Ilyin, is a new leading elite *(sloy)* that will recognize and promote people of "qualitative-spiritual energy."[15] He envisions this "elite" as a group of Platonic dictator-philosophers who go about purposefully christianizing government. At the same time, however, he warns this elite not to overestimate the power of government to transform society, for it is still an "authority approaching from the outside." The elite "is called upon to respect and aid the free creativity of the people it leads, for one can only lead the free; herders are needed only for animals, supervisors only for slaves."[16] Russia, however, also needs a strong middle class, a free and enterprising peasantry, and a "fraternal" working class, according to Ilyin.[17] The operations of government must be most delicately grafted onto the living tradition of the nation; a government contrary to this living tradition cannot help failing.

The first thing that Russia needs in this time of crisis, therefore, is to reconstruct its true national ideal. Russia would have to once again become great in spirit before it could become a great nation. Hence for Ilyin, love of country is an essential component of Christian love. A Christian should see his homeland as a "living treasure, the living breath of the Spirit of God. *The Nation is not God; but its strength of spirit is from God.*"[18] Like the Russian religious philosopher Vladimir Solovyov, Ilyin argues that true love of country teaches humility and repentance, since it is impossible to love other peoples without first loving and understanding your own people. The path to Russian renewal, therefore, lies in "the spiritualization and benevolent enlivening of the Russian national instinct."[19]

Restoring Russia is a task at once patriotic and deeply religious; it is "doing God's work on earth."[20] In his celebrated essay "The White Idea" Ilyin brilliantly weaves these themes together: "Russia is for us not simply a 'territory,' not just a 'people,' and not merely a 'way of life,' 'habit,' or 'power.' She is first and foremost the national vessel of the Spirit of God, our familiar altar and church, our sanctified family hearth. That is why 'homeland' is not for us a term of secular passion, but a true religious treasure. Fighting for our homeland we fight for the ultimate perfection, strength, and freedom of the Russian spirit."[21]

The Church, for its part, should encourage lay people to exercise fully their Christian ideals in the lay world, "to shine forth living religiosity . . . and to give people freedom of inspiration, filling this inspiration with the light of Christian beneficence."[22] In practical terms Ilyin saw this as a return to symphonia, the freely chosen spiritual accordance of the tasks of church and state. Both should serve the same goal — God's work on earth — but by different means and independently of each other.

Ilyin never created a formal system of political thought. Rather, like other religious philosophers, he saw his task as defining a new Russian approach to politics, one that relied heavily on the Slavophile premise of the alternative political culture. This debt to the past becomes readily apparent when one distills the Slavophiles' thought down to its essential components. First, they embraced a limited function for government. The state had no right to intrude into the sphere of private and corporate existence — the realm we would today call civil society.[23] Orthodox Christianity would form its moral core, but it would have to be freely chosen, not imposed. In order to ensure such freedom of choice, complete tolerance of religion must be allowed and the church and the state must remain separate institutions.

Second, the restoration of Russian civil society would require a new national ideal rooted in the traditional values of patriotism and Orthodox Christianity, both essential components of Russian national identity. Only a reconciliation with these values would allow society to finally heal the rift between the intelligentsia and the populace. The new national identity would have to be preserved in the emigration until it could be restored to Russia after the fall of communism. Finally, this national ideal would be most effectively interpreted by either a monarch or an aristocracy bound by tradition. For Russians, democracy could never be an end in itself, but must serve a higher ideal.

To Western ears these prescriptions may sound hopelessly out-of-date and autocratic. It would not do, however, to forget that these thinkers were reacting to the collapse of democratic institutions all around them, first in Russia and then in the countries of Western and Central Europe. Russian neo-Slavophiles sought to identify those values that would enable democracies to withstand the never-ending onslaughts of usurpers and tyrants. They felt that democratic mechanisms could be relied on only if government itself felt committed to the most deeply rooted popular aspirations. These aspirations were reflected in patriotism, expressed both as public conscience and as service to the nation, and in the christianization of public life. The essential task of modern democracy, therefore, was to anchor these aspirations in governmental policy. At a time when many European and American intellectuals succumbed to the intellectual temptations of fascism and communism, neo-Slavophiles reaffirmed the importance of democracy and embedded it in the broadest base of popular support they could conceive of—patriotism and religion. This unreserved commitment to democracy places Russian religious philosophy squarely in the liberal tradition that has found contemporary political expression in the Christian Democratic parties of Western Europe.

As the contours of contemporary Russian politics emerge, it is becoming clear that the interwar generation of neo-Slavophiles did, in fact, succeed in transmitting some of the legacy of Russia's alternative political culture to future generations. As we shall see, their ideas have led directly to the formation of political groups opposed to the communist regime and to the creation of new political parties in Russia today.

The Communist Attack on Russia

From the outset Lenin and the other Bolshevik leaders opposed every appearance of nationalist sentiment that might serve to bolster the old regime.

After the October Revolution the Bolshevik leaders decisively attacked national values, hoping, during a brief but intense period of "war communism," to eradicate traditional values and replace them with feelings of universal proletarian brotherhood.[24]

Thus, during the first two decades of the new regime everything connected with Russian national culture was suppressed. Russian literary classics, such as Pushkin, Lermontov, Tolstoy, Turgenev, and Dostoyevsky, were banned as ideologists of the Russian nobility. When in the 1930s their works reappeared, they had been re-edited to stress their "revolutionary content." The same happened with pre–1917 Russian art, music, painting, and ballet. Many irreplaceable monuments were destroyed because they were "of no artistic or historical value."[25] Thousands of churches were razed, and the few that remained had their bells removed "so that their ringing would not disturb the workers."[26]

The Bolsheviks, to be sure, attacked all national traditions, but Russians were singled out because it had been their culture and institutions that had bound the empire together. In an effort to suppress the national aspirations of the Russians, the Bolsheviks allowed them no separate Party apparatus, no Russian Academy of Sciences, no national university or conservatory. As Hugh Seton-Watson points out:

> From the beginning of their regime the Bolsheviks did their best to discredit most Russian national traditions. To nationally minded Russians, outside or inside the CPSU, it has seemed that Russia has been ruled by non-Russians. Among the top leaders since 1917 has been a high proportion of Poles, Georgians, Jews, Armenians, and even a few Muslims. Traditional Russian culture, in which the Orthodox faith and liturgy and the mythology of paternalistic monarchy played so important a part, was contemptuously rejected in November 1917.[27]

The result, as the contemporary Russian historian Vladlen Sirotkin notes, was a "nihilistic attitude toward our country's past" that belittled patriotism. The father of Soviet legal doctrine, Peter Stuchka, taught this first generation of Soviet citizens that "in our times patriotism plays the role of the most reactionary ideology, whose function is to justify imperialist bestiality and to deaden the class consciousness of the proletariat." Through the early 1930s the very concept of a distinctive "Russian history" was considered antirevolutionary.[28] Russia thus became the only republic without its own history books or its own national encyclopedia, and Russian schools were the only ones that did not require courses in the history of their republic in addition to the history of the USSR.[29]

After 1934 Stalin, however, abruptly reversed his policy and began to emphasize the leading role that Russia should play among the Union republics.

Many Western analysts took this sharp change in attitude as an indication that the regime had altered its course and embraced the very same values that it had been trying so hard to eliminate. With time, the very longevity of the regime was taken as proof that it had developed a base of popular support.

There are several problems with this conclusion, however. Such an abrupt reversal in policy would tend to suggest a calculated decision on Stalin's part to prepare the regime better for the trials ahead — rapid industrialization, possible war — not a gradual merger of communism and nationalism. First, Stalin reckoned that the Soviet regime would be easier to defend if it tapped into certain popular symbols. Second, he imposed clear limits on the type of national symbolism that would be tolerated. Tsarist military heroes, for example, were glorified, but religious figures were not. Although certain authors were restored, other were not deemed useful to the purposes of the regime. Stalin's adoption of a new National Bolshevik tack, therefore, hardly represented an improvement in the status of traditional Russian culture and values, and after his death the aspirations of the alternative political culture re-emerged with renewed force to channel the discontent that many Russians felt with the Soviet regime into civic activism.[30]

Many observers still find it strange, however, to speak of Russian discontent within the Soviet Union. Until the collapse of the USSR most Americans used the terms "Soviet" and "Russian" interchangeably. Among those who understood the distinction, the common wisdom held that the Soviet Union was nothing more than the old Russia in communist disguise. This identification of the Soviet Union as a Russian state reinforced the assumption that if any group of people were likely to support the regime, it would be the Great Russians.

The momentous changes of recent years, however, are slowly beginning to reveal how little was really understood about Russian discontent with Soviet rule. One of the first myths to dissolve in the spotlight of glasnost was that the Soviet regime had forged a stable multinational empire. By mid–1990 seven Union republics out of sixteen had declared de jure sovereignty: Armenia, Georgia, Azerbaijan, Kazakhstan, Estonia, Lithuania, and Latvia. What surprised observers most, however, was that the Russian republic sought to join this list.

It might have come as less of a surprise had Western observers paid more heed to the emergence of a nonofficial strand of Russian national identity inside the USSR. This alternative national identity closely mirrors the responses of other national ethnic groups to perestroika. Each nationality, of course, reacted somewhat differently, but there are common denominators among them. For each the path to self-determination began with the revival of their distinctive national culture and a reinvigorated and highly politicized sense of patriotism that contrasted itself to official Soviet national identity.

Along with other nationalities, Russians too searched for meaning in the devastation of their traditional culture under communist rule. This has required a soul-searching examination of the root causes of this devastation and a reappraisal of old values. This process has been especially poignant for the Great Russians because of their ambiguous status as both colonizers and colonized: they were the main bearers of Marxism-Leninism to other nations, while bearing the brunt of the Marxist-Leninist experiment at home. This ambivalent legacy is aptly described by the French Sovietologist Alain Besançon:

> The alliance with Bolshevism that brought so much satisfaction to Russian nationalism — the pleasure of domination, the accomplishment of Slavophile messianic prophecies, the extension of the language, and so on — has also produced an extraordinary diminution of the Russian nation. Because it has served as an instrument of Bolshevism and has remained closest to the center of power, it has been exposed more than other nationalities to the destructive aspects of the regime. Central, Muscovite Russia, the historical heart of the nation, displays, as far as the eye can see, ruined villages, fallow fields, gloomy towns, and miserable people, destroyed by alcoholism and morally crippled. The essential biological supports of life appear stricken — the birthrate is in decline, the mortality rate on the rise, and there is a frightening lack of sanitary conditions. As for the condition of culture and language, it is better not to talk of them.[31]

The story of how Bolshevism transformed Russia from a relatively prosperous, rapidly modernizing society into a cadaver is one of the most powerful political myths of the alternative political culture. It echoed in the writings of Russia's most talented novelists, playwrights, social scientists, and historians. With the advent of glasnost, however, it became a public indictment of the Soviet system.

When Gorbachev announced, shortly after coming to power, that the Soviet Union was in a "precrisis" situation, many in the West assumed that he was merely trying to shake up the Party cadres to get them to work more diligently. It seems in retrospect that he was understating the crisis. In the previous fifteen years, national income growth had slowed to the point that the country could no longer replace outdated equipment. The impact of declining productivity was most keenly felt in the country's declining standard of living, which for the majority of the population was already at or below the official Soviet poverty level. Estimates by the Soviet State Committee on Statistics (*Goskomstat*) placed the number of people with incomes below the poverty level at the end of the 1980s at between forty and forty-eight million people. Some Russian economists, however, argued that these figures exaggerated the purchasing power of Soviet citizens. Using Western standards for comparison, the economist Aleksandr Zaichenko came to the conclusion that in 1985 only 2.3 percent of all families could be considered rich, about 11.2 percent fell into the middle class, and the remaining 86.5 percent were poor.[32]

To present a better image of the achievements of socialism, Soviet economists frequently used tsarist Russia as a point of comparison rather than the West. Even here, however, not all comparison ran in the favor of the Soviets. Soviet personal consumption in 1988 corresponded to United States levels in 1916, according to Yuri Dikhanov of the Economics Institute of the USSR Academy of Sciences. Whereas between 1913 and 1985 the time needed to buy consumer goods in the United States shrank between five and ten times, in the USSR it remained virtually the same. Zaichenko reveals an even more startling statistic: in 1913 per capita meat consumption in Russia was 40 percent higher than in the USSR in 1988, and in certain regions, such as Vladimir, Vologda, Voronezh, and the Far East, per capita meat consumption was close to, or higher than, American levels today.[33]

For millions of Soviet citizens, however, no amount of money could buy adequate housing or basic medicines because these things were simply not available. By the late 1980s more than one hundred million Soviet citizens still had less than nine square meters of living space. Fifty million people still lived in communal apartments.[34] Health care, once flaunted to demonstrate the superiority of the socialist system, was clearly deficient. Under glasnost the health minister Evgeny Chazov acknowledged that the Soviet Union occupied thirty-second place in the world in average life-span. Thirty newborns out of a thousand did not survive to their first birthday (four times the infant mortality rate in France), and cardiovascular ailments were twice as common as in developed nations.[35] Because more than thirty million Soviet citizens also consumed polluted drinking water, diseases common in the third world, such as hepatitis-B, diphtheria, malaria, and cholera often reached epidemic proportions. When one added to this a decaying infrastructure (65 percent of rural hospitals had no hot water, 27 percent had no sewage systems, and 17 percent had no water at all),[36] it was scarcely surprising to find the USSR Ministry of Health reporting that more than half of the country's 42 million students suffered from health deficiencies that prevented them from pursuing their vocations when they graduated.[37]

Many sought to escape this dismal reality through alcohol, the consumption of which rose dramatically under Soviet rule. According to a confidential report on alcohol consumption prepared by a section of the USSR Academy of Sciences in Novosibirsk, alcohol consumption per capita had nearly tripled between 1953 and 1983. The report concluded that, "unless extraordinary measures are undertaken in the near future, by the year 2000 there will be 80 million alcoholics and drunkards in this country. That is 65 percent of the entire able-bodied adult population." The report's executive summary concluded with these chilling words: "Hitler wrote in *Mein Kampf* concerning policy in the Eastern Slavic territories: 'For them [the Slavs], there is no hygiene, no vaccinations — only vodka and tobacco.' Today we are carrying out Hitler's orders."[38]

Perestroika opened a window on the new Soviet reality for many both inside and outside the Soviet Union. Still, it had clear limits that, despite incessant public pressure, eroded only very slowly. One of the very last taboos breached by glasnost was acknowledgment of the impact that Soviet socialism has had upon Russia proper.

Galina Litvinova, a senior associate of the Institute of Government and Law at the USSR Academy of Sciences, broke through the veil of silence in May 1989 with an article pointing out that social indicators for Great Russians were among the lowest in the USSR.[39] Russians had steadily lost ground to other nationalities in terms of higher education. Before 1917 Russians were near the top of the list; in 1989, however, they ranked sixteenth among the urban population and nineteenth among the rural population. The main reason for this trend, Litvinova claimed, was that there were only half as many scientific research institutions per capita in the Russian federation as in the other Union republics. In addition, the RSFSR ranked last among Union republics in the percentage of the native population admitted to institutions of higher education.[40]

A similarly bleak situation emerges for housing and social infrastructure in the Russian federation. According to the ethnographers Koroteev and Shkaratai, the social infrastructure in major Russian cities was worse than in major cities of most other republics: "Moscow, the capital of the USSR and the largest city in Russia, is in the 70th percentile of the country's cities in terms of the development of its social and cultural infrastructure."[41]

How had this come about? Litvinova revealed that for decades the central government had been shifting funds from the more economically advanced regions to those that were less developed.[42] During the 1930s, a time of particular devastation for the peasantry of Russia and the Ukraine, Litvinova estimated that more than 60 percent of the expenditures of other Union republics was covered by dipping into the All-Union reserve fund. Investments in the economies of Central Asia during the first five-year plans were five to six times higher than investment in the RSFSR. This subsidy is particularly striking in the agricultural sector. Harvest prices for goods in central Russia were ten times lower than in Uzbekistan and fifteen times lower than in Georgia, despite the fact that the goods produced in each region brought similar prices on the world market.[43] Glasnost also revealed that these subsidies continued long after the need to equalize regional economic development had subsided. In 1986 Andrei Illarionov, an economist at Leningrad State University who later served as deputy director of the Russian government's Center for Economic Reform, estimated that although Russia produced goods and services at 11 percent above the per capita national average as a republic, it received goods and services at only 5 percent above the national average. By contrast, the Central Asian states and Georgia received far larger per capita subsidies.[44]

The extent of these subsidies became a subject of intense public scrutiny during the first contested elections for the leadership of the Russian republic in 1989. Boris Yeltsin's opponent, the Party stalwart Alexander Vlasov, was forced to reveal that 68 billion rubles worth of goods had left the republic the previous year, whereas only 10.7 billion rubles worth of goods were received in return.[45] At the same time, the Institute of Economics of the Urals division of the USSR Academy of Sciences issued a report estimating that the RSFSR would have earned 25 billion more rubles in 1988 if trade with other Union republics had been conducted in world prices.[46]

The effects of this policy of bleeding the Russian heartland are evident in the catastrophic decline of the Russian population. Russia is the only republic, aside from Latvia and Estonia, to have suffered a decrease in the percentage of the titular nationality.[47] Even interrepublic migration fails to explain adequately the population reduction in the RSFSR.[48] Litvinova estimated that between 1979 and 1987 the rural population of the RSFSR declined by four million, corresponding to the loss of two to three thousand Russian villages annually.[49] These were not generations that moved to the cities; they have simply died out because Russian women were having fewer children than any other major nationality in the USSR. Between 1970 and 1980 the number of children attending school fell by 20 percent.[50] By 1989 there were fewer children being taught in elementary and middle schools in the RSFSR than in 1940. Since education at this level is compulsory, demographers have concluded that the children needed to fill these schools were simply never born, leading some to make the dire prediction that if present trends are not reversed, the Russian population could decrease by half in two generations.[51]

Thus, glasnost revealed to Russians that seventy years of communist overlordship had left their country in abject poverty and spiritual and intellectual confusion, and, in addition, they were feared and despised as aggressors both at home and abroad. It is hardly surprising that these calamitous revelations should provoke angry cries of genocide, such as in Vladimir Soloukhin's celebrated essay "Chitaya Lenina" (Upon Reading Lenin). Despite glasnost, this essay was first published in the émigré press abroad. It created such a sensation, however, that it was eventually reprinted in the Soviet Union and widely discussed in the Soviet press and on television:

> I can only be astounded at how, even with the best of intentions (maybe, as they saw it), they [the communists] did not regret scattering and, in fact, killing and devouring such a country as was Russia, and such a people as were the Russian people . . . Maybe, later, one could restore the churches and palaces, regrow the forests and clean the rivers, one might even overlook the gutted and disemboweled earth, but it is impossible to restore the destroyed genetic base of the population . . . The more time passes, the more a gaping chasm will emerge in our culture—the severed national roots—and the more thoroughly our own native field will be overrun by foreign growths and small bushes, rather than towering giants the possibility and character of which we can only guess at because they will never mature. They were terminated, unborn, in the very generations before birth. They will never be because their ancestors were killed, shot, starved, and buried in the ground . . .
>
> Slavery merely deprives a people of the ability to thrive, delaying their full growth and spiritual life. Genocide, especially one as thorough as that conducted for decades in Russia, deprives a people of the ability to blossom, it deprives them of the fullness of life and spiritual growth in the future, most especially the distant future. Genetic damage cannot be undone, and this is the most tragic result of the event which we, sobbing with joy, call the Great October socialist revolution.[52]

Although not everyone, of course, blames Lenin for what happened to Russia, by 1990 a quarter million people a year were leaving the CPSU. When subscriptions to Party publications stopped being mandatory in 1989, *Pravda* lost a third of its subscribers overnight. *Kommunist,* the Party's leading theoretical journal, lost nearly 40 percent.[53] Young people were particularly quick to express their discontent—more than ten million had abandoned the Communist Youth League by 1990. A poll taken among nearly ten thousand young people (ages fourteen to nineteen) between midsummer 1988 and March 1989 showed that 40 percent identified "disillusionment with the ideals of socialism" as a leading social phenomenon among young people.[54]

Who Speaks for Russia?

With the ideals they had been taught to believe in tatters, and the threadbare quality of their lives exposed, Russian intellectuals within the USSR increasingly began to ask themselves how the country had embarked upon this ruinous path, and how to search for a way back. The very question, of course, presumed that at one point Russia had been, more or less, on the "right" historical track. This searching resulted in an enormous surge of interest in Russian history, culture, and religion that led large numbers of people directly to the alternative political culture. Western analysts began to take notice of this phenomenon after the publication of John Dunlop's pathbreaking book, *The Faces of Contemporary Russian Nationalism* (1983), dubbing it variously "pseudo-Slavophilism," "the Russian Idea," and "dissident Russian nationalism."[55] By linking Russia's national identity with the potent political and religious symbols of Russia's past, the alternative political culture's unambiguous message was that only by embracing values of the past could "normalcy" be restored to Russia. The modern neo-Slavophiles who emerged from this movement took it as an article of faith that socialism has proven to be antithetical to Russian national interests. For them Russian patriotism means resistance to the socialist experiment conducted on the Russian people since 1917.

The breach between the alternative political culture and the Soviet official political culture first became public in the mid–1960s with the emergence of a literary genre known as the *derevenshchiki,* or "village prose" writers.[56] These writers rapidly dominated the Russian literary scene, and eventually became quite outspoken about their belief that the values of the October Revolution are alien to Russians.[57]

As a group, these writers were highly critical of Soviet industrial and social policies. They argued that the regime's attempts to replace the traditional way of life of rural Russia and strong emphasis on ethical traditions and religious values, with a mass atheist society, had led directly to the drunkenness, corruption, materialism, and demoralization seen today. Viktor Astafyev, one of the most noted village writers, summarized their views as follows:

> What happened to us? Who hurled us into the depths of evil and misfortune, and why? Who extinguished the light of goodness in our soul? Who blew out the lamp of our conscience, toppled it into the dark, deep pit in which we are groping, trying to find the bottom, a support and some kind of guiding light to the future? . . .
>
> We lived with a light in our soul, acquired long before us by the creators of heroic feats and lighted for us so that we would not wander in the darkness, run into trees, or into one another in the world, scratch out each other's eyes, or break our neighbors bones . . .
>
> They [the communists] stole it from us and did not give anything in return, giving rise to the unbelief, an all-encompassing unbelief.[58]

By the end of the 1980s the critique of Soviet mores pioneered by the village prose writers had become almost commonplace in major Soviet journals.[59]

It was adopted by the editorial boards of the national literary journals *Nash sovremennik, Novyi mir, Molodaya gvardiya, Moskva,* and by many regional or specialized journals such as *Volga, Sibir, Rodina,* and *Isskustvo kino.* In addition, *Literaturnaya gazeta, Moskovskie novosti, Pravda,* and *Izvestiya,* the mainstream "mass media," would sporadically publish letters and articles decrying Russia's fate in particular among the Soviet republics.

These writers played a singularly important role in defining and transmitting the values of the alternative political culture. Taking advantage of the greater official tolerance unloosed by glasnost, they began to discuss openly the tension underlying the official and alternative versions of Russian political culture. But the village writers did more than just describe the evil effects of the Soviet approach to economic, cultural, and social development — they rehabilitated traditional prerevolutionary values, thus setting the stage for a public discussion of the alternative political culture.

The turning point came in 1983, when concern over the environmental impact of the project to divert the flow of major Russian rivers from south to north led to the formation of a coalition that included eminent economists, scientists, writers, historians, and artists. Frustrated with their inability to change government policy, they established direct contact with the émigré community in an effort to popularize their concerns.[60]

Opposition to the river diversion project brought together people from widely disparate personal backgrounds. Their critiques of the project, however, demonstrated the existence of a consistent and clearly definable set of alternative values. These included skepticism of technology, a desire to recapture Russia's lost historical and spiritual identity, and opposition to excessive state intervention in personal affairs. These were contrasted with the secular, rationalist course of social development that was taken in the West and spawned Marxism.

As a result of the coalition's efforts, concern for the ecology became a popular rallying cry for Russian nationalists who argued that the ecological balance in nature was similar to the ecological balance within human cultures. The academician Dmitriy S. Likhachev called this "cultural ecology," which he defined as follows:

> Ecology cannot be restricted only to the tasks of preserving the natural biological environment. No less important for human life is the environment created by the culture of our ancestors. The preservation of the cultural environment is a task no less essential than the preservation of nature's environment. If nature is vital to mankind for our biological life, then the cultural environment is just as vital for our spiritual, moral life . . .
>
> Thus, there are two sections in ecology: biological ecology and cultural, or moral ecology. Not observing the laws of biological ecology can result in a

person's biological death, while not observing the laws of cultural ecology can lead to a person's moral death. Between them there is no deep divide, just as there is no sharply defined border between nature and culture.[61]

Thus the struggle to restore the proper balance, to restore "normalcy" to Russian political culture, could be pursued under the guise of protecting the environment, or restoring architectural monuments, or preserving ancient traditions and folklore. Each was an important component in preserving Russia's alternative political culture, and each added to the construction of a non-Soviet, noncommunist Russian national identity rooted in traditions of the past. As Party control weakened, the overtly political significance of these "cultural" concerns became increasingly obvious.

A key role in the creation of Russian nationalist organizations, for instance, seems to have been played by the sixth meeting of Soviet social scientists in 1988, devoted to "The Nation and Social Renewal."[62] Organized with the sponsorship of nearly every major philosophical and cultural association and with the blessing of the Institute of Marxism-Leninism of the CPSU, the meeting had a participants list that reads like a who's who of prominent Russian nationalists: the philosophers Eduard Volodin and Arseniy Gulyga, the mathematician Igor Shafarevich, the writer Georgiy Kunitsyn, the literary critic Vadim Kozhinov, the historian Dimitriy Balashov. There were representatives of the clergy — the sociologist Father Innokentiy Pavlov, and Father Valerian Suslin from Omsk. At the end of this conference the participants issued an appeal to the non-Russian people of the USSR, highlighting how interethnic tension often begins by discrediting the Russian people and ascribing Stalinist traits to them. In reality, the appeal goes on to say, it was the Russians who absorbed the first blows of the Stalinist system. The appeal urges the introduction of republican-level self-financing, opposition to bureaucratic approaches that do not take fully into account national and regional traditions, freedom of conscience for all nationalities, and changing the school curriculum to reflect better the national traditions of all peoples.

A number of new organizations focusing specifically on Russian national concerns were formed shortly after this conference. The idea of a Russian encyclopedia also gathered prominent support. Under the direction of the linguist Oleg Trubachev, the encyclopedia would bring together all that is known of Russian culture at home and abroad (a conscious effort to reintroduce the heritage of the Russian diaspora), and utilize this knowledge to re-educate Russians about their lost historical and cultural heritage. More than three hundred academics signed up to participate in the project, which is to be completed by the year 2000. Interestingly, the very first section planned will be a series of essays on Russian philosophers, pointedly including émigrés.[63] Nineteen eighty-eight also saw the establishment of the first Russian Popular Houses, an initiative of the Russian Cultural Fund. Such houses were to be set up across the country to disseminate and gather information about lost Russian arts and crafts and spiritual music, as well as to publish books "good for heart and soul."[64]

In 1990 the prominent Russian nationalist Ilya Glazunov was named the first rector to the newly established All-Russian Academy of Painting, Sculpture, and Architecture. According to Glazunov, the academy's purpose was to "resurrect and preserve love for the Fatherland, for its great past and its present, in young souls; and to strengthen our feeling of unity with the great civilization of Europe."[65] Glazunov also helped found the Association of Russian Artists *(Tovarishchestvo russkikh khudozhnikov),* whose program is typical of the many Russian national organizations that arose during this period:

> We appeal to you, brothers in spirit and supporters living inside or outside of Russia, to assert all your strength and talent in the task of reviving, educating, and strengthening the national self-awareness, moral and spiritual force of the Russian people, in the name of and for the future well-being of our great historical Fatherland, of its governmental and cultural foundations.
>
> Our Homeland, uniting the fates of the Russian, Ukrainian, Belorussian, and other peoples, who for centuries lived in harmony, has survived terrible and tragic events. The result has been not only the destruction of cultural monuments, and the economic and political crisis of the governmental system, but also the destruction of that which is the foundation and beginning of all social and political institutions — the national self-awareness of the individual. The lack of respect and lack of understanding for our own national particularities lead to lack of respect for the national traditions and principles of fraternal peoples.[66]

Simultaneously, there was a noticeable change in the attitude toward Russian national concerns among informal political groups, with the Moscow Popular Front and segments of the Democratic Union in Leningrad taking a greater interest in these issues.[67]

By 1991 the debate between National Bolsheviks and neo-Slavophiles had become a prominent feature of the political transition from the Soviet to the post-Soviet era. The removal of Article 6 from the Soviet Constitution, with its reference to the Party's "guiding" function in Soviet society, allowed social commentators and editorial boards across the country to engage openly in what one writer aptly called a "cold civil war."[68]

Perestroika and the "Cold Civil War"

The opening salvo of this war was fired on August 4, 1989, when the economist Mikhail Antonov, the sculptor Vyacheslav Klykov, and the mathematician Igor Shafarevich sent an open letter to the RSFSR Writers Union complaining about the journal *Oktyabr*'s publication of Andrei Sinyavsky's "Walks with Pushkin" and Vasiliy Grossman's *Forever Flowing*. They were particularly incensed by G. Vodolazov's introduction to Grossman's novel which, they said, represented an attempt to sanitize Russian history by artificially separating the policies of Lenin and Stalin. The authors complained that the journal displayed a consistent policy that could only be termed "Russophobic." Sinyavsky, the critics claimed, forces the reader to choose between living in a free world or co-existing with Russia in totalitarianism. Grossman, in turn, was said to emphasize Russia's uniqueness as a "thousand-year-old slave" whose special mystique is to destroy all that she touches. The fact that these words had been published in *Oktyabr*, the organ of the Russian Writers Union, was particularly galling.[69]

The embattled editor of *Oktyabr*, Anatoly Ananyev, promptly responded that his literary freedom was under attack. Grossman's story is not about Russian history, he said, "it is against Stalinism, it is against any form of violence."[70] In an editorial, *Literaturnaya Rossiya* replied that the debate is not at all about Sinyavsky or Ananyev, "but about Pushkin, about honor and dignity. [It is] about ethical and aesthetic values, the displacement of which has implications not only for us but for our descendants . . . There must be moral standards—one's relations to country, to parents, to children, and to national treasures, among them Pushkin . . . Indifference is fatal for us today and in the future. We honor this criterion, because without it life on this earth would be terrifying."[71]

In this "cold civil war" each side saw itself as defending an essential truth that must be revealed to the populace. The stakes were high precisely because this was no ordinary literary debate, but a distillation of conflicting reasons for the failure of the socialist experiment and how that failure ought to be corrected.

A few tried to take the middle of the road. While extolling Grossman's literary merits and praising his work as the first to publicly link Lenin and Stalin, the writer Peter Krasnov, the historian Vladlen Sirotkin, and the literary critic Igor Vinogradov nevertheless questioned Grossman's historical assumption that Lenin and his companions were just helpless pawns of the Thermidorian Revolution. Unable to overcome the "slave mentality" of the Russian populace, they were devoured in the maw of an increasingly repressive system constructed to reform that populace. Grossman, they pointed out, did not condemn Lenin. Quite the contrary, he tried to exculpate Lenin and thereby salvage the intellectual integrity of Bolshevism.

This attempt to salvage the last remnants of Bolshevism, said Krasnov, is the real battle cry of today's neo-Westernizers, and to prove his point he cited from Vodolazov's introduction: "I consider that people who wish to assist humanity's progress should not be thinking about how to 'replay' October and Leninism, but about how to 'replay' the years 1929 and 1937, relying on the values of October and Leninism." Krasnov suggested that one instead begin by questioning Lenin's motives, and then go back further to the origins of this "project" to remake humanity that so enthralled Russian Marxists. For Krasnov and other neo-Slavophiles true reforms must be rooted in a return to national values, "using all that is best and organically tied to our past consciousness, with a balanced exchange of knowledge and experiences with other peoples."[72]

In contrast, for Ananyev and other neo-Westernizers, there is nothing to be gained in restoring the past: "There is no healthy conservatism [in Russia], as in England, no conservative culture—there are only extremes." Ananyev specifically rejected the notion that Russia's pre–1917 heritage can play a positive role in reforming Soviet society: "Under the guise of national thought arises repressive thought."[73]

Clearly, this debate is only peripherally about literary censorship, an issue incidentally resolved in Ananyev's favor by a finding of the Supreme Soviet. It is, in reality, a debate between those who feel the Bolsheviks' objectives were fundamentally desirable but were thwarted by historical circumstance, and those who view the objectives of the October Revolution as inherently evil and as inevitably leading to totalitarianism. Oddly enough, the latter group is often labeled "conservative" in the West, even though it promotes a much more radical critique of socialism.

This debate is indeed reminiscent of the debate between Westernizers and Slavophiles during the nineteenth century, but it is cheapened by mutual lack of respect, and by the attempt of each side to adduce blame for the current state of affairs. Many neo-Slavophiles insist that their opponents accept responsibility for the fact that the ideals they cherished are to blame for the death of millions. Neo-Westernizers (and National Bolsheviks) retort that it is the other side's obstinate unwillingness to criticize the inequalities and injustices of the tsarist past that prevents progress today.[74]

Ultimately, of course, this debate cannot be resolved, it can only be mitigated by democratic institutions and a culture of civic discourse. Its origins lie in vastly differing conceptions of Russia's national ideal that will no doubt persist and even gather strength in democratic Russia. What most Western analysts term the "revival of Russian nationalism" was actually the final, public phase of neo-Slavophile efforts to establish an alternative Russian national identity. By the time Western analysts took note of this, however, it had already reached the stage of formulating political alternatives. Noting the explicit political implications of the revival, some in Russia even referred to this movement as "the Russian Party," a term once used by Dostoyevksy and his contemporaries to describe the early Slavophiles.[75] This term, though not quite accurate in an organizational sense, does reflect the partisan attitude of this group—they are for Russia and against the USSR. The neo-Slavophile political culture, and its "Russian Idea," thus presented a profound conceptual challenge to Soviet rule.

What then is this Russian Idea? It is, first and foremost, enlightened patriotism. As chairman of the Soviet Cultural Fund and editor of the journal *Nashe nasledie* (Our Heritage), Dmitriy S. Likhachev is one of the visible proponents of the Russian Idea. In his frequent appearance in journals and on radio and television he draws attention to the distinction between patriotism and nationalism:

> Patriotism is the most benign of sentiments. It is not even a sentiment—it is the most important side of our personal and social spiritual culture, when a person and his whole country rise above themselves and strive for more than individual goals.
>
> Nationalism, by contrast, is the most unfortunate of the burdens of humanity. As with every evil it hides itself, living in the shadows and only pretending to be the product of love for one's country. It is in reality the result of anger and hatred toward other people, and toward that portion of one's own people which does not share nationalistic views.[76]

As the French scholar Françoise Lesourd has pointed out, much of Likhachev's work has been devoted to establishing a new concept of Russian national identity that will heal the rift between Petrine and Muscovite traditions in Russian political culture.[77] Advocates of the Russian Idea in the Soviet Union have consciously adopted the term "patriot," because they feel it distinguishes them from both the official ideology of communist internationalism and the pseudo-liberal imitation of the West, with its skepticism of patriotic and religious sentiment.

The ideal of enlightened patriotism (or liberal nationalism) is certainly not new to the West. John Stuart Mill described it as a prerequisite for popular self-expression.[78] Rousseau, Herder, and Bolingbroke believed that as each culture developed its own genius and self-understanding, it would be inspired to greater understanding and kindness toward other nations with similar strivings. This view was shared by Nikolai Karamzin, and later by the famed historian Sergei Solovyov and his philosopher son Vladimir Solovyov.[79]

The partisans of the Russian Idea see the affirmation distinctive of national cultures as essential to individual liberty. While firmly rejecting the glorification of the state, they promote what they perceive as "authentic Russian values" in contrast to the artificial values foisted on the people by the regime. These values amount to a restoration of what Ksenya Myalo has called "the broken thread" of national consciousness, including popular participation in the political process and religion as the basis for ethics.[80]

Far from threatening Russian democracy, the proponents of the Russian Idea sought a much more radical restructuring of society than that envisioned by perestroika. It is the neo-Slavophiles who pointed out the abnormality of Russian historical development after 1917, and who urged a return to an "organic" history that reflects the accumulated experience of the Russian people. Prominent Russian neo-Slavophiles were at the forefront of uncovering the crimes of the Stalin era, but they did not stop there. They were the first to blame the official ideology for the decimation of the peasantry through forced collectivization. They charged the regime with destroying the spiritual foundations of life through the persecution of religion. More consistently than any other group in Soviet society, neo-Slavophiles traced Stalinism back to the original conception of socialism promulgated by Marx and Lenin. In sum, it is the neo-Slavophiles who have made the doctrines of patriotism, religious piety, and constrained autocracy the core of their political agenda. Communism lost its social base of support in Russia thanks in large measure to the devastating critique of "real socialism" provided by the neo-Slavophiles.

The success of the Russian Idea in forging an alternative conception of Russian national identity also helps to explain the striking absence of popular support for the CPSU when it belatedly attempted to democratize itself after 1989. Having purged itself of dissident voices fifty years ago, the Party now had no popular base of support upon which to draw. The well-known fact that some of Gorbachev's closest advisers, including Fyodor Burlatsky and Aleksandr Yakovlev, opposed any open reliance on Russian patriotism further undermined perestroika's efforts to achieve broad-based support.

Perestroika's failure can thus be ascribed in large measure to Gorbachev's inability or unwillingness to go beyond that peculiar hybrid, National Bolshevism, which attempted to do to nationality what the regime had done to religion—create and use its superficial "Soviet" version of the alternative political culture to undermine national traditions.

As with religion and autocracy, the attempt to co-opt national identity succeeded in part, most notably in the populace's positive image of the USSR as a world power. Still, after seventy years of communist rule, one is struck, as Fred Barghoorn says, by "the strident tone of much Russian nationalist discourse [that] bespeaks frustration rather than self-confidence or contentment."[81] If communist values and Russian values had merged during this time, one suspects that the results would be more obvious. One might expect to see a widespread disdain for prerevolutionary Russian political and social figures, particularly for the tsar. One would expect a decrease in religious fervor, particularly among the young and better educated. One might expect Russians to be eager exporters of their revolutionary social model to other countries. At the very least, Russians should have given up the search for personal profit and material gain. Instead we see precisely the opposite. The reason for this, of course, is that Marxism-Leninism is not a national ideology. On the contrary, it is quite adamant about the fact that people should eventually forsake their national and religious heritage in favor of a loyalty to their socioeconomic class. Voluntary adoption of Marxism by any nation would thus be tantamount to national suicide.

In *The Faces of Contemporary Russian Nationalism,* John Dunlop mentions in passing that the various facets of Russian nationalism have in fact already had quite a long period of gestation, "interrupted," as he puts it, by the October Revolution.[82] Perhaps the best evidence for this longevity is the explosion of Russian political and cultural self-awareness that took place as soon as government censorship eased. The publicity the neo-Slavophiles gave to the high price the Russian people paid for communism exacerbated the latent tensions between the alternative political culture and the official ideology and explains, ultimately, why the debate over Russian nationalism emerged with such force in the 1980s, and why it will continue to play an important role in Russia's political future.

5

Russia's Alternative Political Organizations: The Re-emergence of Civil Society

Socialism will develop to extremes in all its phases, to the point of absurdity. Then once again a cry of rejection will erupt from the great bosom of a revolutionary minority, and again a decisive struggle will begin in which socialism will take the place of present-day conservatism and be defeated by a future revolution, as yet unknown to us.
— Alexander Herzen

There will come a time when the White movement will adopt the forms of a patriotic order and give birth to a national political party. — Ivan Ilyin

Having surveyed the three central components of Russia's alternative political culture and traced how each sought to restore civil society, we must now assess their political impact. Opposition to the Soviet regime began the day after the Bolshevik coup of November 7, 1917. It led to a bitter struggle between the Bolsheviks and their supporters — the "Reds" — and the supporters of the Provisional Government and their allies — the "Whites." This civil war effectively ended in November 1920 when General Peter Wrangel, the last commander of the White Volunteer Army, ordered the evacuation of all civilian and military personnel from the Crimea.

Yet despite the Whites' total military defeat and decades of vilification in the Soviet media, the last two decades saw a marked upsurge of interest in the White movement among young Russians. White Army memorabilia became highly prized. White Army songs, memoirs, historical novellas, anything associated with the "lost cause" was romanticized. Shortly after leaving the Soviet Union in 1975, the dissident Aleksandr Udodov wrote that "the White struggle in Russia has not been forgotten. Even the tone of Soviet films in recent years has changed markedly. Caricatures of the White officers have disappeared . . . As a concession to public opinion, the White officers are shown as intelligent, valiant, and honest opponents. The sympathy of the viewers is entirely on their side."[1]

Seven years later, an open letter to the participants of the White movement from the great-grandson of the commander of a Red Army regiment offered further evidence of this remarkable shift in public attitudes:

> I decided to write this letter so that, perhaps at the sunset of your days, it would be pleasant for you to learn that you have not been forgotten, that long decades of Soviet propaganda have not been able to expunge you from the popular memory; that the youth in Russia see in you knights without fear or reproach and deem that you did not struggle in vain . . .
>   Looking back into the dark past, covered with lies, we come to this conclusion: Time, history, and perhaps even a majority of the Russian people were on the side of the Communists. Truth, honor, and Russia were on your side.[2]

The ideals of the White movement had somehow survived, a testament to the fundamental incongruity between the values of the regime and those of a significant portion of the populace, between official Soviet political culture and the Russian alternative political culture. If there is a strand linking contemporary political groups to the past, therefore, it originates in the ideals of the White movement.

The White Idea

Vladimir Brovkin favors a chronology of three phases with respect to the Russian civil war, corresponding to the social forces that dominated during each period.[3] Such a periodization highlights the diversity of the social forces involved in the civil war. The first phase, roughly comprising 1918, is characterized by the disintegration of order in the country and the rise of local sovereignties. The Bolsheviks' main opponents during this period were the right Mensheviks and the Socialist Revolutionaries, who set up a rump Constituent Assembly in the city of Samara on the Volga. The second phase, roughly the first half of 1919, is characterized by the military successes of the White Armies. Resistance to the Bolsheviks spread quickly throughout the country. Its very spontaneity led to difficulties in coordinating the White effort. The most important group, both numerically and strategically, was the Volunteer Army in southern Russia commanded by Generals Alekseyev, Kornilov, Denikin, and Wrangel. In just six weeks these ten thousand volunteers managed to occupy a territory populated by more than fifty million people. Brovkin attributes their remarkable success to the peasant rebellions that helped clear the way for White forces. By the autumn of 1919, however, the momentum of the Whites had slowed considerably due to poor coordination, personality conflicts between their leaders, and peasant apathy.

The third and final stage of the anti-Bolshevik struggle took place after the defeat of the White Armies, says Brovkin. Powerful peasant insurrections swept the country in late 1920 and early 1921.[4] The scope and power of these peasant uprisings forced Lenin to introduce a "New Economic Policy" (1921–1928) and accommodate a modicum of free enterprise and private peasant landownership. The peasantry thus succeeded, at least temporarily, in forcing the Bolsheviks to leave the countryside alone. It was not until a decade later, after Stalin had consolidated control over the Party, that the Bolsheviks could begin their second major assault on the peasantry — collectivization. At this point, however, the peasantry no longer had any allies to assist them, and organized resistance was futile. Nevertheless, the horrendous cost of collectivization — at Yalta, Stalin remarked to Churchill that ten million had died in the process of resisting collectivization and in the resultant famine of 1932–1933 — shows how bitterly Soviet policies were opposed by the rural population, and how much they resembled a foreign occupation.[5]

Many reasons are adduced for the failure of the Whites. Some historians emphasize the brutality of their conduct, while others stress the conflicts that plagued the military leadership. Whatever the reasons, they mask a considerable consensus on fundamental values within the White movement. A comparison of basic documents from the various White Armies shows that, despite tactical disagreements, the Social Revolutionaries, Constitutional Democrats, and Mensheviks who supported the White cause all agreed on the political principles they were struggling to uphold.[6]

The first principle upon which all agreed was the unity of the Russian empire. This unity, however, was to be based on "national-cultural self-determination" and would allow for extensive local autonomy. Most groups, though not all, interpreted this to mean a federal system of government. Second, all groups agreed on the need to restore all "liberties and institutions of true popular government, namely the Constituent Assembly, zemstvos, and municipal dumas."[7] Third, with the exception of General Krasnov's forces in the Don region, all groups agreed on the legitimacy of the February 1917 revolution. The White movement thus saw itself as fighting for the restoration of legitimate authority, which for the vast majority meant the recently elected Constituent, not the monarchy. The Constituent Assembly was deemed the sole appropriate arbiter of Russia's future precisely because it was popularly elected. Even General Krasnov, one of the few advocates of restoring the monarchy, later adopted a constitution for his region based on the fundamental laws of the Russian empire *after* 1906, that is, after the institution of a constitutional monarchy.[8]

Lastly, all groups agreed on the preservation of civil liberties and the rule of law. The provisional statutes for civil administration for the regions occupied by the Volunteer Army list these rights in great detail:

7. In the regions occupied by the Volunteer Army, Russian citizens enjoy inviolability of person, residence, private correspondence. No one is to suffer restriction or loss of freedom except through due process of law. Search and arrest can be carried out only in cases provided for by law and in a manner defined by law.

8. Freedom of the press is recognized. The procedure of inspecting the press and of [establishing] responsibility for crimes and misdemeanors committed through the press . . . [is] to be defined by law.

9. Russian citizens may assemble peaceably and without arms, and likewise organize societies and unions for purposes not contrary to the law. The manner of using these rights of civil liberty is to be defined by law.

10. Property is inviolable. Compulsory expropriation of immovable property, when necessary in the interests of the state and of society, will be carried out in accordance with law and with fair compensation.[9]

Unlike the communists, therefore, the Whites never viewed themselves as being above the law. One example is the White policy on land distribution. Criticized for favoring restoration to former landlords, in fact White leaders refused to make promises on the disposition of the land, believing that such issues should be resolved by the Constituent Assembly. Their policy was to halt the willful expropriation of personal property and to leave the land in the hands of the de facto tenants.[10] White leaders recognized that adherence to this principle would cost them public support, but they saw it as necessary if Russia was to become a law-governed state.

The White political vision for Russia was thus highly consistent. It recognized the diversity of political, ethnic, and social groups in Russian society, and sought to reconcile these within the framework of a constitutional order under the rule of law. This clearly distinguished them from the Bolsheviks, who counted on a dictatorship of the proletariat to establish social control. As Brovkin notes, "The Whites' ultimate goal . . . remained that of imposing state authority on separate identities rather than that of blending all into one."[11] Put another way, the Whites understood the need for a civil society distinct from the state, whereas the Bolsheviks did not.

An inability to translate this vision into a coherent policy, however, doomed the White cause. The monarchy's disgrace had weakened the authority of traditional institutions, and although the intelligentsia insisted that the Constituent Assembly would hold the key to a legitimate transition of authority, having just been elected it was an unknown entity to most of the populace, with no constituency outside of the intelligentsia to support it. The weakness of national institutions, combined with the general decay of the fabric of society, sealed the fate of the Whites.

It is not correct, however, to infer from the defeat of the Whites that Bolshevik ideals were more popular. With perestroika, Soviet historians have felt freer to contradict the official version of the inevitability of the October Revolution and the Bolshevik victory. Vladimir Shishkin, for example, argues that "it is difficult to imagine a time in the entire history of Russia that was pregnant with so many variants from which to choose as 1917."[12] He and his colleague P. V. Volobuev note at least six possible alternative scenarios: 1) a peaceful transition to democratic socialism; 2) a revolutionary form of proletarian socialism; 3) a reformed capitalist system; 4) a military dictatorship supported by the bourgeoisie; 5) a restoration of the monarchy; and 6) popular insurrection and anarchy. A seventh possible outcome, a multiparty democratic political system, says Shishkin, seemed the most likely at the time, since forty-two million people had just participated in the elections to the Constituent Assembly, two-thirds of them voting for the "bourgeois" parties.[13] Another revisionist historian, V. Startsev, argues that a moderate reformist path involving a number of political parties would have been the most probable, had the Bolsheviks been thwarted in their armed uprising in Petrograd.[14] But the true depth of the Russian alternative political culture's attachment to civil society may ultimately be measured by the fact that political resistance to the regime continued in the emigration and resurfaced whenever possible inside the USSR. In each arena different segments of Russian society sought to re-establish the progress toward civil society broken off by the October coup d'état.

A New Generation in Exile

Nearly two million Russians found themselves outside of the Soviet Union after the end of the civil war. During the first two decades of exile they maintained vibrant communities abroad that included Russian theaters, schools, and universities. As late as 1936, 108 newspapers and 162 Russian journals were regularly published abroad.[15] There were also many political parties and groupings, which fell into three main categories: the first prepared itself for the renewal of military campaigns inside Russia; the second continued the political bickering that had weakened the White effort, now augmented by recriminations about who had lost that effort; and a third tried to come to terms with the reality of Bolshevik rule and to explain what it meant for Russia.

It was this last group that proved to be the most enduring. Under the tutelage of an extraordinary group of Russian religious philosophers exiled by Lenin in 1922, a distinctive strand of neo-Slavophile Russian thought flourished among the European capitals of the interwar period. Its contribution to Russian political culture has survived to this day in the political movement called the Popular Labor Alliance of Russian Solidarists, best known by its Russian acronym — NTS.

The NTS was founded in 1930 in Yugoslavia as the Popular Labor Alliance of the New Generation (NTSNP). It was born of a rebellion among émigré youth dissatisfied with the passivity of the older generation and desirous of more active engagement in the struggle for a new Russia. These *nats-malchiki* (nationalist boys), as they were condescendingly called by the older generation, embraced patriotism as an antidote to international communism and favored romantic idealism to the West's emphasis on secular rationalism.

What distinguished the NTS most from other émigré groups of the interwar period was its forthright acceptance of the fact that the civil war had been lost and that Russians must now live with a new, Soviet reality. In a clear challenge to the older generation, the inaugural edition of the NTS newspaper *Za Rossiyu* stated: "We reject all restoration, we accept the revolution as an accomplished fact."[16] For the young émigrés, however, the search for an alternative ideology clearly could not succeed unless it involved Russians on both sides of the border. From its outset, therefore, the organization sought to disseminate its ideas inside Soviet Russia by any means possible.

The first dispatch of leaflets by balloon was attempted in 1935. Soon afterward a school was organized near Warsaw to train volunteers to cross the heavily guarded Soviet-Polish border illegally, and in 1938 six men made the attempt. The Soviet press soon took notice of these efforts, and on December 6, 1938, Radio Moscow reported the first arrest of NTS saboteurs in the capital.[17]

By calling themselves a "new generation" NTS members sought a way distinct from both atheist communism and the rationalist liberalism that seemed incapable of comprehending disinterested dedication to higher ideals. To NTS members Western democracies seemed invariably to devolve into demagoguery, mudslinging, and social fragmentation. One early NTS publication described liberal democracies as "ruled by masses who are depraved by demagoguery and by corrupt parliamentarians . . . unable to create the maximum favorable conditions for the development of man."[18]

In fact, the young émigrés blamed liberalism for the social fragmentation that had led to the October Revolution, since such was the conclusion of one of their favorite publicists, Ivan A. Ilyin. Before the revolution Ilyin had been a professor of law in Moscow and an elected member of a peasant executive committee in Tula province. He had welcomed the February revolution, and viewed the Constituent Assembly as "a government of national self-preservation . . . the realization of popular democracy [*narodovlastie*]."[19] Exile to the West, however, had made him much more critical of liberal democracy. He deplored the Russian intelligentsia's lack of support for Russian nationalism, and in his later writings argued that Russia's resurrection from communism would only occur through a conscious embrace of its national and religious heritage.

A gifted orator and prolific writer, Ilyin wrote an influential pamphlet, "The White Idea," which became a manifesto for the émigré remnants of the White movement. In it he argued that the young generation bore the responsibility of visualizing and embodying the Russian ideal. Only by preserving that ideal could the damage inflicted by Bolshevism eventually be undone. Although he never joined the NTS—to protect it from the "sins and prejudices of the past" the Second Congress of the NTSNP passed a resolution stipulating that no one born before 1895 could join—he had a strong influence on its young leaders.[20]

One sees this influence in the contempt for "vote chasing" and political parties, and in the emphasis on service and personal commitment to Russia. National service, Ilyin said, was a spiritual quality transcending ethnicity. Russia needed not a fascist ideal of service to the secular state but rather an eternal ideal for which the state was just a temporary vessel. Because the Bolsheviks attacked all national values, the young émigrés embraced their "Russianness." Preservation of national heritage, language, and culture abroad became prime duties for young NTS members. The NTS also stressed the religious component of Russian identity, and saw the Russian Orthodox Church as playing a prominent role in postcommunist Russia. Finally, the NTS stressed the importance of government in providing appropriate conditions for individual prosperity. The government should discourage excessive self-gratification and encourage public service. Economic laissez-faire was rejected as inappropriate, and unearned income (profiteering) as intolerable.[21]

It seemed for a while as if the NTS might find its sought-after combination of idealism, nationalism, and anticommunism in fascism. After a fact-finding mission to Italy, however, Executive Secretary M. Georgievsky reported that fascism had turned out to be "just another dead-end street."[22] Nor did German national-socialism hold any appeal for the young émigrés, particularly after their favorite ideologist, Ilyin, was forced to flee to Switzerland in 1938 to avoid arrest by the Gestapo. Eventually, however, the NTS developed its own hybrid political ideology, known as "solidarism," based on an Orthodox understanding of social and economic teachings pioneered by the Catholic Church. After World War II, NTS members would increasingly identify themselves as simply "Christian Democrats," a designation given a certain legitimacy by the fact that during the 1980s the group attended, as official observers, several regional Christian Democratic Party conferences in Germany and France.

Prior to World War II, however, the group limited its political program to a six-point platform adopted at its first Congress. The platform included a call for the restoration of personal freedoms and the rule of law, a "sound self-interest" in international policy, self rule for national minorities, private ownership of land, and free choice of economic relations. These basic components of any civil society, however, were to be tempered by a strong government that stood above parties and classes and regulated the economy to protect those too weak to fend for themselves. On all essential points, however, NTS objectives corresponded to those of the White General Lavr Kornilov, founder of the White Volunteer Army, with whom they consciously sought to identify. The political ideals of the White movement had thus survived the revolution and been adapted to new circumstances by the younger generation. This sense of continuity was reinforced by the direct support of key figures close to the Whites, including Ivan Ilyin, Peter Struve, and Vasiliy Shulgin.[23]

How might Soviet citizens, deprived of contact with the outside world for more than a generation, respond to these ideas?[24] World War II provided an opportunity to compare the popularity of the political agendas of the official ideology and the alternative political culture.

The Russian Liberation Movement

When the German Reich invaded Soviet Russia on June 22, 1941, many welcomed it as a liberating army. In less than a month the Germans had captured more than 200,000 prisoners. Entire units crossed over to the Germans.[25] From the very outset of the war, therefore, the German Army was in the unusual position of having several hundred thousand enemy volunteers, eventually known as *Hilfswillige* (HiWis). A leading British authority, Catherine Andreyev, conservatively estimates that at its height there were nearly 1 million former Soviet citizens fighting in the German Wehrmacht, and another 3 million forced laborers.[26] By contrast, the leading German expert on the subject, Joachim Hoffman, states that by the end of 1941, 3.8 million Red Army personnel had voluntarily surrendered to the Germans, and the total involved in the German war effort numbered 5.24 million.[27] Wartime is usually an opportunity for an embattled leadership to rally the country. Exactly the opposite occurred in the Soviet Union during the first six months of the German war effort, however, as Soviet soldiers either refused to fight or joined the German forces in astounding numbers.

Sensing the strength of popular opposition to the Bolsheviks, the deputy chief of the political department of the Ostministerium, Dr. Otto Bräutigam, in October 1942 wrote a memo urging that a "Russian De Gaulle" be sought to lead an opposition movement to the Soviet regime. Several possible candidates were approached, including Stalin's son Yakov, but the military's choice eventually fell upon Major General Andrei A. Vlasov, who had been captured four months earlier.

The idea of forming a Russian army of liberation had actually come to Vlasov independently, shortly after his capture.[28] While in a select German prison for high-ranking officers, he and Colonel Vladimir Boyarski composed a memorandum which, they claimed, reflected the views of most Soviet senior officers. They wrote that the war was being lost by the Soviets because of the lack of popular support for the regime. Stalin, however, would continue the war no matter what the cost, just to save his own skin. A military force composed of Russian prisoners of war would gladly fight Stalin, but only if they were treated as allies, not as mercenaries. Such a force, they said, could become the nucleus for the creation of a new social and political system, which most Russians desperately wanted.[29]

The authors' claims might be dismissed as a thinly veiled attempt to ingratiate themselves with their captors but for the fact that they refused to place themselves unconditionally at the service of the German Reich. Indeed, at one point in their memo they disingenuously suggest that anticommunist Russian forces might be better off allied with Great Britain and the United States! It is clear from this memorandum, and from his subsequent difficult relations with the German High Command, that Vlasov viewed opposition to Stalin not as treason but as a patriotic duty that would be understood by every Russian. Regardless of the Germans' decision, Vlasov repeatedly told them that the course of the war would eventually turn against them, forcing them into an alliance with an independent Russian army.

After much internal debate, the German High Command gave its tentative approval to the idea, whereupon Vlasov immediately asked to see the political programs of émigré groups. The only one available was the NTS Program Outline (called *Skhema*), which had been prepared for just such a contingency.[30] Written by some of the founding members of the NTS, and amended by new recruits inside German-occupied territories of the USSR, this document formed a valuable bridge between the experience of the young émigrés and their Soviet counterparts. It emphasized a mixed econ-omy, a classless society, the rule of law, civil rights, and a government above party divisiveness. Under the influence of new members inside the USSR, however, it made no mention of any social role for the Church, and empha-sized the right of nationalities to self-determination.

This NTS *Skhema* served as the model for almost all subsequent political documents by the Russian Liberation Army (known as ROA in Russian) that Vlasov headed. Significant portions of the "Smolensk Declaration" (1943) and the "Prague Manifesto" (1944) were drafted by NTS members, with entire passages lifted from the *Skhema*. Several of Vlasov's closest advis-ers were members of the NTS, including Generals Trukhin and Meandrov, key staff at the Dahbendorf officer training school, and Alexander Kazantsev, the editor of the RAL newspaper *Volya*.[31] Despite their very different back-grounds, the young émigrés and the Soviet officers instinctively sensed that they had much in common — both were suspicious of democratic liberalism and political parties but agreed on the need to guarantee civil liberties, free-dom of movement for the peasantry, private property, and the rule of law. The NTS term *natsionalno-trudovoi stroi*, or "popular labor system," was soon adopted as the official RAL vision of Russia's future.

The remarkable coincidence between the views of Russian émigrés in the NTS and many Soviet officers of the Russian Army of Liberation testifies to the survival of basic political-cultural values despite twenty years of separa-tion. In a famous passage from *The Gulag Archipelago*, Aleksandr Solzhenit-syn describes the impact of his "first contact" with a young émigré his own age who had fallen into Soviet hands:

> I found it interesting in the extreme to picture through his life all those compa-triots of my generation who had landed outside Russia . . . They grew up, so to speak, in the shadow of the indelible misfortune which had befallen their families. Whatever country they grew up in, they looked on Russia alone as their Motherland. Their spiritual upbringing was based on Russian literature, all the more beloved because to them it was the beginning and end of their Motherland . . .
>
> We would often lie beside one another on the wooden bunks. I tried to understand their world as best I could, and our encounter revealed to me a concept confirmed by later encounters — that the outflow from Russia of a sig-

nificant part of her spiritual forces, which occurred in the Civil War, had deprived us of a great and important strand of Russian culture. Everyone who
really loves that culture will strive for the reunion of both streams, the one at
home and the tributary abroad. Only then will our culture attain wholeness.
Only then will it reveal its capacity for benign development.[32]

The true test of the survival of Russia's alternative political culture under
Stalin, however, would be to see whether these ideals could find support
among a broad swath of the population. Convinced that they could, Vlasov
in 1943 prepared his first programmatic political declaration, the "Smolensk
Memorandum." Addressed to all the people of the Soviet Union and signed
by a "Russian Committee" ostensibly based in Smolensk, the appeal begins
with the blunt assertion that "Bolshevism is the enemy of the Russian
people." It blames wartime losses not simply on Stalin's personal dictatorship, but on "the rottenness of the whole of the Bolshevik system." The
appeal calls upon the Russian people to rise up and destroy Stalin's regime,
and to establish in its place a new Russia based a thirteen-point program.
Five of these points deal specifically with civil rights. They include the abolition of collective farms and the "systematic transfer of land into the peasant's
private ownership," the dismantling of the secret police, the introduction of
"genuine freedom of religion, conscience, speech, assembly, and the press,"
and the inviolability of persons and their homes. Finally, there is a pledge to
free national minorities and release all political prisoners. The next largest
section deals with guarantees of social welfare and clearly shows the impact
of Soviet rhetoric. Included here are relatively amorphous concepts such as
the "opportunity for the intelligentsia to work freely for the well-being of
the people," "social justice," and "protection from exploitation of all working
people," as well as the right to education, leisure, a secure old age, and pen-
sions for war veterans. A final section calls for restoring the national infrastructure and traditions destroyed by the Bolsheviks, specifically, rebuilding
factories, support for independent commerce, trades, and crafts, and the rebuilding of towns and villages. The one jarring note to what might otherwise be termed a social-democratic social agenda is point twelve, which calls
for the "abrogation of the one-sided payments to the Anglo-American capi-
talists" agreed to by Stalin.[33]

The "Smolensk Memorandum" was rejected by the German higher authorities. In a manoeuvre designed to force a change in German policy, however, dissidents within the German Ostministerium arranged for the memorandum to be "mistakenly" dropped over German-occupied territory in
January 1943. The leaflet immediately aroused tremendous interest on both
sides of the front. Smolensk, where the committee was supposed to be located, was flooded with letters and people seeking to join the committee.[34]

From that moment on, Andreyev writes, "Soviet citizens within the Third Reich began to consider themselves members of a Russian Liberation Movement, and the individuals serving in the Wehrmacht sewed insignia onto their uniforms to indicate their unity of purpose with the Russian Liberation Army."[35]

To capitalize on this favorable response and to further test the popularity of the anticommunist message inside Russia, the Germans finally allowed Vlasov to make two trips inside occupied Soviet territory. The first, in February 1943, took him to Smolensk, Bobruysk, and Mogilev. The second, in May 1943, took him to the northwest regions of Pskov and Luga. By all accounts Vlasov was greeted with great enthusiasm and his speeches warmly received. At Luga, excited crowds broke through the police cordon. Vlasov stressed that Russia would never submit to foreign domination, but explained to his audiences that the German nation would help Russians overthrow the Stalinist dictatorship just as the Russians had once helped the Germans get rid of Napoleon.[36]

Vlasov had clearly tapped into a wellspring of popular discontent, yet despite the obvious potential of such a movement, on June 8, 1943, Hitler personally vetoed the idea of an allied Russian army. Vlasov's impudence in claiming the Germans as allies so offended the Fuehrer that he had Field Marshal Keitel issue the following directive:

> In view of the absolutely shameless statements of the Russian war prisoner General Vlasov, on a trip to Army Group North, which occurred without the Fuehrer's knowledge and without my knowledge, it is ordered that General Vlasov be immediately returned under special guard to a prisoner-of-war camp, which he is not to leave again for any reason. The Fuehrer no longer wishes to hear Vlasov's name in any connection except propaganda operations in whose implementation the name but not the person of General Vlasov will be needed. Should General Vlasov appear once more in public, he is to be handed over to the Secret State Police [the Gestapo] and rendered harmless.[37]

Amazingly, the German High Command seems to have been blithely unaware of just how much its war effort already relied upon the HiWis. Despite this setback, Vlasov continued to work on his project, apparently encouraged by a meeting arranged in the Ostministerium by sympathizers working with the military plotters seeking to assassinate Hitler.[38]

Vlasov's prediction that the Germans would have to accede to his demands for equal treatment was eventually fulfilled, but only in September 1944. After a meeting with Reichsminister Heinrich Himmler, he was finally given an opportunity to set up a government-in-exile, called the Committee for the Liberation of the Peoples of Russia (KONR in Russian). On November 14, 1944, KONR issued a political declaration, known as the

"Prague Manifesto," which repeats many of the points made earlier in the "Smolensk Memorandum," with a few interesting additions and clarifications. The equality of all nationalities and their right to self-determination were made more explicit and moved up from point number six to point number one. The condemnation of England and America, inserted in the Smolensk declaration at German insistence, was replaced with the simple statement that Russia desires "friendly relations with all countries and the greatest possible development of international co-operation." Government measures to strengthen the family and guarantee "genuine equality for women" were promised, and the inviolability of private property was guaranteed, but only if "earned by labor."[39]

Even at this late date, with the tide of the war clearly favoring the Soviet Army, the response to this appeal for an anti-Bolshevik liberation movement was astounding. An estimated 2,500–3,000 volunteers daily requested enlistment in the Russian Liberation Army. On November 30, 1944, 470 joint telegrams were registered by Vlasov's chancellery in Berlin-Dahlem. A total of 43,511 signatures were appended, and another 172 claimed to speak for "all" the internees in the camp. Hoffman estimates that on that one day more than 60,000 inmates volunteered to join the Russian Liberation Army. By the end of November 1944 that number had risen to more than 300,000, and by January 1945 to more than 1 million.[40] In December the Presidium of KONR announced that it could not possibly accommodate all the requests it had received, and it urged those wishing to volunteer to serve the cause by continuing their work in industry or agriculture.

It might be argued that these inmates sought only to escape their desperate situation in German prison camps. Offers to join the new army, however, came in equal measure from those already fighting in the German Army and those working as forced labor in factories or on farms. Moreover, it does not explain why so many were willing to risk death at the front rather than await their imminent liberation from prison by the rapidly approaching allies. It seems clear from the overwhelming response to the "Prague Manifesto" that its political objectives did indeed meet with broad popular support, and that Hoffmann is essentially correct when he terms the Russian Liberation Army "a true patriotic uprising" among the millions of Russians who had escaped Soviet control.[41]

What does the Vlasov movement reveal about the continuity of Russian political-cultural ideals? Was it "the continuation of the White Idea in the struggle for a national Russia," or was it more akin to the Kronstad rebellion of 1921 — a movement born of Soviet values that accepted the October Revolution but saw it betrayed by Stalin?[42] The majority of Soviet citizens had been raised with a very negative image of the White cause. Hence, any movement that aspired to have a broad social base within the Soviet Union would need to distance itself from this image. Still, the record suggests that though many in Vlasov's entourage originally viewed the émigrés with suspicion, the two groups soon recognized the basic similarity of their political outlooks. From the outset, both groups repudiated Bolshevism and wished to establish basic civil rights and restore the land to the peasantry. The influence of two decades of socialist upbringing, however, is evident in the emphasis on the responsibility of the state to promote social welfare and in the idea, held by some ROA leaders, that the original soviets had been democratic institutions.

A major role in integrating the two political visions and in highlighting the similarities between them was played by the younger generation of émigrés, particularly those in the NTS. Although originally skeptical of their ability to understand Soviet reality, Vlasov eventually came to admire the group. The political agenda of the Russian Liberation Movement was clearly inspired by the NTS *Skhema,* which, in turn, was a conscious effort to combine White émigré activism and Soviet socialist reality. The ability to reconcile key elements of both émigré and Soviet Russian cultures in such a remarkably short time underscores the fundamental continuity of political culture both inside and outside the USSR. Despite its failure, the Russian Liberation Movement demonstrated that a political platform calling for the restoration of civil liberties, private property, and national self-determination still appealed to millions of Soviet citizens after more than two decades of Stalinism. The fundamental aspirations of Russian political culture for the restoration of civil society may have been driven underground, but it had not been eradicated.[43]

Khrushchev's "Thaw" (1956–1961)

Although sporadic military uprisings against Soviet rule continued into the early 1950s in the western Ukraine, massive military opposition of the kind envisioned by Vlasov was no longer feasible.[44] The country was too exhausted from decades of turmoil and conflict. In addition, Stalin's self-serving embrace of national symbols had given Russians hope that the social truce instituted during the war might continue. The calm that had descended on Soviet society between 1945 and 1953 was generally seen as evidence of a reconciliation between the regime and the populace, but the tenuous nature of this truce was abruptly demonstrated in the literary and political "thaw" that followed Khrushchev's speech to the Twentieth Party Congress on the atrocities of Stalin's crimes.

Although the extent of literary opposition to the regime is well known, there is still disagreement among observers over whether these writings reflected a widespread counterculture, or only the meanderings of a small coterie of disgruntled scribblers. The latter argument is belied by the simultaneous emergence of opposition among other segments of society. Indeed, between 1953 and 1963 there were spontaneous prison riots, student discussion groups, and even a few general riots, occurring in Temir-Tau, Novocherkassk, Minsk, Krasnodar, and Kaunas.[45] Moreover, the writers who challenged Party orthodoxy saw themselves as presenting the views of the populace to the political leadership, and were viewed as threatening for that very reason.

The first few years of the Khrushchev regime were particularly encouraging to national minorities. There was a pragmatic attitude toward local nationalism, the rehabilitation of victims of nationalist purges, a more positive evaluation of cultural patrimony, and the reopening of many national cultural and scientific institutions. Like Gorbachev, Khrushchev apparently believed that large portions of the intelligentsia and the populace might join in the renovation of socialism. He became frightened, however, when the Hungarian revolution rejected socialism outright. The Soviet political elite's ambivalence about pursuing reforms is captured in the following passage from Khrushchev's memoirs:

> On the one hand we really did allow an easing . . . and relaxed our controls, and the people started to express themselves more freely both in conversation and in the press . . . But there were two views on this: it reflected our inner feelings and we wanted it; on the other hand, there were people who did *not* want this thaw, for fear that it might produce a flood which would inundate everything and which would be difficult to deal with . . . For this reason, we, as it were, restrained the thaw . . . Things that were undesirable to the leadership would have overflowed the restraining barriers, and such a tide would have . . . swept away all the obstacles in its path. The fear was that . . . the leadership . . . would not be able to lead and direct into Soviet channels the creative forces which would be let loose, nor to ensure that the output of these creative forces would serve to strengthen socialism. This concern was good, a good instinct, but perhaps a bit cowardly.[46]

The civic activism that emerged during this period, therefore, was a spontaneous and disorganized reaction to the changes Khrushchev himself had hinted at. Over the coming decade this spontaneous outburst gradually became more organized, first as a movement for human rights and then as the demand for full political participation in society. This first taste of glasnost left a lasting impact on "the generation of the 1960s" and encouraged some to hope that the top Party leadership might someday again seek broader public support.[47]

Three types of political response to the thaw emerged in Russian society after 1956. The first, the dissident movement for human rights, demanded the rule of law. Its most prominent voice was Andrei Sakharov. The second, the Russian nationalist movement, called for the abandonment of communism and a return to Russia's prerevolutionary heritage. Its most prominent spokesman was Aleksandr Solzhenitsyn. The third, the movement of socialism "with a human face," called upon the CPSU to reform itself from within. This strand, represented by the historian Roy Medvedev, provided an early critique of the "Stalinist" model of socialism and helped to promote Mikhail Gorbachev.

Human Rights (1969–1979): Forerunner of Political Dissent

The human rights movement is the aspect of dissent most familiar to the West. Despite its limited membership and short life-span, it played an important role in developing a civic consciousness among the populace. Khrushchev's revelations about Stalin at the Twentieth Congress of the CPSU in 1956 had shattered all illusions of Party infallibility. Politically active young people reacted to these revelations by committing themselves to the support of basic human rights as a means of preventing further abuses of government power. Among the earliest landmarks of the struggle for human rights was the "Civic Appeal" distributed at Moscow State University in 1965 by a group calling itself "Resistance."

Several hundred people responded to the group's call for a peaceful public rally in support of political prisoners. They met in Pushkin Square in Moscow on the evening of December 5, 1965, the day of the signing of the first Soviet Constitution.[48] These gatherings later became a yearly event in the life of the dissident community. Their appetites for freedom whetted by Khrushchev's "liberalization," the students demanded the freedom to organize independent literary journals and form independent discussion groups and clubs. The government reacted swiftly, arresting the organizers and expelling the students. Underground journals, however, survived and became increasingly political. In 1966, Yuri Galanskov, the founder of one of the first underground literary journals to circulate among students at Moscow University, *Phoenix,* began a new journal to address social and political issues. *Phoenix–66* thus became the country's first samizdat (self-published) underground political journal.

In 1967, however, Galanskov and three of his assistants were arrested and tried for anti-Soviet conspiracy and ties to the Russian émigré organization NTS. This was the first nationally publicized trial of regime opponents since the infamous Stalinist "show trials" of the 1930s. The regime tried to discredit the young students by suggesting that they were in the pay of émigrés and foreign intelligence services. Despite widespread public protests against the trials, all four were convicted and given long prison sentences.[49] Galanskov, seriously ill at the time, died on a prison operating table in 1972.

As a result of arrests and repressions, part of the dissident youth movement disintegrated, while another part went underground. The invasion of Czechoslovakia in 1968, however, saw an upsurge in the intelligentsia's support for human rights. That year marked the appearance of Andrei Sakharov's *Memorandum on Peaceful Coexistence,* as well as the first issue of the *Chronicle of Current Events.* The involvement of the intelligentsia forever altered the character of the movement. Whereas the youth had been guided by emotions and idealism, the intelligentsia organized itself with greater caution, conditioning its aims to what it perceived as the realistic limits of the situation. The methods it employed were carefully devised to conform to Soviet law. The approach chosen was the promotion of human rights, ostensibly guaranteed by the Soviet Constitution. The call for human rights was thus portrayed as nothing more than a call to respect the Constitution.

The first human rights organization, the Initiative Group for the Defense of Civil Rights, was established in 1969. Its first action, an open letter protesting the arrest of Major General Peter Grigorenko, set the standard for all subsequent human rights activities. First, the group appealed to the West (in this case to the United Nations) rather than to the Soviet government. The Initiative Group claimed that it had to appeal abroad because "the hope that our voice will be heard, that is, that the government will stop its lawlessness, has vanished."[50] Instead of mobilizing domestic public opinion, the group would mobilize Western public opinion to pressure the Soviet leadership. By drawing international attention to human rights violations in the USSR, the group also hoped to mitigate the punishment the state could inflict. At the time, most foreign governments were not receptive to the idea of coercing the Soviet leadership into respecting human rights. The United Nations, for example, never replied to the group's appeal.

Second, the group's aims were overtly reformist rather than revolutionary. It pledged loyalty to the Soviet system and emphasized its lack of organizational structure. In order to avoid even the appearance of opposition, the Initiative Group never offered any programs or plans for the government to implement. It characterized itself as apolitical and never went further than admonishing the government to "respect its own Constitution."

Third, the Initiative Group did not seek new members. Rather, within a nucleus of approximately fifteen people, it initiated petitions. Between May 1969 and January 1970 the group sponsored five letters on human rights violations, but its activities ceased shortly after the arrest of part of its leadership and the emigration of the rest.

The cause of the Initiative Group, however, inspired others. Between 1970 and 1975 three new organizations appeared: the Human Rights Committee (the Sakharov Committee), Group–73 (Amnesty International), and the Public Group to Assist in the Observance of the Helsinki Accords (the Moscow Helsinki Group). The aims and methods of the Sakharov Committee, best known for its most distinguished member, the physicist Andrei D. Sakharov, reflected the academic background of its founders. Valeriy Chalidze, the editor of the committee's journal, *Obshchestvennye problemy* (Social Problems), stated that the committee's purpose was "not to disclose and demand but to study thoroughly and recommend, with a consideration for the real conditions of the problem and a consideration of the problems of the state in this area."[51]

The committee's appeal to the Fifth World Congress of Psychiatrists on April 4, 1971, is a classic example of this strategy. Members asked the Congress to direct its attention to the problems and rights of the mentally ill, and to the "possible unlawful use which might be made [of psychiatry] as a means of political repression of one's beliefs."[52] They further requested that a standing commission be set up to study psychiatric practices around the world, and that it systematically publish its findings. The cautious phrasing of this appeal is noteworthy when one recalls that at the time the incarceration and forced psychiatric treatment of several noted dissidents, including Ivan Yakhimovich, Nataliya Gorbanevskaya, Viktor Fainberg, Peter Grigorenko, and Vladimir Kuznetsov, had already been well documented in the West.[53] Not surprisingly, some dissidents rejected the purely analytical approach taken by the Sakharov Committee. Writing in the leading samizdat publication, *The Chronicle of Current Events,* the noted religious author Anatoly Levitin-Krasnov welcomed the committee's appearance, but predicted that young people would not be satisfied with "professorial and purely academic appraisals of learned liberals." He urged the broader opposition community to cooperate with the committee but not to limit itself to the style of the human rights activists.

Despite its limited scope, the Sakharov Committee was much more successful than the Initiative Group in attracting international attention. By 1971 it had become affiliated with the International League for the Rights of Man in New York and with the International Institute on Human Rights in Strasbourg.[54] Yet even though the committee attracted some of the most prestigious names in the Western scientific community, this was not enough to change Soviet government policy. Once it became obvious that this essential aim would not be fulfilled, the committee's membership declined.

The next step in the evolution of dissent was the creation of the Moscow Helsinki Group. Between May 1976 and May 1978 the Moscow Helsinki Group produced fifty-one numbered documents and several open appeals to Western leaders, but none directed at the Soviet government. This recognition of the futility of appealing to Soviet authorities stands in sharp contrast to the hope of the Sakharov Committee members that the regime would respect its own Constitution. The new group's position was summarized in a memorandum on the potential impact of the Helsinki Accords on human rights in the Soviet Union:

> An analysis of the internal politics of the Soviet Union with regard to the rights of man convinces one that the Soviet government does not intend to uphold the international obligations it undertook at Helsinki.
> If the movement for human rights in the USSR could considerably broaden its informative work within the country and toward the West . . . [and] if the Western public . . . actively supported the human rights movement in the USSR, then the Soviet rulers would be forced to curtail their repressive policies, which would in turn help the spontaneous realization of democratic rights. The unlikelihood of such a development, however, should not undermine our efforts, since it is precisely our efforts that increase its likelihood.[55]

The Moscow Helsinki Group also took the unusual step of issuing appeals to the various nationalities of the USSR to form local Helsinki monitoring organizations. Such groups were formed in the Ukraine, Lithuania, Georgia, and Armenia. Although all groups ascribed to the principles voiced in the initial declaration of the Moscow Group, they reflected regional concerns as well. The Ukrainian Helsinki Group, for example, cited the need for Ukrainian autonomy. Its membership formed a curious mixture of nationalists (Levko Lukyanenko), "True Marxists" (General Peter Grigorenko), and religious activists (Peter Vins), linked, it would seem, by only one transcendent concern — Ukrainian patriotism. The Armenian Helsinki Group cited the need to reunite part of Azerbaijan with Armenia, and reassert the priority of the Armenian language.

In retrospect, it is striking just how many of the issues that emerged publicly during the latter half of perestroika can be traced back to the early human rights efforts of the 1970s. The alternative political culture was already beginning to co-opt the agenda of these "apolitical" organizations. A prime example of the way in which human rights fostered the development of a broader social opposition can be found in the independent labor movement that emerged at the end of the 1970s.

The roots of an independent workers' movement go back to the 1950s, when, as individuals, workers first sought redress of their grievances. These appeals all went unanswered, so they united to collectively petition social,

Party, and government institutions, as well as trade union and central newspapers. Having reached the conclusion that there was no institution in Soviet society that defended the interests of the workers, they decided to organize their own independent trade union "to have the right to officially and juridically protect our rights and interests, to gather all those whose rights have been unjustly restricted, in any matter, in a common struggle for their rights, as enumerated in the new Constitution of the USSR." The founding statement of the Free Labor Union of Soviet Workers (February, 1, 1978) was signed by 43 workers and claimed to represent more than 200. An addendum to the union's "Charter" listed the names, addresses, and professions of 110 candidates for membership and added that several more had asked that their names be withheld.

The intelligentsia's initial response to the workers' movement was hesitant. The Moscow Helsinki Group issued a cautious letter supporting the aims of the workers, while at the same time distancing itself from union. The workers, by contrast, were eager to collaborate with the human rights movement. In their first open letter to foreign newsmen, they cited several types of human rights violations in addition to violations of workers' rights.

The Free Labor Union managed to issue some twenty documents before its leaders were arrested. The workers were not about to give up so easily, however, and in October 1978 a new labor union, the Independent Interprofessional Workers Union (IIWU), succeeded the old one. It claimed more than two hundred members, including those remaining from the former Free Labor Union.[56] This time the workers decided to operate on a semicovert basis, advertising only the names of the ten council members, rather than all the members' names. Beyond the violation of professional work norms, the IIWU also espoused the defense of the social, political, and cultural rights of any worker asking for its protection. Despite arrests and threats, the IIWU remained active for several years, gathering and disseminating information on the violations of workers' rights. After the collapse of communism, some of its leaders emerged to take a prominent role in the independent, postcommunist labor unions.[57]

By the end of the 1970s, the limitations and weaknesses inherent in the human rights movement had become apparent. First, the movement had far too narrow a base of support. Although other strata of society supported the human rights activists as individuals, its backbone and core leadership remained the scientific and literary intelligentsia. This small coterie of individuals still tended to view the majority of the population as politically unsophisticated and reactionary. Second, the lack of organizational structure among groups led to a more rapid disintegration of the organizations than would otherwise have been the case. This organizational fluidity was an advantage when gaining adherents and deflecting government reprisals. It proved, however, to be a serious weakness in coordinating support. A third weakness was the almost exclusive focus on garnering Western support. This orientation implied a pro-Western, liberal sentiment which alienated many nationalists and traditionalists and was easily exploited by the regime to portray the human rights activists as traitors.

Finally, the human rights movement lacked a clear objective. How does one implement an abstract concept such as human rights? To suggest, as Valeriy Chalidze had, that "these changes take time" is no response to pressing social needs. What's more, it presupposes that the regime will act in good faith. This faith in the "reasonableness" of the Soviet leadership eroded much more slowly among the intelligentsia than it did among other segments of the population, leaving the intelligentsia unprepared to undertake concrete political steps to change the regime. One also gets the impression reading the documents of the various human rights groups of the 1970s that very few activists thought through what an enormous change for Soviet society the observance of human rights would entail. This conceptual inadequacy was first highlighted in an insightful samizdat article published in 1971 entitled "Strategy and Tactics."[58] Its author, V. Tretyakov, argues that human rights organizations and underground political opposition groups really form different stages of the same movement. In effect, if human rights groups succeed in establishing a favorable climate for reform of the system, they have fulfilled their purpose and should give way to the next phase, in which the political opposition would confront the regime. Tretyakov foresaw the path that the restoration of civil society would take. As the human rights movement came to an end in the late 1970s, it would be replaced by a political opposition with a much more confrontational stance. Because of the disillusionment generated by the activists' failure to achieve results, no new human rights volunteers emerged after 1979 to take the place of those arrested.

At the time, the demise of the human rights movement was commonly attributed to increased repression and to the lack of civic consciousness in Russian political culture. But the certainty of repression had never before prevented new volunteers from taking the place of those arrested. The reason the human rights movement had faltered now was that, after a decade of struggle, its concerns were too narrow and too apolitical to achieve any real success. The most significant weakness of the human rights movement was that it offered no political alternatives to the existing regime.

A glance at samizdat literature during the heyday of human rights organizations shows that underground civic aspirations had outgrown the narrow and passive agenda set by the leadership of the human rights movement. While human rights organizations were still engaged in supplication, independent civic groups were increasingly discussing issues of religion, history, and national self-awareness. The idea of working *within* the existing political system thus came to be seen as a hopeless dead end by the rest of the opposition, which by the end of the 1970s appealed to human rights activists to broaden its appeal. Three documents stand out as pre-perestroika attempts by a nascent civil society to address the inadequacies of the human rights movement and propose solutions.

The first, written in May 1980, just one month after the birth of "Solidarity" in Poland, argues that independent trade unions in the Soviet Union had failed because they had focused too much on human rights violations among workers, and too little on what practical assistance could be offered to them. The strictly apolitical approach advocated by human rights organizations, the authors contend, was inappropriate because the Soviet government would never recognize independent workers' groups. Dissidents and human rights activists might be of help to workers, but only if they agreed to work conspiratorially, in opposition to the regime.

The second document is an in-depth opinion survey of fifteen activists conducted in Moscow at the end of 1981.[59] The consensus that emerged from this broad spectrum of opposition activists was that, with the demise of the human rights groups, underground political activity had become inevitable. They urged other activists to broaden the popular appeal of the movement beyond the intelligentsia and to pay more attention to the everyday demands of average citizens.

The third document is an appeal from a group of samizdat distributors written in April 1983.[60] Here, too, the key theme is broadening the network of samizdat distribution. The authors believe that the time for appeals to the government has past. Instead, individuals must act independently and, if necessary, illegally to disseminate information as widely as possible.

Recent revelations regarding the extent of samizdat, the rapid emergence of informal groups in 1988 and 1989 (more than sixty thousand in less than two years), and the electoral success of several noted dissidents in the first competitive electoral campaigns in 1989 seem to confirm that it was the *strategy* of human rights groups, not the *idea* of human rights, that was rejected in the early 1980s.[61] The end of the human rights era also helped clear the way for direct political opposition to Gorbachev, most spectacularly in the case of independent labor unions, whose early weaknesses, incidentally, mirror those of the human rights movement. When these unions reemerged in the late 1980s, they were much more politicized and quickly captured widespread public support.[62] What Western observers generally perceived as the end of opposition was thus in reality a search for new, more successful tactics by which to revitalize civil society.

The human rights movement served an essential function in raising civic consciousness in society. Given its reluctance to appeal to the broader Russian public, however, it could only be a preliminary step on the road to restoring civil society. In order to become a movement with broad public support, it needed to be anchored in the values of the alternative political culture. This task began in the 1960s with the formation of neo-Slavophile political organizations.

Neo-Slavophile Politics: ASCULP and the NTS

Politically, the 1960s are characterized by the slow but steady growth of neo-Slavophilism. The most obvious manifestation of this return to tradition appears in the rise of "village prose" writers, who dominated the editorial boards of leading literary journals. Another indication that this was a broad-based social phenomenon, however, lies in the expansion of the movement to preserve historical and cultural monuments. The All-Russian Society for the Preservation of Historical Monuments (VOOPIK), which in 1965 had only three million members, a decade later had nineteen million, and by the mid–1980s had more than thirty-five million.[63] In 1971 nearly fifty million Soviet citizens visited ancient Russian towns and cultural centers for the holidays, nearly twice as many as in 1964.

Of the three strands that promoted the restoration of civic culture after the 1960s, therefore, the neo-Slavophile revival clearly had the broadest base of popular support. Its greatest weakness, however, was its ambivalence about clearly identifying and confronting the source of Russia's malaise — the Party-state ideocracy — for fear of undermining Russia's territorial integrity. This ambivalence about Russia's "imperial heritage" divided the Russian nationalist opposition at home just as it had divided the White emigration. It is difficult for many Russian nationalists to recognize the separatist aspirations of minority nationalities because they believe that the current frenzy for independence is only a passing phase that does not truly represent the will of the majority.

The neo-Slavophile critique is rooted in the cultural movement that emerged in Russia in the 1960s known as *pochvennichestvo,* a term that derives from the Russian word for "the soil" *(pochva),* an allusion to the peasantry, in which traditional Russian values are rooted. The two most active neo-Slavophile political groups inside Russia were the All-Union Social Christian Union for the Liberation of People (ASCULP) and the Popular Labor Alliance of Russian Solidarists (NTS).

ASCULP is one of the most fascinating organizations to appear in the Soviet Union because it so completely rejected Soviet political culture. Its constitution describes it as a "secret, supra-party military-political organization founded by common agreement for the liberation of the fatherland from the tyrannical totalitarian regime, and for the establishment of a social-Christian order."[64] The original founders were four students who had all arrived at the conclusion that the cult of personality was an organic part of the communist system and not, as Khrushchev had suggested, simply the result of Stalin's character flaws. Their search for alternatives to the communist system led them to re-examine Russia's past and present, and especially its Christian heritage.

According to the ASCULP, contemporary conflict was the result of the opposition of Christian and non-Christian world views. Communism, the "sickly birth child" of capitalism, could be overcome only through the "christianization of all public life." This christianization ought not to be confused with an authoritarian theocratic regime, however, since "Christian religion recognizes each individual personality and the brotherly relations between men as the highest and absolute value." The goal of the Social Christian movement, therefore, was to "remold the faceless communist collective into a people spiritually free, independently active, and fraternally interconnected."[65]

The organization survived for three years, from 1964 to 1967. During this time it accepted twenty-eight members and thirty candidates for membership in several cities, among them Irkutsk, Tomsk, Siauliae (Lithuania), Volgograd, Moscow, and Petrozavodsk. They ranged in age from eighteen to forty-three. Twenty of the twenty-eight full members had university or senior high-school instruction. The group also drew from a wide swath of Soviet society, including the sons and daughters of laborers, intellectuals, even Soviet officials. All had studied in Soviet schools and seemed in every respect to be rather typical products of the Soviet educational system. What had led each of them to view the Soviet regime as Russia's worst enemy? At his trial Mikhail Sado explained:

> After the cult of Stalin, the cult of Khrushchev was already in the offing, while in the country the situation continued to worsen. Slavery, authoritarianism, dishonesty, injustice were everywhere manifest.
>
> The products of industry were of poor quality. Excess waste had become habitual. Bribery and collusion assumed colossal proportions. In the rivers fish died, in the woods animals [died]; agriculture showed a picture of the most complete ruin. Kolkhoz workers earned twenty-five to thirty rubles a month for back-breaking work. I myself saw the poor people there, bent over from morning to evening under the rain to collect potatoes. Still, the potatoes often remained in the fields. At the same time, Khrushchev and his family traveled around the world making idiotic speeches that aroused the shame of any Rus-

sian worthy of the name. Discontent rose. The prices of meat and milk products increased. Grain we bought abroad. This is what Russia had been reduced to! Other catastrophes followed: In the country, a state of tension had developed that exploded in popular revolts against Soviet rule in Novocherkassk, Kara-ganda, Tbilisi, Krasnodar, and other places.

I was convinced that we were on the brink of chaos that could throw the country into anarchy at any moment.

Tell me, citizen judges, what could a son of his country do in these condi-tions? Russia is my homeland, my mother. Could I possibly sit and watch calmly as my mother died?[66]

Although Khrushchev's reforms of the early 1960s seemed to offer hope for a peaceful evolution, they were soon abandoned. The "thaw," however, had already left its seeds in the minds of these young students. As Evgeniy Vagin, the chief ideologist of the ASCULP, put it, "After this book of Sol-zhenitsyn's [*One Day in the Life of Ivan Denisovich*] the idea of an under-ground anticommunist organization ceased to be something abstract, but assumed a living reality. It became absolutely clear that things could not go on as before."[67] The group decided that only a "military-political" opposi-tion would force the regime to change. Members were willing to relinquish armed struggle only when the country had embarked on the path of full democratization.[68]

Despite their lofty declarations, in reality, the group represented little more than a youth circle. ASCULP rejected the notion of everyday political struggle and placed before its members just two tasks — the growth of the organization's membership, and self-education. Their ultimate goal, "the es-tablishment of personalism," was something they thought might be accom-plished in fifteen or twenty years.[69]

Personalism derived from the teachings of nineteenth-century Slavophile and early-twentieth-century *Vekhi* authors. It attempts to chart a middle course between the extremes of individualistic, materialistic capitalism and collectivistic, atheistic communism. According to its main proponent, Niko-lai Berdyaev, one of the contributors to the *Vekhi* anthology, "personhood" is a spiritual-religious category whose essence pertains to the spiritual rather than to the material world. Because of this, personal worth is "the highest and absolute value." As distinct from individualism, "which is the antithesis of the Christian idea of interrelationship of people," Christian personalism presupposes social interaction and mutual obligation.[70] The social projec-tion of Christian personalism was developed by émigré Russian religious philosophers such as Sergei Lewytzkyj. ASCULP stressed the continuity of Russian political thought and, quite independently, developed a philosophy and historiography remarkably similar to that developed by the NTS in exile.

In its program, a lengthy document of fifteen chapters, ASCULP adapts this neo-Slavophile Russian historical and philosophical tradition to the task of devising a governmental structure that is in tune with Russian political culture. The government, it says, must be "theocratic, social, representative, and popular."[71] It should be divided into four branches: the legislative (the Popular Assembly); the executive (the head of state and his cabinet); the judicial (the Supreme Court); and the guardian (The Supreme Synod). The Popular Assembly is to be elected by proportional representation of city and country communities; the heads of state are to be chosen by the Supreme Synod and then confirmed by popular vote. The Supreme Synod, which is one-third members of the Church hierarchy and two-thirds leading figures from among the populace, is to be the spiritual authority of the nation. It has no administrative or legislative function but may veto any misuses of political power.[72]

The program favors a "personalist form of property" that unites labor and the means of production "under the jurisdiction of the individual." "Self-directed personalist collectives," organized into national corporations, are to be the driving force in the agricultural life of the country, balancing the needs of the market against the welfare of the majority.[73] Despite these caveats, strongly reminiscent of the early views of the NTS and the Vlasov movement, the program's authors saw private property as the "material guarantee of true independence of the individual" and insisted that both land and capital be privatized.[74]

The ASCULP program thus differs little from its Western European Social Christian counterparts except, perhaps, for the explicit ethical guidance to be provided through the Supreme Synod. This addition is a fascinating reflection of the role that religion plays in the traditional conception of Russian political culture. Although in every respect these young men were typical products of their Soviet environment, their brief encounter with the works of Russian religious philosophers of the early twentieth century led them intuitively to construct what can best be described as a modern version of the Muscovite "liturgical state."

Within this highly moralistic state, however, all basic human rights were to be guaranteed by the Constitution: free trade (point 22); free development of cultural and scientific organizations (point 65); freedom of information (points 29 and 64); free and private educational facilities (points 27 and 65); independence, as opposed to separation, of church and state (points 31 and 32); freedom of religious worship (point 33); independence of the judiciary from the government (point 34); and an electoral system and guaranteed right of opposition (point 49). What's more, points 53 through 72, entitled "The Rights of Man and of the Citizen," form a basic bill of rights.

Ultimately ASCULP was really more of a brotherhood than a serious revolutionary organization. As the dissident Vladimir Osipov notes, its members were simply a bunch of young people who wanted to help Russia revive its "authentic" historical and religious traditions.[75] This makes the draconian sentences imposed upon these young activists especially noteworthy. The four original organizers were tried for "treason" and received sentences ranging from eight to twenty years. Igor Ogurtsov, the group's leader, served twenty years in prison. One can only infer that the regime wished to make an example of this particular group to other would-be neo-Slavophile activists.

The second political organization in this tradition, the NTS, emerged from the Second World War as the only organization that united a prewar pedigree traceable to the White movement with extensive contacts with Soviet citizens through the Vlasov movement. Despite the death of more than two hundred NTS members in Nazi and Soviet concentration camps during the war, the NTS had matured from a small, émigré-based organization to one that had established a small but continuous physical presence inside the Soviet Union.[76]

After the war the political ideology of the NTS shifted decisively toward Western Christian Democracy. Its latest program, adopted in 1975, is scarcely distinguishable from its Western Christian or democratic counterparts. The organization also sought to extend its appeal to all the peoples of the USSR by recognizing the right of each titular nationality to complete independence. In view of the economic interdependence achieved by the USSR, and the historical ties that traditionally link many of its peoples, however, the NTS considers such a dismemberment neither desirable nor beneficial, and strives to preserve national unity within a federal state.

The 1975 program is also flexible with regard to the precise form of government of this federation. The executive branch is to be dedicated to the values of solidarism, and situated above all political strife, so as to guarantee the proper functioning of the legislative and judicial branches. The legislative system calls for four chambers of parliament: a National Assembly elected by universal suffrage, an upper house composed of delegates of diverse administrative units, a regionally elected Council of Peoples proportionately representing the various nationalities of the Soviet Union, and a Council of Labor to discuss the problems of laborers and the economy.[77]

In the economic sphere, the NTS proposes a division of the national economy into three sectors, all complementing one another. The nationalized sector deals with the exploitation of natural resources and is in charge of heavy industry, power production, transportation, water works, forestry management, and so forth, but is strictly limited in the exercise of its powers by the legislature. The private sector includes a significant portion of light industry and commerce. The public sector, which is controlled locally, should provide for fuel, gas, electricity, local transportation, and town planning. Finally, in agriculture, a major portion of the land is to be returned to private ownership, although some model enterprises will be maintained by the state. The NTS devotes an entire section of its program to cultural and spiritual life, as well as to education. Creative freedom, freedom of worship, and the right to an education are to be guaranteed and supported by the state.

The NTS strategy for achieving a popular revolution, adopted in 1949, was known as the "molecular theory." Briefly, it involved the creation of a decentralized underground network within the USSR composed of a large number of very small units of two or three persons each. For safety, these units would not maintain direct contact with one another, but would make their presence known by certain symbolic acts. All groups, however, would follow the same basic strategy and carry out instructions relayed by short-wave radio, leaflets, and sometimes by courier from the revolutionary headquarters outside the USSR.[78] When society reached its revolutionary saturation point, these "molecules" would spontaneously bond into larger groups and emerge to publicly oppose the regime.

In keeping with the "molecular theory," the NTS sought to keep its membership in the Soviet Union secret. Nevertheless, after the deaths of two prominent personalities in the dissident movement, Yuri Galanskov and Aleksandr Galich, the organization revealed that they had been members.[79] Galanskov was one of the leaders of the independent youth movement in the early 1960s, and editor of the first underground political journal, *Phoenix–66*. Galich, a renowned playwright and poet, had been a member of several human rights organizations in the USSR before being forced to leave the Soviet Union in 1974. He joined the NTS shortly after leaving the Soviet Union and died unexpectedly in 1976. Although many others were arrested or implicated with the NTS by the Soviet press, no confirmation has ever been given, allegedly to protect other members of the organization in the USSR. The chairman of the NTS executive bureau, Boris Pushkarev, however, recently stated in an interview published in Russia that from 1960 to 1990 his organization maintained some two thousand underground contacts within the USSR.[80] Today some two-thirds of the NTS's organizational staff operates inside Russia.

The Soviet secret police, the KGB, has made several attempts to assassinate or kidnap NTS leaders living in the West. In addition, the Soviet media has produced a constant drumbeat of articles, television program, and books devoted to discrediting the organization. After a brief respite, this propaganda production resumed and increased, so that from the mid–1970s to the mid–1980s some fifty articles yearly were devoted to the organization and its activities in the Soviet media. Oddly enough, all this negative advertisement served to create an image of the NTS as much more formidable and resourceful than it actually was, to the extent that in 1967, at a speech commemorating the fiftieth anniversary of the founding of the KGB, Yuri Andropov designated the NTS as a prime enemy of the Soviet regime.[81] It seems odd that the Soviet regime should spend such enormous resources to thwart an organization that numbered only a few hundred active members worldwide. The fact that the Soviet leadership paid any attention at all to this quixotic band of revolutionary intellectuals certainly does not stem from their technical or numerical resources.

Two factors appear essential to understanding both the longevity of the NTS and the regime's visceral response to it. First, the group succeeded in attracting replenishments from each succeeding generation of émigrés by emphasizing political and cultural ideals that transcended the fractious environment of émigré politics. Second, the regime responded not to the *actual* impact of the organization but to its *potential* impact. Its ideals had indeed helped to crystalize the thought of many dissidents in the USSR. The monarchist Aleksandr Udodov, who spent most of his young life in various Soviet prison camps, mentions that he first heard of the NTS in 1962 when, "in its search to get out of the swamp of liberal-democratic lies and the darkness of communist deception, Russian youth came to conclusions often amazingly close to the philosophy of solidarism and the program of the NTS."[82] Nothing indicates the truth of this better than the striking similarity between the NTS and ASCULP programs. Their philosophical premises are nearly identical, despite the fact that each developed entirely unbeknownst to the other, one in the Russian diaspora, the other inside the Soviet Union. This potential was partly realized in the early 1980s, when NTS activists helped to politicize the labor movement and forged alliances with center-right anticommunist political parties such as the Democratic Union and the Christian Democratic movement.[83]

In 1980 the NTS presciently noted the existence of what it termed "constructive forces" at every level of society, even the secret police and the top Party elite. The patriotic sentiments of these individuals, it argued, could be tapped to promote peaceful reform inside the country. In 1987, when Gorbachev amnestied a large number of political prisoners, including several members of the NTS, the organization decided it was time to name open representatives in the USSR. At the same time it released a document devoted to identifying the measures necessary to assist the transition from a collapsing system to a democratic state. This document, called "The Path toward the Future Russia," was widely circulated among informal political associations and within the newly forming electoral blocs, in particular the Interregional Deputy's group of the 1989 Congress of Peoples' Deputies. After 1988 NTS members regularly participated in public gatherings and demonstrations organized by various informal political groups. In 1990 it sought to obtain the legal authority to publish its journals, *Posev* and *Grani*, in Russia, a process that was finally completed in 1993. Today, the NTS sees its purpose as

> facilitating the self-organization of a new, fraternal civil society and overcoming the Soviet legacy . . . The union [NTS] has always been simultaneously a social and political organization. Likewise today our long-term political authority will depend on the real assistance that our groups in different localities can bring to people. Only this participation in daily affairs at the local level will allow people to sense those interests that they will be called upon to assert in future political life, and will create the basis for specific political and legislative proposals.[84]

NTS groups now exist in more than 40 Russian cities. They have helped establish farmers' cooperatives in the Ulyanovsk and Irkutsk oblasts, private schools in Tobolsk, history museums and clubs in Petrozavodsk and Barnaul. They participate in labor movements in Kuzbass and the Urals. They have helped to set up credit cooperatives in St. Petersburg, Vyborg, Barnaul, Novosibirsk, and Samara. NTS members have served as advisers to the Russian government, and the organization took an active part in gathering signatures for a referendum on privatization of landownership, gathering 130,000 of the 2.5 million total.[85]

In addition to its own periodicals and books, which can now be purchased inside Russia, the organization continues to receive considerable coverage from national and local media, most of it now favorable. Since 1990, there have been more than three hundred press and journal articles about the NTS and dozens of radio and television interviews with members. The media presence of the NTS seems strongest in St. Petersburg, where the newspapers *Smena* and *Nevskoe vremya* regularly publish resolutions of the NTS Council, and St. Petersburg Radio devotes air time to the organization's leaders.

The NTS chose not to participate as an organization in the December 1993 national elections, although several individuals affiliated with the organization were elected to the new parliament. Aleksey P. Mannanikov, a former deputy of the Russian Supreme Soviet, was elected to the Federation Council, and three others made it to the Duma: the lawyer Aleksey N. Sarychev from Barnaul, the former deputy from Novokuznetsk (Kemerovo) Bella Denisenko, and the youngest member of the Duma, twenty-three-year-old Mark Feigin of Samara.[86] The organization does, however, intend to register as an official political party in Russia and to campaign actively in future elections at the local level.[87]

By the end of 1993 this organization, formed by émigré youths in the wake of the collapse of the White movement, had become a visible presence in postcommunist Russia, thus fulfilling Ilyin's prophecy that the White movement would one day give birth to a national political party inside Russia.

The Party's "Loyal Opposition"

The third important strand of political opposition could be characterized as the Party's "loyal opposition." It originated in the unofficial Marxist discussion groups that sprang up after Stalin's death but, unlike many of the young participants in that spontaneous movement, the "loyal opposition" clung to the view that the October Revolution had been a great step forward for humanity and for Russia. Under Lenin's leadership, members argued, the country had prospered and reached new heights of socioeconomic equality and freedom. Socialism's current troubles could be traced to Stalin's dictatorship, which usurped the authority of the democratically elected Soviets and destroyed the democratic principles of Leninism. The thaw allowed for greater criticism, but fell short of completely restoring Leninist principles. Under Leonid Brezhnev, the country was slowly rebureaucratized and re-Stalinized. The solution for Marxist-Leninists like Roy Medvedev was to retain the major achievements of socialism, such as collectivized agriculture, central economic planning, and a benign one-party system, while gradually introducing a more humane conception of modern socialism that would allow for greater dissent.

Only a few of the underground Marxist discussion groups and organizations that sprang up in the late 1950s and early 1960s managed to take on a more formalized character. One such group was "The Union of Communards," organized among Leningrad students. It recruited its members primarily from among the Communist Youth League (Komsomol) and the militia. As members of the militia and Komsomol, they were confronted daily with the worst aspects of Soviet society, such as drunkenness and vandalism. Their discussions revolved around the possible reappearance of Stalinism and the degeneration of Marxism in Soviet society. They pledged to re-establish "true Marxism." At the time of its dispersal in 1965 the union reportedly had more then 250 members; its leaders, Valeriy Ronkin and Sergey Chalmaev, each received ten-year prison sentences.[88]

Marxist student groups met with the greatest support during the middle and late 1960s, when the reforms pursuant to the Twenty-second Party Congress were still fresh in the public eye and it seemed that the Party might evolve democratically. By the end of the 1960s, however, it was clear that even the Marxist opposition would have to go underground if it wished to survive.

After 1970, almost a decade passed before there was a new Marxist youth circle. Then, in 1978, four young people were arrested for organizing the Revolutionary Communist Youth Union and for attempting to organize an All-Union Conference of Leftist Groups in October of 1978. The union published an underground journal, *Perspectives,* which included theoretical articles and information about political and religious persecution.

The July 1976 issue of *Perspectives* described the government of the USSR as a single, capitalist monopoly exploiting the populace. There was no socialism at all in the USSR, claimed the Youth Union. In reality the people were constantly being robbed by the ruling Party class. The journal accused Lenin of treason to socialism and Stalin of fascism. As an alternative to the communist dictatorship, the group proposed a socialist democracy with full freedom of private enterprise and creativity. In this instance, the arrest of the union organizers Tsurkova and Skobov did not still the protest. On December 5, 1978 (Constitution Day in the USSR), two hundred students from local high schools, Leningrad State University, Leningrad Pedagogical Institute, and other schools gathered near the Kazan Cathedral in Leningrad to protest the arrest of Tsurkova and Skobov, as well as the suspension of other students at the above-mentioned institutes.[89] This response was but one indication of the change in attitude toward the regime that had occurred in the country since Stalin's death.

Although this organization was similar in tone to previous Marxist organizations, there was an important difference between the Revolutionary Communist Youth Union and its predecessors. The union rejected all of Soviet history, averring that the CPSU has never had anything to do with either Marxism or socialism. Even Lenin was disinherited. No longer was the CPSU considered reformable, rather, it was seen as totalitarian and dictatorial to the core. The Youth Union willingly divested itself of the name of "loyal opposition" and consequently stood condemned by both official and unofficial Marxists loyal to the Party.

The latter group derived support from segments of the scientific-technical intelligentsia and highly placed Party advisers. The existence of such political rifts within the CPSU had been the subject of speculation for years. Khrushchev himself made Stalin's attack against "true Leninists" within the Party the main drama of his "secret speech" to the Twentieth Party Congress in 1956. Many Western Sovietologists agreed that something akin to interest groups had emerged within the Party hierarchy after Stalin's death. Scholars such as Moshe Lewin, Jerry Hough, and Stephen Cohen have argued that reformers within the Party had a significant impact in promoting social change, and some even traced their impact to the early 1960s.[90] In 1985 the recent émigré Alexander Shtromas convened a provocative conference on the survivability of the Soviet system, making a strong case for the existence within the Party elite of what he termed a "second pivot."[91] The existence of such a group was indirectly confirmed by Roy Medvedev, who in the 1970s had distributed his political diary among a segment of the Party elite.[92]

As a rule, the technical intelligentsia shunned organizations and programs, fearing that they smacked too much of political opposition. A notable exception, however, was the "social-democratic agitation pamphlet" *Seyatel* (The Sower). This publication, which appeared in 1971, set as its goal "the formation of a Social-Democratic Party in Russia."[93]

The *Seyatel* group condemned the current state of affairs in the USSR as the "purest state capitalism." According to *Seyatel*, the development of state capitalism in the USSR had undergone three phases. First there was the Bolshevik period, from 1917 to 1927, which *Seyatel* described as "indisputably progressive." The achievements of this period included laying the basis for a centralized economy, achieving "the necessary flexibility in the political field," and the "well-known level of intellectual freedom and informational diversity." Second, however, came the Stalinist period, from 1927 to 1953, marked by the "flowering of administrative state capitalism . . . in its most ferocious and crude expression . . . The system rigidified completely, lost its flexibility, and became absolutely soulless and inhuman."[94] Although the third and current phase marked the end of Stalin's excesses, the system had thus far proved unable to return to its previous flexibility.

In order to achieve "socialism with a human face" the very essence of the system must be altered. In words strikingly similar to those of Solzhenitsyn and later Vaclav Havel, the *Seyatel* group appealed to all members of the intelligentsia to undertake a "moral revolution . . . Without this moral upheaval we will never move an inch."[95] Ultimately, the *Seyatel* authors proposed a scientifically regulated society:

> There must exist an independent organ formed of specialists, experts, and learned personalities who are occupied with the elaboration of the basic principles of the economic and political system, and with the basic principles of public life . . . This "institute of scientific experts" will fulfill the primary legislative function. Relative democracy [absolute democracy being incompatible with the needs of modern industrial society] is guaranteed by a democratic organ which is given only the rights of supreme supervision, observation, and [public] information.[96]

Economic reform should "carefully introduce elements of the NEP — small private-property holdings in agriculture and the social services." The main elements of centralized state planning, however, should be maintained, but, "in accordance with Lenin's wishes, broadened and given legislative functions."[97] To prevent the formation of a new class elite, *Seyatel* proposed that differences in individual incomes not be allowed to exceed three to five times (in exceptional cases five to six times) the minimum income.

By the early 1980s, similar themes were being ascribed with increasing frequency to specialists and analysts working within the CPSU apparatus. In 1983 a memo critical of central planning was distributed at a restricted seminar sponsored by the economic department of the CPSU Central Committee and the Academy of Sciences of the USSR. It was later revealed that the memo, subsequently known as the Novosibirsk Memorandum, had been authored by Tatyana Zaslavskaya and Abel Aganbegyan at the request of the CPSU general secretary Yuri Andropov. The document placed the blame for the current economic malaise squarely on central planning and argued ominously that, without serious structural reforms, "the system of productive relations . . . [would continue to fall] behind the level of development of productive forces" — the classic Marxist recipe for revolution.[98] At the time, however, the report's recommendations were rejected as too radical.

Less than two years later, a "Manifesto for Renewal," also attributed to mid-level Party functionaries, appeared.[99] This manifesto stressed the urgent need to reform the economy and prevent the Soviet Union from becoming a second-rate power. It also urged specific political changes, including freedom of the press, freedom of religious expression, private land usage for agricultural production, private trade, and "alternative political organizations" whose ultimate aim should still be the building of a socialist society. This last idea was eventually adopted by Gorbachev's leading advisers in the form of the "Popular Fronts in Support of Perestroika," whose purpose, as Tatyana Zaslavskaya bluntly put it, was to overcome local resistance to perestroika.[100]

By 1985 the stage was thus set for a constituency within the Party eager to renew and deepen the de-Stalinization process abandoned by Khrushchev. Having achieved positions of influence, however, these mid-life reformers were often unwilling to sacrifice their personal welfare for the quixotic opposition of the dissident movement. Indeed, they often justified their lack of public support for the human rights groups on the grounds that real reforms in Russia had always occurred from above. Their chance to act came with the appearance of Mikhail Gorbachev.

Successes and Failures of Perestroika

When Gorbachev finally rose to the top leadership position in 1985, the malaise of Soviet society was already quite palpable. As Robert C. Tucker noted early on, "People en masse have stopped believing in the transcendent importance of a future collective called 'communism.' They have stopped believing in the likelihood of the society arriving at the condition and the desirability of trying to achieve it through the leading role of the Communist Party, or themselves as 'builders of communism,' which is how the official party programme defines Soviet citizens."[101]

Gorbachev's reforms began with a series of clamorous failures. His alcohol program was a flop. He soon had to abandon two of the four original elements of his reform program, namely, quickening production *(uskorenie)* and production accountability *(podotchetnost)*. Glasnost, the third component, was originally envisioned purely as a tool for managerial accountability, something akin to whistle-blowing.

In order to overcome the vested interests of Party bureaucrats and managers, Gorbachev had only one constituency he could rely on to support greater openness — the intelligentsia. To gain their allegiance he allowed glasnost to expand into previously prohibited areas of history, religion, and culture. The intelligentsia eventually embraced the concept, not for the objectives Gorbachev intended, but in order to restore as much historical and cultural knowledge to the population as they could during this second "thaw." Although Gorbachev subsequently tried to limit glasnost, this proved as bootless as sweeping back the tide.[102] Having lost control over his own policy, Gorbachev found himself in the awkward position of having to defend it, lest his ineptitude call into question his own political leadership.

Public opinion eventually galvanized in support of his beleaguered programs of perestroika and glasnost because of the spontaneous political activities of tens of thousands of independent organizations, known in Russian as *neformaly*. For the first time since the 1920s, unofficial political activity had gained a public voice. In 1987, in a heavy-handed attempt to control the direction of civil society, Gorbachev advisers recommended the creation of front organizations that were to act as political action committees, stirring up support for Gorbachev.[103]

Gorbachev and his advisers, however, sorely underestimated the political acumen of the populace. From the very outset it was clear that the people were less interested in supporting perestroika than in taking advantage of it for the restoration of civil society. It also soon became apparent that these organizations would not long remain "informal," but would evolve into political parties.

The astounding growth of informal political associations — thirty thousand by the end of 1987 and more than sixty thousand by early 1989 — belies the commonly held view that Russians had no sense of civil society before Gorbachev.[104] Unsanctioned political activity spread so quickly (by 1989 more than fifteen million people claimed membership in an informal group) because it built upon previous opposition attempts to restore civil society. The evolution of "informal" political activity, in fact, mirrors the three distinct political agendas that had driven political opposition since Stalin's death: human rights groups, such as *Grazhdanskoe dostoinstvo* (Civic Dignity), sought to institutionalize respect for the rule of law in Soviet society; Russian nationalist groups, such as *Otechestvo* (Fatherland), worked to promote Russian history and religion and to preserve the environment; while Marxist groups, such as *Perestroika–90,* became the public backbone that Gorbachev and his advisers had hoped would dominate, but which always remained a distinct minority. Each of these three strands in Russian political life was an extension of previous efforts to re-establish civil society. The human rights movement encouraged legal and civic awareness by exemplary personal sacrifice. Neo-Slavophiles and nationalists sought to restore a positive sense of Russian patriotism and civic responsibility for the environment, while the opposition within the CPSU, led by a younger generation of leaders, promoted the idea that the Stalinist model of socioeconomic relations had failed. Despite their ideological differences, each strand agreed on the need to limit the state's intrusiveness into the private sphere, an essential precondition for modern civil society.

The scope of spontaneous political activity during this period shatters the myth that the revival of civil society is attributable solely to the efforts of Mikhail Gorbachev. In fact, only a small minority of these informal political organizations defined their purpose as supporting perestroika, and even fewer saw themselves constrained by it. It is more accurate to say that society took advantage of the appearance of an innovative and uncautious leader like Gorbachev, and that the disintegration of the political authority of the Communist Party occurred not as the result of his policies, but as the result of deeply rooted social impulses that capitalized on his mistakes.

The traditional concept of Russian political culture simply cannot explain the sudden eruption of civic activism among millions of people. The magnitude of this political involvement is clearly the result of the cumulative efforts to restore civil society by previous generations, a debt acknowledged by activists in the informal political movement.[105] For young people in particular, the effort to re-establish a linkage with Russia's political heritage quite often led beyond the Soviet period, to the political ideas of the White movement, to Russia's pre–1917 political parties, or even to monarchy.[106]

Gorbachev deserves enormous credit for refusing to crack down on society (as the Chinese leadership did in Tiananmen Square) when it became apparent that it would not willingly embrace socialism. His policies, intentional or not, must also be given credit for emboldening reformers within the Party apparatus and for permitting an atmosphere in which even anticommunist ideas could be aired. But the more popular portion of political activism clearly had intellectual roots outside of Gorbachev's official program of reform. Moreover, it was politically active well before Gorbachev came to power in 1985. Gorbachev was never able to place himself ahead of political developments in society because he did not understand how fundamentally different the political aspirations of Russia's alternative political culture were from his own. In the end, Gorbachev appears much like Nicholas II — the last representative of a dying regime, struggling desperately to preserve an ideal that society had long since discarded.

6

Back to the Future of Russian Politics

The tragic fate of the Russian people by no means indicates that the whole stock of creative energy and creative ideas has collapsed . . . [History] flows on in varied psychic
reactions in which thought at one time contracts and at another time expands, which at
one time sinks into the depths and disappears from the surface . . . So it will be with us
also. The havoc which has taken place in spiritual culture among us is only a dialectic
moment in the destiny of Russian spiritual culture . . . All the creative ideas of the past
will again have their creatively fruitful importance. Spiritual life cannot be extinguished;
it is immortal.   —Nikolai Berdyaev

A healthy nationalism will become the determining force in Russia's renaissance in the
near future . . . Uvarov's increasingly mentioned triad—"Orthodoxy, autocracy, nationality"—illustrates its eternal consonance with the views of those striving to preserve the
nation and the state.   —Sergei Lykoshin

There have been not one but two revolutions in Russia since 1991. The
first, Gorbachev's resignation, like Tsar Nicholas II's abdication in February 1917, formally ended the old regime. The second revolution, the
decommunization of Soviet society, however, has only just begun. It will
involve more than just renaming former cities and streets and reorganizing
state institutions. For Russia to survive as a state it must redefine the purpose
of its existence. It must, in the words of Russian Foreign Minister Andrei
Kozyrev, "search for a new identity for a great nation—great in history, in
its territory, in its resources."[1] To be effective this identity must coincide
with key elements in Russia's past, adapting the principles of democratic
government to the ways and customs of the peoples of Russia. Modern neo-
Slavophiles call this finding a "Russian path" toward democracy and economic prosperity, much as the Germans and Japanese had to find theirs after
World War II.[2]

As important as economic prosperity is, piecemeal efforts to establish democracy in Russia that focus exclusively on economic issues are bound to

fail. Just as crucial to the ultimate success of Russian democracy is the country's spiritual and national revival, which seems to arouse more suspicion than understanding in the West. As often happens in American foreign policy, the euphoric mood of 1991 (post–August coup) has already given way to a "new pessimism" about Russia, which sees only two possible futures for the country: first, that Yeltsin will eventually be replaced by an authoritarian and aggressive anti-Western political leader; or second, that Yeltsin himself will become such a leader. All of Russian politics is frequently reduced to an unresolved struggle between pro-American "Westernizers" and reactionary, anti-American "Slavophiles," epitomized, according to U.S. Ambassador to Russia Thomas Pickering, in the conflict between Yeltsin and Zhirinovsky.[3]

This stark contrast between reform and reaction is as false as the simplistic historical analogy to Westernizers and Slavophiles, yet it is fed by the all-too-common view that Russia is "a nation with no history of democratic political culture in its 1,000-year existence."[4] Here is where an interpretive approach to Russian political culture can be useful. By illuminating the historical roots of Russia's democratic aspirations, it can cast the future in a different light, uncovering interpretations and ramifications of current political events that would otherwise be overlooked.

The adoption of a broader framework for political culture can also offer a way to get beyond the quagmire of recriminations that has engulfed post-Soviet studies. In the two years that have passed since the official end of the Soviet Union, there have been many essays on the conceptual failures of Sovietology, but little consensus on what should be done to fix them. Indeed, much of the terminology currently in vogue — "post-Soviet," "Eurasian," "Newly Independent States," "FSU" — indicates more than a little nostalgia for those halcyon days when it was possible to ignore national differences among the populations of the region and treat the USSR as a single unit.

Lastly, a new set of assumptions about Russian political culture also has obvious implications for Russia's role in the post–Cold War world and for its relationship to the West. The seventy-year struggle against communism has reinforced antimodern and anti-Western views among those who see Marxism as a Western import. For some in Russia (and Eastern Europe), the struggle against communism has thus become synonymous with the struggle against Western influence. Does this mean, as Samuel Huntington has recently suggested, that Russia and the West are therefore destined to clash over values fundamental to each civilization?[5] Or is there an alternative political culture resilient enough to combine the best aspects of modernity and Russian tradition and culture? Some tentative answers to these questions can be gleaned by looking at how the three major aspects of political culture discussed in this book—autocracy, religion, and nationality—are responding to the challenges of postcommunist society.

Constrained Autocracy Restored

In many ways the most crucial issue in Russian politics today is how to establish a legitimate political authority. The dissidents and democrats who took over from Gorbachev after the failed coup of August 1991 captured the popular imagination but lacked any institutional power base. In a matter of months, therefore, the old nomenklatura was able to reassert control, first over local politics, then among the industrial managers, and finally in the Supreme Soviet. Slowly but surely, the opponents of reform were whittling away at Yeltsin's powers as chief executive.

Opinion surveys show that the vast majority of people viewed this tension between the executive and the legislature as an undesirable state of affairs. Moreover, public frustration over the political impasse between Yeltsin and the Supreme Soviet was clearly directed at the latter.[6] The most consistent demand among average citizens was for a political authority that could quickly and effectively enact reforms, halt the disintegration of the country, and restore law and order to the streets. In other words, there was a strong desire for someone to "take charge."

Yet this was clearly not a desire for a new dictatorship. An extensive survey of more than ten thousand Russian citizens in eleven regions of the country conducted in 1993 shows that though nearly half favored a "firm hand" in government, this meant "regulation of the economy and protection of the individual against high-handedness and lawlessness, accompanied by the preservation of political freedoms . . . The last thing they have in mind is to wind up in the iron embrace of some homegrown Pinochet who would pave the way to the kingdom of the market through arrests, exile and executions."[7]

Most Russians thus seem to prefer something that could be termed a modern version of constrained autocracy. This is exemplified in Russia's newly adopted Constitution, which is consciously modeled on the Gaullist Constitution that established the Fifth Republic. This Constitution, while providing for a system of checks and balances among the branches of government, creates a powerful yet constrained executive subordinate to the will of the people. The very first words of the new Russian Constitution highlight the difference from the previous version. The Soviet Constitution begins:

> The Great October Revolution, accomplished by the workers and peasants of
> Russia, under the leadership of the Communist Party headed by Lenin, over-

threw capitalist and landowner rule, broke the chains of oppression, established the dictatorship of the proletariat, and created the Soviet state, a new type of state, the basic instrument for defending the gains of the revolution and for building socialism and communism. Humanity thereby began the epochmaking turn from capitalism to socialism.[8]

This document clearly places the purposes of the Russian state in the context of a global, ideological mission mandated by the leadership of the Communist Party of the Soviet Union. By contrast, the preamble to the present Russian Constitution reads:

We, the multinational people of the Russian Federation, united by a common destiny on our land, affirming human rights and liberties, civil peace and concord, preserving the historically evolved unity of the state, preceding from generally recognized principles of the equality and self-determination of peoples, honoring the memory of our forebears, who handed down to us love and respect for the fatherland and faith in goodness and justice, revitalizing the sovereign statehood of Russia and affirming the unshakable nature of its democratic foundation, striving to ensure the well-being and prosperity of Russia, proceeding from our responsibility for our homeland to present and future generations, recognizing ourselves as part of the world community, adopt THE CONSTITUTION OF THE RUSSIAN FEDERATION.[9]

In the current Constitution it is the people who retain sovereignty, constitute the state, and authorize it to act on *their* behalf. Furthermore, this Constitution does not simplistically adopt the doctrine of a separation of powers, but combines it with aspects of the Russian tradition of constrained autocracy. This tradition has generally been skeptical of totally separate and contrasting spheres of authority, preferring a more organic view of the state to the Anglo-American division of powers.

After disbanding the Supreme Soviet, President Yeltsin reconvened the Constitutional Assembly on November 9, 1993, and accepted a number of compromises to his draft which increased the legislature's authority while preserving for the president the role of guarantor of national stability.

Under the new Constitution the president has wide-ranging powers that include the right to select government ministers, key officials, and most judicial appointments. These are all, however, subject to confirmation by the Duma, the lower house. Federal judges and the prosecutor general must be confirmed by the Federation Council, or upper house. The Duma may also voice its disapproval of government by holding a vote of no confidence. Though the president is not obliged to abide by this first vote, if a second vote of no confidence is held within three months, the president must either appoint a new prime minister or hold new elections.

As in other parliamentary democracies, the Constitution grants the president the right to introduce legislation. The Duma must approve all matters relating to economic policy and the budget, whereas the Federation Council must review any item affecting the constituent parts of the federation (for example, border clashes, the use of armed forces, and state-of-emergency declarations). Matters pertaining to the national budget, taxes, financial and monetary policy, and national defense must be reviewed in both houses, and presidential vetoes can be overridden by a two-thirds majority of both chambers. In the current Duma only a third of the seats are controlled by strong supporters of reform. Still, this should be sufficient to sustain presidential vetoes in the Duma. In the Federation Council, by contrast, Yeltsin seems to have more support, which should allow the passage of key legislation. Finally, the Constitutional Court has the authority to oversee compliance with federal laws and to resolve jurisdictional disputes within the federation.

Like the Gaullist Constitution of 1958, Russia's first postcommunist Constitution was designed to meet the needs of a deeply divided society. The extensive powers of the president serve to break legislative logjams and allow, if necessary, for legislation to be passed by decree. This Constitution, as Carl Linden puts it, "clearly strikes the right chord for many if not most Russians . . . There is probably a strong resonance between the strong executive office and the autocratic tradition of Russia's past."[10] And precisely because it corresponds well both to Russia's current political needs and to its political culture, the Constitution could well provide a framework for stabilizing Russian politics.

Perhaps even more important for the long-run success of the *constrained* autocratic tradition in Russia, however, is the resurfacing of the ancient principles of Russian federalism embodied in the zemstvos. Their most popular advocate has been Aleksandr Solzhenitsyn, who, in his widely disseminated 1991 text *Rebuilding Russia*, reminded readers of this indigenous tradition of self-government and suggested how it could be revived today.[11] Since then there has been a burgeoning of local attempts to recreate the zemstvos, particularly in Siberia. In February 1994 these attempts reached a new plateau when a conference of prominent Siberian and Far Eastern religious activists meeting in Novosibirsk issued an appeal to convene an All Russian zemskiy sobor, the first in more than three hundred years.[12]

Given the challenges Russia faces, it is not surprising that most Russians favor a strong yet constrained form of autocratic government. Still, as evidenced by the consistent support shown for a market economy and for political pluralism, one can be fairly confident that what Russian voters want is not a return to the past but a more orderly transition to the future.[13]

The Revival of Symphonia

The prominence of Russian Orthodoxy is another dramatic sign of the changes that have occurred in Russia, as the country moves from being an officially atheist state to a theist society. Nearly a third of those who once considered themselves atheists now declare themselves believers, with the conversion rate particularly high among the young and well-educated. Interestingly, this is largely a rediscovery by Russians of their own religious heritage, Eastern Orthodoxy. The percentage of non-Orthodox converts has risen by only a scant 2 percent.[14]

One extensive study of religious beliefs in Russia conducted just prior to the collapse of the Soviet Union shows that more than three-quarters of the population have a "great deal" of confidence in organized religion, while only 7 percent feel that it has too much power.[15] The study, organized by Father Andrew Greeley, notes that on these issues Russia is, respectively, first and last among twenty-one nations in his worldwide survey. Two-thirds of Russians say they would support prayer in public schools, and three-quarters would ban antireligious literature (as would 68 percent of atheists!). A quarter also believe it would be good if people with strong religious beliefs held public office.[16] Interestingly, the same survey indicates marginally greater tolerance of nontraditional sexual orientation and behavior among religious believers in Russia than among their American counterparts.[17] This suggests that many Russians make a clearer distinction than Americans between the public role of the Church and its role in establishing guidelines for personal morality. This would be consistent with the notion that the rise in religious self-identification is more the restoration of a historical notion of the Church's role in public life than it is the wholesale adoption of a religious world view.

Many Western observers, however, are troubled by the official attention being bestowed upon Russian Orthodoxy. Citing the ostensible Russian tradition of subservience to the state, they believe that religion might form a virulent amalgam with chauvinism in support of expansionist policies. This prospect seems compounded by the fact that the Moscow patriarchate has resisted all serious efforts at internal renewal, and by the sympathy toward the Russian Orthodox Church being voiced by nationalists and excommunists.[18]

The reality of church-state relations in postcommunist Russia, however, shows little sign of subservience. Throughout the dramatic events of the past two years, the Russian Orthodox hierarchy has tried to remain above the political fray, with two notable exceptions: first, when it came to the support of President Yeltsin during the August 1991 coup attempt; and second, when it attempted to act as an intermediary during the conflict between the president and the Supreme Soviet in October 1993. These were both reluctant engagements, clearly aimed at averting bloodshed and preserving social harmony and Russian unity.

A small but vocal dissident strand among the Orthodox clergy has challenged this political passivity of the hierarchy. These clergymen see it as favoring the status quo and hindering the expansion of democratic, Christian values in Russian society. The most prominent dissident voice in this group is that of Father Gleb Yakunin, who, just prior to the December 1993 elections, was stripped of his priestly authority by the hierarchy for disobeying the patriarch's decree that clergy not participate in elections to the new Duma. For Orthodox dissidents this action has only served to highlight the need for a more active political engagement among Christian clergy and laymen.

To meet this need several political organizations have formed, the most important being the Russian Christian Democratic Movement (RCDM) headed by Viktor Aksyuchits, and the Russian Christian Democratic Party led by Aleksandr Chuev. Both aspire to the role played by Christian Democratic parties in Western Europe. Popular approval for these parties has oscillated between only 5 and 18 percent, yet even after the December 1993 elections, their true electoral potential is still unknown, since neither party registered in time for the elections.[19] Although both had obtained the 100,000 signatures required to be placed on the ballot, these were not obtained in at least 7 different regions of the Russian federation, as the law requires.[20]

Father Yakunin briefly joined the RCDM, but left it in December 1991; he has since become a prominent spokesman for "Russia's Choice," the secular, proreform party headed by Yegor Gaidar. By contrast, Father Vyacheslav Polosin, one of the original founders of the RCDM, appears to represent the views of many clergy who, albeit concerned about daily politics, seek first and foremost to reinstate the traditional Orthodox ideal of symphonia in church-state relations. As chairman of the Commission on Freedom of Conscience and Religious Belief of the Supreme Soviet of the Russian Federation, Polosin shut down the State Council for Religious Affairs and helped craft the new legislation governing relations between the state and religious organizations, widely regarded as the most significant piece of legislation of the first session. Not long before becoming chairman, Polosin published a lengthy essay entitled "Reflections on Theocracy" in the émigré journal *Grani*.[21] It provides an interesting insight into the way some Orthodox clergymen view the role of the Church in postcommunist Russia.

Polosin explores why Christianity is essential for a free society in Russia.

Freedom per se, Polosin contends, is an abstract and amorphous ideal, too easily corrupted. To have a stable moral foundation it must be rooted in the Christian Truth. Likewise, the Christian concept of the individual must lie at the heart of the legal system, so as to allow "all the values of the law to be founded upon the value of the individual, and [individual] freedom and development. In this way the legal system will be first concrete, second free, and third humane."[22] But beyond infusing the law with the spirit of Christianity, legal and confessional institutions must be kept strictly distinct. Only complete jurisdictional separation will preserve the impartiality of the law, as well as the Church's own canonical sovereignty, and allow it to become again "a free agent of theocracy on earth."[23]

Theocracy, as Polosin defines it, is the harmony of God's will with man's. It lies in stark contrast to the principle of autocracy, which he defines as willful individual self-assertion. Although Polosin acknowledges that a pure subordination to God's purpose is impossible in this world, he still feels that it can best be approximated through the mediation of the Church, which represents, in Orthodox thinking, the only pure and communal (sobornyi) source of God's will. A true Church, faithful to canonical traditions, would make the theocratic ideal possible because anyone in society could turn to it for social guidance. Unfortunately, Polosin says, the Soviet regime forced the Moscow patriarchate to adopt many "illegal and uncanonical" practices.[24] Now the only way to restore the Church's true identity would be to model a council on the last fully free Russian Church Council, held in January 1918.[25] In his essay Father Polosin, in essence, restates the symphonic ideal of church-state relations. The Church's social stature, he correctly points out, was greatly enhanced when it openly embraced this ideal, and he urges the Moscow patriachate to do so again.

But does symphonia strengthen or weaken Russian democracy? Some religious authorities have pointed to the serious ecclesiastical dangers of confusing the missions of church and state.[26] Symphonia, however, aspires not to become merely a national church, but rather to forge a close and intimate relationship between church and state, while preserving the self-sufficiency and independence of each. In other words, it seeks not a "civil theology," but a sanctification of all aspects of human life, including political life. Of course, any engagement in this task is fraught with the potential errors of serving lesser goals (national, political, sectarian), yet Orthodoxy's vision of Christendom demands nothing less.

Is Orthodoxy, therefore, at all compatible with modern democracy? Contemporary American Orthodox theologians such as Stanley Harakas point out that Orthodoxy is not inherently wedded to any particular political system. For example, in a secular society such as the United States, where there is no patriarchal presence to mediate with the state and a "high wall" separates church and state, the Church can still fulfill its role through the social engagement of its flock. Its members can work as free citizens to raise social consciousness, shape public values, and nudge society along toward Christendom.[27] Harakas's approach, by the way, is nearly identical to Kartashev's earlier call for a symphony between church and *society*, and is perfectly consistent with Orthodox tradition, reiterated in the Circular Letter of the Eastern Patriarchs (1848), that it is "not the patriarchs and not the [Church] councils . . . [but] the very body of the Church, that is to say, the people themselves" who are the supreme interpreters of its tradition.[28]

Attempts by individual clergymen (even the most highly placed) to assert their own particular visions of proper church-state relations, therefore, should not be confused with the true, ecclesiastical definition of symphonia. From an Orthodox perspective, when either the church or the state oversteps its proper boundaries symphonia simply ceases to exist. When it becomes impossible to pursue the symphonic ideal in the real world, the Church must patiently wait for a better time when, as Anton Kartashev put it, the state will have demonstrated its worthiness to the Church. Until such a time, the Church must "stand on its own two feet" and live "divorced" from the state, so that it may fulfill its proper spiritual mission unfettered by the state.[29]

Symphonia, therefore, automatically presumes the kind of strict distinction between the purposes of secular and spiritual authority that many observers deem essential to modern, pluralistic democracies. Father Polosin's efforts, both theological and practical, illustrate that symphonia in contemporary Russia not only accepts but demands such a distinction. In the Russian context symphonia is vital to forging a political-cultural environment that is *both* Russian and democratic.

To be sure, the symphonic ideal has been honored more in the breach than in reality over the course of Russian history. It is nevertheless remarkable to find that it has survived at all and is even emerging as a potent symbol of modern Russian socioreligious aspirations. Its very survival bespeaks a highly defined sense of religious and cultural identity that well-intentioned reformers ignore at their own electoral peril.

In 1990 the writer Vladimir Soloukhin caused a sensation by crossing himself before a large public gathering. Just four years later it is unimaginable that a major public event could begin without a blessing. Even the State Duma holds weekly prayer services for parliamentarians and their staffs.[30] This is, perhaps, not so surprising when one reflects that the Russian language is saturated with Christian terminology and symbols: the week ends with the "Sabbath" and begins with the "Resurrection," and the word for peasant is, essentially, "Christian." The revival of interest in pre–1917 cultural values will no doubt encourage the Church to assert even greater moral authority, and maybe even a form of tutelage over many areas of social policy and education.[31] This tutelage, however, will be quite distinct from partisan political sponsorship, which the Church will always seek to avoid. The feelings of unease that some in the West feel about religion's playing such a prominent role in society may, ultimately, simply reflect the fact that Russia is trying to recapture a religious heritage that the West has already all but abandoned.

Nationalism and Patriotism

The revival of national pride is frequently associated with chauvinism, anti-semitism, and xenophobia. But the exhilaration that people feel in recapturing the national heritage denied them under communism is not at all the same thing as chauvinism. Although the emergence of extremist groups such as Pamyat and the obstreperous, chauvinistic bombasts of Vladimir Zhirinovsky make Russia seem especially vulnerable, a healthy democracy needs a strong sense of patriotic identity as much as it needs to avoid nationalist extremism.

In *The Magic Lantern,* Timothy Garton Ash argues that national pride was a vital step in the process of individual political emancipation in Eastern Europe.[32] The same has been true of the Soviet Union. In the Baltic States, the Ukraine, and Russia independent civic action and new political parties emerged only *after* the flame of patriotic fervor had been rekindled. A patriotic consensus thus seems to be a necessary precursor to political pluralism in communist regimes, and the greatest weakness of Russian democracy to date has been its failure to embrace patriotism, thereby driving many into the arms of extremists. The failure of perestroika, for example, can be attributed in large measure to Gorbachev's condescending assumption that it would be sufficient to offer yet another utopian vision of a brighter future for all mankind. His neglect of specifically Russian national interests led directly to a fatal lack of popular support for his policies.[33]

Boris Yeltsin's rise to political prominence, by contrast, owes much to his reliance on Russian themes. His first campaign for the Russian presidency was built around "restoring Russia," and, in a noted speech to students at the Higher Komsomol School in Leningrad on November 12, 1988, he was the first Soviet leader both to speak out against the urge to "idealize and deify Lenin" and to praise Aleksandr Solzhenitsyn for his contribution to the dismantling of Stalinism.[34] Indeed, although Yeltsin is often labeled as a "Westernizer," his policies and pronouncements could as easily be characterized as neo-Slavophile. Like the nineteenth-century Slavophile reformers Yuri Samarin and Dimitriy Shipov, Yeltsin embraced change not for its own sake, but for the sake of restoring Russian greatness.

The themes of Russian unity and concern for Russian welfare were also promoted by Yeltsin's vice president, Aleksandr Rutskoi. During the first year of Yeltsin's presidency Rutskoi's visible endorsement of Russian patriotism served, paradoxically, to protect the president from direct criticism by the more extreme nationalist groups. Rutskoi's arrest following the October crisis alienated not only extremists but many moderate conservatives as well.[35]

The options of neo-Slavophiles were then further narrowed by the fact that eight parties with more than the 100,000 signatures were denied registration for the December 1993 elections. Of these, five represented moderate conservative or "patriotic" views — the Constitutional Democratic Party, the Russian Christian Democratic Movement, the Russian Christian Democratic Party, the Party of Consolidation, and the National Republican Party.[36]

The exclusion of such a significant number of moderate, conservative parties from the ballot no doubt contributed to the weak showing of the patriotic center in the December elections. The available alternatives — voting for the communists or voting for Sergey Shakhray's Party of Russian Unity and Concord — each had serious drawbacks. Many patriots remain skeptical of communist pledges of democracy and feared that the communists might again be manipulating Russian nationalist sentiment to serve the interests of the nomenklatura. Shakhrai's party, though clearly attuned to patriotic values, had close ties with the government. Several of its key figures were members of Yeltsin's inner circle; no less than four ministers (Shakhray, Shokhin, Soskovets, and Kalmykov) headed the party list. Voting for them, therefore, could scarcely be considered a vote against Yeltsin. As a result, many registered their protest by voting for Vladimir Zhirinovsky, the only candidate in the field with a clearly nationalist agenda and no apparent ties with the old communist establishment.

Although many Russian patriots are still ambivalent about allying with the communists, the sharp antagonism that existed under Soviet rule is clearly receding. The prospects for this "Red-Brown" alliance, as it has been dubbed by reformers, have been the object of considerable speculation. It is too early to predict whether the December elections foreshadow a reanimation of Soviet imperialism, or whether patriotism tempered by Christian ideals can reshape Soviet institutions into ones that reflect Russia's alternative political culture. It is worth noting, however, that the present Communist Party leaders have turned their backs on Marxism-Leninism, and now refer to themselves as "social democrats." They have embraced Russia's cultural and religious heritage, and declare themselves in favor of political pluralism and a mixed economy. Indeed, the only apparent disagreement between reformers and the communists during the last campaign was over the speed with which changes ought to proceed. Such pragmatism is a good indication of the progress that Russia has made on the road to political pluralism.

As Russia struggles to define a new national and political identity, however, we can still expect Russian politics to be highly conscious of ethnicity. Many of the country's problems after all relate directly to its identity as a nation: territorial integrity, respect for the civil rights of Russians in the "near abroad," the definition of Russia's new foreign policy. In the long run, Yeltsin's presidency will surely be seen as coinciding with the first phase of a process of geopolitical realignment among the diverse regions within the Russian federation, as well as adjacent to it. At the end of this process some of these regions will have established closer ties with Russia, while others will have drifted away. Polls taken in the central and eastern Ukraine (not including the Crimea, which has shown consistent support for rejoining Russia) show that opposition to the dissolution of the USSR nearly doubled in the year since independence was declared.[37] By 1994, 55 percent of Belorussians favored restoring the USSR, whereas 63.3 percent said Belarus and Russia should form a single nation.[38] Over the coming decade, therefore, some more intimate form of union than that currently afforded by the CIS is likely to embrace the Slavic core of the USSR.

The December 1993 Elections

The parliamentary elections held in December 1993 confirmed the Russian public's continuing concern with all three facets of the alternative political culture described above. In the West the results have usually been interpreted as a setback for democracy because the advocates of a rapid transition to capitalism failed to receive an absolute majority. In fact, however, these results point not to a defeat of democratic values but to a shift in the public's emphasis: away from exclusive concern with economic revival and toward spiritual and national recuperation.

The reasons behind this shift are not difficult to understand. Former Prime Minister Yegor Gaidar's economic policy relied on sharply curtailing monetary emissions and freeing prices on almost all consumer goods. The hope was that unprofitable factories would shut down and force workers to seek new, more productive forms of employment. Many managers, however, decided to call the government's bluff and continued to produce unneeded goods, running up huge deficits. The Russian Central Bank, meanwhile, supplied them with all the credit they needed by printing more money. The result was a vicious cycle: government subsidies fed inflation, inflation dampened foreign and domestic investment, without investment factories continued to require government subsidies, and so on.

Despite setbacks, however, the Russian economy has made considerable progress toward recovery. Wages more than doubled in dollar terms between December 1992 and December 1993, from $40 monthly to $104 monthly. More than 40 percent of all Russian workers (70 percent of industrial workers) are now employed by the private sector, where real earnings are significantly higher.[39] By January 1994, food purchases, which had consumed 70 percent of family income in January 1993, had fallen to only 40 percent.[40] Meanwhile, personal savings deposits increased more than fivefold, to more than three trillion rubles, leading Russian banks to compete for a lucrative new market—small investors.[41]

By the end of 1993, 6.5 million apartments (nearly 20 percent of the total) had been privatized, and despite the absence of a law governing landownership, more than 44 million families laid claim to private plots.[42] By the end of the first round of privatization in June 1994, more than 139 million Russians had invested their government-issued privatization vouchers, a participation rate of more than 94 percent. In addition, 70 percent of Russian industry (20,000 of 28,000 large or mid-sized industrial enterprises and 90,000 small firms) had been sold off.[43] The second stage of privatization, set to begin in mid–1994, envisions the sale of an additional 20 percent of state industry through direct cash auctions, and the removal of many previous restrictions on the purchase of shares in state companies by foreigners. Foreign investors have responded to these changes by investing portfolio money in Russian shares at a rate of $500 million a month since the passage of the Executive Order on privatization in July 1994. Moscow brokers now believe that money has stopped leaving Russia and begun to flow back into the country, as investors seek to capitalize on the explosive growth in stock prices.[44] Summing up the economic progress to date, the government announced that the percentage of people living below the poverty line had fallen by nearly half between February 1993 and February 1994.[45]

Despite—or, perhaps, because of—the collapse in industrial production, the progress of the Russian economy still seems dramatic when compared with that of the Ukraine, Belarus, and the Central Asian republics. Still, the disruption of interrepublic economic ties, the government's inability to pay workers due to a shortage of funds, and the lack of Western aid to provide basic unemployment benefits for the large numbers of people employed in state firms (unemployment officially reached 10.4 percent in June 1994 and could double in 1995), have all contributed to the popular perception that economic reforms are to blame for the people's misery.[46]

Yet despite the unevenness of the economic recovery, popular enthusiasm for the transition to a market economy has remained remarkably consistent, with most people still supporting the introduction of key market features.[47] What they reject are the half-hearted and often contradictory means the government has used to achieve them. Government ineptness and the conditions imposed for Western assistance have proved an especially popular rallying cry for the opposition. Demands for even stricter monetary restraints are increasingly difficult to justify to the electorate when, despite the fact that the inflation rate was cut by more than half over the course of 1993, only 1 dollar in 7 of economic assistance promised to Russia in 1993 by the Group of Seven industrial nations was actually received. Of the 2.5 billion dollar aid program pledged by the U.S. Congress, for example, less than 1 percent had actually been spent by early 1994.[48]

The Russian government's response has been to reconsider its approach to economic reforms. One early advocate of "shock therapy," Sergey Vasilyev, head of the government's Center on Economic Reform, claims that Russia is heading toward a situation typical of Latin American countries in the 1960s and 1970s; that is, significant state intervention in the economy, high inflation rates, and economic stagnation. Although disappointed, he sees Chernomyrdin's economic policy after the election not as an attempt to reinstate government monopolies, but as regulated state intervention in the economy, with the government controlling financial flows, profit margins, and subsidizing credits.[49]

Paradoxically, the very fact that the government now feels compelled to respond in some way to voters' discontent shows just how far Russian democracy has come. The December 1993 elections illustrate just how much the terms of Russian politics have changed in the two years since the end of the Soviet Union. Today there is no major national party that argues for the restoration of centralized economic planning. There is no party that promotes the use of military force in restoring the former Soviet Union (even Zhirinovsky's Liberal Democratic Party is careful to avoid outright statements that anything more than economic pressure will be needed). There is no party that claims for itself alone a monopoly on truth and political power. Despite their differences, all of the parties now in parliament, including the reconstituted Russian Communist Party and Vladimir Zhirinovsky's misnamed Liberal Democratic Party, claim to accept the premise that Russian politics should be conducted in a framework of economic and political pluralism, under the rule of law.

Moreover, it is not entirely clear that the radical reformers lost the December 12 elections. On May 4, 1994, *Izvestiya* published the findings of a special commission, appointed by President Yeltsin's administrative staff, to analyze the results of the elections. This independent study group, headed by Aleksandr Sobyanin, found that no fewer than nine million fraudulent votes had been cast. The overwhelming majority of these votes were cast for candidates of Vladimir Zhirinovsky's Liberal Democratic Party, the Communist Party of the Russian Federation, and the Agrarian Party, which was closely allied with the communists. Had the results of the election been recorded accurately, Sobyanin projects that the composition of the first postcommunist State Duma would have been as follows:

Current Seats	*Revised Estimate*
Russia's Choice 40	no fewer than 58
Liberal Democratic Party 59	no more than 36
Communist Party of the Russian Federation 32	no more than 28
Yavlinsky-Boldyrev-Lukin Bloc 20	no more than 23
Women of Russia 21	no more than 19
Party of Russian Unity and Concord 18	stays the same at 18
Democratic Party of Russia 15	no more than 16
Agrarian Party 21	no more than 14
Russian Movement for Democratic Reforms 0	no fewer than 12[50]

With reformers holding no less than 50 percent of the total seats, as compared with 30 percent today, such a parliament would probably have favored even more radical political and economic reforms.

Rather than contest the outcome of the elections, however, both reformers and their opponents have apparently decided not to upset the fragile status quo. The main reason for this is that the same analysis also found that only 46.1 percent of the electorate participated in the referendum on the new Constitution, well below the 50 percent required for its approval. Under the present political distribution of power, therefore, each side retains what it wants most: the president and his supporters have a viable Constitution, while the opposition gets control of the agenda of parliament.

This tentative political equilibrium is symbolized by the highly touted "Civic Accord" *(Dogovor ob obshchestvennom soglasii)* signed on April 28, 1994. This accord, signed by nearly every major political and social organization, obliges signatories to extend federal decentralization while preserving the territorial, political, and legal integrity of Russia. It also calls upon the executive and legislative branches to avoid confrontation and to see the present Duma out to the end of its term. It establishes a number of specific legislative goals in the areas of tax reform, structural economic reform, and labor and banking laws that the president would support.[51]

Although the accord has been dismissed as window dressing by its critics, Yeltsin's supporters have portrayed it as the first step in the formation of a new political tradition.[52] But perhaps the best indication of the accord's viability as a sort of mutual nonaggression pact is the proliferation of similarly high-minded accords among Yeltsin's opponents.[53]

A continuation of this trend toward political stability, however, cannot be taken for granted. One of the most troubling aspects of the December elections is the fact that half of the eligible electorate did not even bother to vote. Indeed, the percentage of people participating in the new, pluralistic institutions of government has declined with each call to the polls. The Russian people clearly need to regain confidence in their institutions of government, or they will simply refuse to join in the political discourse. To become self-sustaining, Russian democracy must broaden its electoral base, which will have the added benefit of counterbalancing the extremes of left and right that now dominate Russia's lower house, the Duma.

Much of the common wisdom in both Russia and the West, however, continues to portray the majority of Russians as indifferent or even hostile to democratic values. It argues that Russia's lack of a middle class dooms popular democracy; hence, Russians support a "democratic dictatorship." It would be more accurate to say that the small middle class that now exists does not trust the government to represent its interests. It prefers to elude government scrutiny rather than defend its interests in the public arena. Only when the people are confident of the accountability of the Russian government will they invest the effort to influence the political system.

Many Russian moderates have likened their country to a runaway locomotive. The first task, they say, is to slow the engine down so that the passengers can be sure of arriving safe and sound. As much as Russia needs economic revitalization, it needs even more desperately to deepen the slender thread of political accountability established by the December 1993 elections. A sense of public trust must be established before the government can embark on any more painful economic restructuring. The postelection slowing of economic reforms, according to the moderates, thus serves to affirm the principle of government accountability to the people. Whether the people's choice is sound economics is, of course, an entirely different matter.

This does not mean that reforms have been derailed. The speaker of the Russian parliament, Ivan Rybkin, the leader of the Agrarian Party now allied with Russian communists, has said that on economic policy fully three-quarters of the deputies support further privatization of the economy. "Today in parliament," Rybkin declared, "everyone is against the country being transformed into some social welfare agency. We have to concentrate on protecting only those who cannot stand up for themselves."[54]

Even the Duma's controversial decision to amnesty the August 1991 coup plotters and those who fought in the October 1993 dissolution of the Supreme Soviet, widely reported as a slap in the face to Boris Yeltsin, appears to have been a move supported by moderates in both the executive and the legislative branches. On the one hand, Speaker Rybkin argued that the pardon would allow the country to put the past behind it. A prolonged trial, particularly of the latter group, would only have undermined the authority of the president and the Constitution by reminding the nation of Yeltsin's weak legal basis for dissolving the old Supreme Soviet.[55] On the other hand, Sergey Shakhray, who rose to public prominence as the government prosecutor during the 1991–1992 trial of the CPSU, played a leading role in drafting the latest amnesty law, and in April 1994 he was rewarded with a promotion to the post of deputy prime minister. It also appears, in retrospect, that a promise was extracted from those amnestied that they would no longer engage in political activities of any kind.[56]

The Regions and Russia's New Political Consensus

Despite the relative novelty of multiparty politics in Russia, two long-term trends are already emerging that will decisively shape the course of post-Soviet Russian politics. The first is the inexorable shift of political and economic power from the center to Russia's eighty-nine federal regions. The second is the emerging consensus around a new ideology that combines patriotism with the free market.

The area beyond Moscow and St. Petersburg remains as unfamiliar to most Western observers as Africa was to Stanley and Livingstone. In the Soviet period travel to these regions was severely restricted, while today the lack of Western amenities makes these regions unpopular among correspondents, academics, and businessmen, who prefer the larger cities of European Russia.

Ignorance of the countryside, however, is just as common among educated Russians. Despite a recent report that by the fall of 1993 Russia's regions had amassed nearly 60 percent of the federal authority in their hands, literature on Russia's regional elites is still very scarce.[57] The political significance of the provinces is thus growing rapidly, and at the expense of the two historical capital cities.

The call for regional autonomy arose largely as a response to the chaos of the center. The period between 1989 and 1992 can best be characterized as a tug of war between the regions and the center over autonomy as the regions, fearing the effects of chaotic decentralization, sought to prepare for the worst by lessening their dependence on Moscow. The search for a viable form of federalism was finally given substance in the Federation Treaty of March 31, 1992, whose basic tenets continue to guide Russian policy. Under the Federation Treaty, Russia's regions are encouraged to claim as much sovereignty as they can manage, provided that they "recognize their responsibility for the preservation of the historical state unity of the peoples of the Russian federation."[58]

What this means in practice has since been elaborated in the state treaties signed between Russia and Tatarstan on February 15, 1994. These treaties, which are to become a model for relations with Russia's other autonomous regions, give Tatarstan a great deal of latitude in setting its own tax rates and retaining the lion's share of revenues collected from income taxes, corporate profits, and the value-added tax. The National Bank of Tatarstan will also have the right to distribute its own credits and to set its own interest rates, as long as the rates average out to the Russian Central Bank's discount rate. In return, Tatarstan has agreed to stop defining itself as a "sovereign state" and a "subject of international law," although it retains the right to enter into international trade agreements without having them approved by Moscow.[59] The result, according to the presidential adviser on nationalities Emil Pain, has been the transformation of Tatarstan from one of the most troublesome regions from the perspective of preserving Russia's territorial integrity (the only region that refused to sign the Federation Treaty altogether) into one of the most tranquil.[60]

Before 1992 it was widely argued that republics and regions would reap enormous economic benefits from independence, but this has turned out not to be the case. Disillusioned, Russia's regions today strive to preserve a modicum of political and economic autonomy, while strengthening their role as players at the national level. This helps to explain the inordinate influence of Sergey Shakhray's Party of Russian Unity and Concord in the Russian government (four ministries, including the vice prime ministership, were held by the party as of the summer of 1994). Although it garnered less than 7 percent of the total vote, it was very popular in several of Russia's autonomous regions.[61]

What most regions inside the Russian federation clearly do *not* want, therefore, is complete independence, for it serves no useful purpose. It is far more convenient to retain certain links with central authorities, and to blame Moscow for local economic turmoil. Moreover, secession is politically unpopular these days—it smacks of further dividing Russia and severing the ties that people have become accustomed to.[62]

Not surprisingly, Russia's regions differ widely in their political sympathies. Nevertheless, a careful examination of the regional electoral distribution of the December 1993 elections shows some interesting patterns. The opposition (Liberal Democratic Party, Agrarian Party, and the communists) did well in Russia's agricultural heartland: the central "black earth" regions, including Kursk, Lipetsk, Tambov, Bryansk, Rostov, Vladimir, Krasnodar and Stavropol, Penzen, Orenburg, and Mordovia. Along with the large factory towns where Yeltsin's privatization decrees have been fought tooth and nail by local nomenklatura, these form the regional core of opposition to reforms. The federal government's inability to push through a coherent land law and reluctance to privatize large-scale industries have only entrenched the positions of the elite and the suspicions of the populace.

By contrast Russia's Choice, the leading proreform party, did well in urban centers and in those regions where local governments encouraged the transition to a market economy. Outside of Moscow and St. Petersburg, the radical reformers did especially well in Kaliningrad, Archangel, Murmansk, Khabarovsk, and the Siberian Far East. The first two have profited from their status as port cities and free-trade zones, while the latter have benefited from expanded contacts across the border with China.[63]

It is worth emphasizing one new and, for the opposition, troubling development. The party that Marx and Lenin thought would appeal most to the urban proletariat has been abandoned by city-dwellers and embraced by collective farmers. In a democratic Russia, however, rural regions simply do not have the electoral clout to oppose the country's transformation. Given Russia's inexorable urbanization, the power of the old political leadership within rural regions is clearly declining. It is an apposite historical irony that, having destroyed the peasant's traditional way of life, the Communist Party now finds its fortunes tied to this least productive, least innovative, and most rapidly shrinking remnant of its former political empire.

Russian federalism will therefore most likely resemble a pattern all too familiar in the West, where regional elites lobby the government, seeking subsidies for ailing local industries, monies for cleaning up the environment, military conversion, and other local problems, all the while attempting to reject federal encroachment. Already there is considerable discussion of the importance of regional lobbies in the Duma today, where the deputies' bloc "New Regional Leaders" has emerged as the second largest voting coalition.

In time, the creation of a new regional elite within the political system will unify Russia's political landscape by leading to the formation of multiregional economic associations. Eight such associations have formed since the end of 1990, and they now encompass nearly all of Russia's eighty-nine federal regions.[64] Interestingly, even the usually recalcitrant regions of the Chechen republic and the northern Caucusus have been eager to foster closer economic ties.

Over the next twenty to thirty years, therefore, it seems likely that most conservative regional elites will lose their strangle hold on power, driven by the unavoidable pluralization of political and economic life and the pressures of economic integration. Already, large-scale industries and collective farms are being forced to compete with their more productive private counterparts since neither the executive branch nor the legislature can subsidize them any further. Regional elites who resist will find their economic doldrums compounded by the exodus of young people to other, more prosperous regions.

On both counts, therefore, the appearance of new regional elites will reinforce the emerging consensus in favor of a new national ideology that combines patriotism with the values of the free market. A key feature of this new consensus is that it simultaneously appeals to broad segments of the urban and rural populations.

Postelection surveys show that the two pivotal issues that defined voter sympathies in the December 1993 elections were market reforms and the unity of the Russian state. Because the voters were faced with an unfamiliar list of candidates and a complex set of platforms and agendas, pollsters found that on most specific issues, be it attitudes toward land privatization, the rising crime rate, or the restoration of all or part of the USSR, their responses closely followed the attitudes they expressed toward market reforms generally, and toward the preservation of state unity.[65] The December elections can thus fairly be judged as a referendum on issues, and the characteristics of an emerging consensus on political values can readily be seen if the results are placed within a matrix that charts each party's attitudes toward patriotic and national concerns alongside their views on individual and economic freedom.

From this matrix, it becomes apparent that Russian political values in 1993 bear little resemblance to the stereotype of Russian political culture. Cosmopolitan collectivism, inculcated for more than three generations in the guise of socialist internationalism, has almost no measurable support. *Not one of the parties that stood for election in December 1993 falls into this category.* Indeed, there are so few notable Marxist-Leninist political organizations left in Russia today that one recent survey of communist voting patterns wondered whether there would be such a party left in Russia by the year 2000.[66]

In communism's place, a solid consensus has emerged in favor of a world view that combines patriotism with a market-oriented economic system. The matrix illustrates that nationalist[67] or patriotic parties officially garnered three-quarters of the popular vote (squares A and C), while the parties that favored strong legal guarantees for private entrepreneurship and were generally perceived as favoring continued economic decentralization officially garnered more than two-thirds of the vote (squares A and B). By contrast, par-

Cosmopolitanism

Free Market/Individualism | State Control/Collectivism

B. (Cosmopolitan-Capitalist)

Russia's Choice	15.51%	[21.1%]
Russian Movement for Democratic Reforms	4.08%	[n.a.]
Total	19.59%	[25% or more]

D. (Cosmopolitan-Collectivist)

None

A. (Patriotic-Capitalist)

Liberal Democratic Party	22.92%	[12.9%]
Women of Russia	8.13%	[6.88%]
Yavlinsky-Boldyrev-Lukin Bloc	7.86%	[8.2%]
Party of Russian Unity and Concord	6.73%	[6.37%]
Future of Russia: New Names	1.25%	[n.a.]
Cedar	0.76%	[n.a.]
Total	47.65%	[c. 35%]

C. (Patriotic-Collectivist)

Communist Party	12.40%	[10%]
Agrarian Party	7.99%	[5.2%]
Democratic Party of Russia	5.52%	[5.98%]
Civic Union	1.93%	[n.a.]
Dignity and Charity	.70%	[n.a.]
Total	28.54%	[c. 23%]

Patriotism

Russian political values according to the December 1993 elections. *Sources:* A. B. Zubov and V. A. Kolosov, "Chto ishchet Rossiya?" *Polis*, no. 1 (1994), pp. 93–112; Dimitriy Kuznets, "Osoboye mnenie kandidatov," *Segodnya*, no. 89 (December 7, 1993), p. 2; "Izbiratelnye bloki: kto est kto," *Rossiyskie vesti* (December 11, 1993), p. 2; "Mody sezona 'Dekabr' 93: ptitsy schastya zavtrashnego dnya," *Molodost Sibiri*, no. 45 (November 1993), p. 5; and "K itogam referenduma i vyborov 12 dekabrya 1993g. v Rossii," *MEMO*, no. 4 (1994), pp. 51–63. The official percentages are taken from the *Bulleten Tsentralnoy izbiratelnoy kommissii Rossiyskoy Federatsii*, no. 1 (12), 1994, and appear first. Sobyanin's estimates, which follow in brackets, are reported in Larisa Aidinova, "Falshivye vybory, mertvye dushi?" *Vek*, no. 18 (May 13–19, 1994), p. 3.

ties that paid little or no attention to patriotic sentiments during the campaign (squares B and D), or that favored significant restrictions or delays in privatization (squares C and D), did poorly. It is a further sign of the times that all parties emphasized the importance of legalizing private-sector initiatives.

Interestingly, the revised election results submitted by Sobyanin do not significantly alter this consensus. About the same percentage favor economic decentralization, while patriotism's appeal falls to just under 60 percent. The distinctive amalgam of promarket patriotism displayed in square A still emerges as the most popular. Its fall from 48 percent to 35 percent of the popular vote can be attributed to a net shift in votes away from Zhirinovsky's Liberal Democratic Party to Gaidar's more radically oriented Russia's Choice.

The new Russia's main political ideology might thus be called "promarket patriotism," and it remains popular in numerous surveys conducted since the December elections. A 1994 survey of eleven Russian regions, for example, found that though 89 percent of those polled described the country's situation as "dangerous, critical, or catastrophic," only 20 percent described their personal situation as poor, and 63.8 percent indicated a desire to undertake personally some form of entrepreneurship.[68] Apparently people continue to attribute the collapse of the economy to the ineptness of the political elite (hence the extremely low regard for politicians of any stripe), rather than to the failings of market systems generally.

The reason behind the popularity of promarket patriotism becomes more understandable when one realizes that it is directly traceable to the seeds sown by Russia's alternative political culture. Andrey Zubov and Vladimir Kolosov, two analysts with the Russian Academy of Sciences, have argued that this particular combination dominated Duma politics during the decade before the October Revolution.[69] On the right it included chauvinistic parties such as the Union of the Russian People and its offshoot the "Chamber of the Archangel Michael," while on the left it encompassed the Constitutional Democrats and Progressives. During the productive third and fourth sessions of the Duma, it was exemplified in the dominance of the moderate "Union of October Seventeenth," or Octobrist Party. It is interesting to note that soon after the opening of the first post-Soviet Duma, individual deputies from disparate parties united to form the parliamentary bloc "Union of December 12," a name that consciously sought to evoke the political consensus forged by Russia's leading prerevolutionary party.

The results of the December 1993 election thus confirm the resilience and continuing impact of Russia's alternative political culture. The theme of an effective but constrained authoritarian rule as a guarantor of Russian national traditions and state unity suffused the campaign and became as important as economic issues. But can the alternative political culture succeed in combining tradition with modernity? Can it help forge a stable, democratic, yet distinctively Russian political and economic system? Although the challenges are enormous, and the resistance of an entrenched bureaucracy daunting, there are signs that a democratic culture is becoming institutionalized in Russia.

Patriotism and the Metamorphosis of Russian Communism

While the collapse of communism has captured the world's imagination, just as dramatic has been the revolution in popular attitudes toward the state. In response to the question, "What, in your opinion, should be government's role in the life of our country?" the majority now respond that the government should guarantee only a minimum standard of living, and anyone wishing more should earn it himself.[70] This coincides with the findings of other surveys conducted in 1993 and 1994 which point out that, though the initial enthusiasm for reforms has all but vanished, it has been replaced not by opposition to reforms but by a proreform inertia, which the sociologist Yuri Levada aptly terms "reforms without reformers."[71] Some analysts have even argued that the speed with which political skepticism has replaced political romanticism is proof of the fundamental soundness of modern Russian political attitudes.[72]

Could this reflect the creation of a new social contract, replacing vertical relations with government with horizontal ties throughout Russian society? Like Russian moderates, those in the West who have applied social contract theory to post-Soviet politics emphasize the need for stable and respected political institutions that will give Russians "the confidence necessary for them to believe that their time of troubles will eventually end."[73] They point to the existence of a high degree of consensus on the need for democratic and nonviolent resolution of conflicts, and economic reform. Moreover, they say, most of the reforms initiated by President Yeltsin could not have been undertaken without consistent popular backing, manifested repeatedly in referenda and elections since 1991. To succeed, however, a social contract must also reflect deep-seated political and cultural values that are given concrete, institutional form. Fortunately, the interpretive approach to political culture gives us the tools by which to ascertain which institutions and interest groups are likely to become the anchors of such a social contract.

There is nothing unique about the criteria for effective democracy in Russia. According to Barrington Moore, democracy involves "a long and certainly incomplete struggle to do three closely related things: 1) to check arbitrary rules, 2) to replace arbitrary rules with rational and just ones, and 3) to obtain a share for the underlying population in the making of rules."[74] What will be distinctively Russian, however, are the institutional forms this struggle will take. To flourish, Russia's new political institutions must reconstruct democratic processes to fit the Russian cultural environment. The easiest way to accomplish this is to institutionalize those aspects of the alternative political culture that have proven their resilience over time. Failure to do so weakens the ability of democratic institutions to tap into popular roots and to rely on popular support. Emigré Russian religious thinkers of the interwar period attributed the weakness of democratic institutions in both Russia and Europe to this fatal gap, and a number of contemporary Russian conservatives have echoed their warnings.

For many Western observers, schooled in traditional Sovietology and political culture theory, herein lies the fatal flaw of efforts to democratize the Soviet system: they believe there are no popular or historical roots to Russian democracy. An interpretive approach to political culture not only allows these roots to become apparent but, as the only bridge that spans the Soviet period and links Russia's pre–1917 past with the present, highlights the vital role that the alternative political culture must play in the creation of stable, democratic institutions.

The need to reinforce the links between patriotism and democracy is still too rarely recognized. In Russia, radical Westernizers, suspicious of the state, have been quick to abjure the proper and necessary functions of state authority. Then they blame the populace when their ideal of rapid integration with the West is rejected. By contrast, nationalists and excommunists have been too quick to accuse their opponents of selling out the country's interests. The polarization of Russian politics is thus the direct consequence of a failure to reinforce the linkage between patriotism and democracy and to create, through this linkage, a moderate, enlightened patriotism that could provide a coherent concept of the Russian national interest.

Western analysts have also too often viewed patriotic fervor as antithetical to democratic principles. It cannot be denied, however, that reforms have succeeded best in those countries where anticommunist movements were able to rely on strong patriotic sentiments. In Poland, the Baltic States, Hungary, and Czechoslovakia the call to restore traditional values gave a sense of pride and hope to the opposition institutions, and the ability to label the imposed values as "foreign" allowed them to be more quickly and decisively rejected.

Russia had no such rallying point, and, as a result, the end of communist rule has been accompanied by a difficult and painful reassessment of Russian national values, which has divided key constituencies necessary for a successful reform. Russian commentators often liken the present situation to the seventeenth-century "Time of Troubles," when Russia's survival as a nation seemed in doubt.

Russia's best hope for a stable and democratic political future lies in shoring up the middle ground between extremes, where a sensible, enlightened patriotism can take root. Viktor Aksyuchits, a people's deputy from a working-class district in Moscow, and a founding member of the Russian Christian Democratic Party, defined enlightened patriotism as "first and foremost, love of one's people, one's history, and one's culture. But like all true love it excludes nationalistic conceit, conflict, and chauvinistic hatred." The term has since been adopted by prominent political personalities, from Deputy Prime Minister Sergey Shakhray to former Russian Ambassador to the United States Vladimir Lukin. Although it originated in the conservative, neo-Slavophile wing of the Russian political spectrum, its popularity clearly now transcends the narrow confines of party politics.[75]

But will enlightened patriotism hold together such a deeply divided society? Is it enough to allow a new social contract to take root? There are grounds for cautious optimism, one of the most important being the ongoing transformation of the Communist Party, once undisputed hegemon of the Soviet party-state, into an ordinary political party. Many analysts are skeptical that this remnant of the former CPSU has truly embraced political pluralism. They point to the participation of the Communist Party leader Gennadiy Zyuganov in the outlawed National Salvation Front, and fear that the leadership's embrace of patriotic verbiage is merely a gambit designed to cover hegemonic aspirations.

The potential of the communists to reconstitute themselves into a pluralistic party, however, may have been underestimated. The process of structural and intellectual deconstruction of the Party has actually been under way for a number of years. Although the removal of Article 6 of the Soviet Constitution on March 14, 1990, officially ended the Party's monopoly on power, its popularity had already been sinking rapidly. In 1989, 37 percent of the populace said they were prepared to trust the Party, but a year later only 8 percent were still willing to do so.[76] A survey published in *Moscow News* in May 1990 revealed that only 18.8 percent of the electorate would have voted for the CPSU had free elections been possible.[77] Between October 1988 and July 1991, the CPSU lost nearly a quarter of its total membership, while after the August 1991 coup attempt the Party's level of popular support sank to just 2.3 percent, comparable to support for Marxism-Leninism.[78]

Most significant, however, was the disaffection of the elite. One of the first extensive, open-ended interview studies of the Russian elite, conducted in June 1991, showed that only 1 percent of this group fully agreed with the statement, "Socialism, as Lenin understood it, can be the basis for the renewal of society," whereas 51 percent completely disagreed with it. Eighty-five percent fully agreed with the statement, "The CPSU should not be a privileged party," whereas only 1 percent somewhat disagreed (there were no respondents in complete disagreement).[79] Considering that 63 percent of this group had been members of the CPSU (compared with 9 percent of the total population), the prospect for the CPSU's retaining power did not look good even before the failed coup.

After the coup, Yeltsin banned the Party on the grounds that it had usurped the authority of the state. The CPSU responded by appealing to the Constitutional Court. The trial, which lasted more than a year, further eroded communist support. Although people were more or less evenly split on whether Yeltsin's decision had been correct, by a margin of four to one they agreed that the Communist Party had been more harmful than useful.[80] The Constitutional Court's ruling on November 30, 1992, sought to provide a modicum of justice to both sides by ruling that Yeltsin had indeed acted properly in disbanding the national governing bodies of the CPSU for their role in conspiring against the state. The justices, however, also found that the millions of rank-and-file communists had not engaged in the conspiracy and therefore had a right to reconstitute the Party.

As a result, today there is no longer one Communist Party, but several different communist groupings, loosely allied. Their initial disorganization seems to have been overcome just in time for the December 1993 elections, at which the newly formed Communist Party of the Russian Federation sought to present a united front of mainstream communist organizations.

Just how different is the CPRF from its predecessor? Critical of Soviet socialism, the Party now strives for what it terms "popular socialism" *(narodnyi sotsializm)*, characterized by true democracy, federalism, and the rule of law.

Popular socialism, it is now averred, respects all forms of ownership, but actively promotes "popular" *(obshchenarodnaya)* ownership. Such ownership is distinguished from state ownership in that the use and administration of property is accomplished primarily by workers' collectives, under the supervision of duly elected popular representatives. Although the CPRF supports economic planning for the rational distribution of resources, it opposes any interference in the decisions made by individual factories, or among factories of different sectors of the economy, or within distinct regions of the country. Lower-level economic relationships are to be determined strictly by the market, which is termed "an important complementary stimulus to the growth and effectiveness of production."[81] The methods used to reach popular socialism must be peaceful and constitutional.

Critics within the Party have complained that what is missing from this new communist manifesto is as important as what is included. The concept of class struggle has been replaced with the search for patriotic consensus. As proof they cite Zyuganov's condemnation of Soviet social science for having "almost untaught us how to think of contemporary reality in terms of common national interests, viewing the nation as an organic force *(sobornuyu silu)*, and not only as an arena where social groups struggled."[82] This emphasis on social accord and patriotism, critics contend, blurs the lines of class enmity and encourages the dangerous illusion that political conflicts among classes can be reconciled peacefully. They accuse the current leadership under Gennadiy Zyuganov of having forgotten Lenin's commandment that parliamentary participation be viewed only as the means to an end, not the end itself.[83]

Although reformers like Zyuganov now appear to be in control, they are still opposed by powerful voices within the CPRF. The most notable are Anatoly Lukyanov, the former chairman of the USSR Supreme Soviet and a recently amnestied August 1991 coup plotter, and two members of the Central Executive Committee of the CPRF, Ivan Boltovskiy and Boris Slavin. The strength of the latter group can be seen in the Party's refusal to sign the Civic Accord, despite Zyuganov's initial indication that it would.[84]

The gradual "social-democratization" of the Communist Party, however, seems irreversible. Because the Party is now a conglomeration of loosely affiliated, regionally based political groupings with socialist leanings, Party leaders no longer have the power to simply dictate its interests to regional Party organizations. They must learn to accommodate local interests or lose support. This point was brought home to the Party's leadership when it opposed participation in the December 1993 elections. It was quickly forced to reverse its decision when eighty-five out of eighty-nine regional organizations insisted on participating.[85]

The need to respond to base constituents makes this Party something quite different from the CPSU during its heyday, and there is every reason to believe that it truly reflects the desires of a particular constituency in Russian society. As a party, therefore, its political success now depends on retaining its rather conservative electoral base, while showing that it can also forge an electoral coalition broad enough to govern. One result of these conflicting requirements has been that, while professing undying opposition to the government and the Constitution, the CPRF has promoted many compromise legislative packages in the new Duma and voted alongside reformers to defeat no-confidence motions against the Chernomyrdin government.[86] Consummate pragmatists, the current Communist Party leaders are intent on rebuilding a strong state structure. What to call the ideology best suited to this task seems for them a matter of philosophical speculation, far removed from practical politics.

As the economy privatizes even further, and old command methods become more useless, the Party's claim that it can wield the levers of power more effectively than anyone else will appear increasingly implausible to the electorate. It will be interesting to see how the Party responds to this challenge — by moving closer to socialist democracy, or by returning to more ideologically entrenched positions. Both patterns have been evinced by the Communist parties of Western Europe. It will also be crucial to watch internal Party politics closely to see how much the Party has truly abandoned democratic centralism, and to see how it performs in regional, as well as national, political coalitions.

Contemplating Russia as Part of the West

Watching the daily struggles of Russia's fledgling democracy, we can easily forget how much has changed since 1991. The rapid march of small-scale privatization, which has created more private stockholders in Russia than in the United States, is just one example of why the restoration of Soviet-style communism seems utterly implausible. Although the precise path that the restoration of Russian democracy will take is far from certain, it is not entirely unpredictable. Surveys and election results suggest that the values of Russia's alternative political culture are consistently viewed with sympathy by a large portion of the population. A study conducted by the Interlegal Research Center in January 1993 reports that although "national-patriotic" organizations could rely on the steadfast support of only 10 percent of the population, the potential of the "patriotic idea" was much higher. More than 40 percent of the population shares this ideal, but is frightened away by the extremist rhetoric of current nationalist leaders.[87] It is safe to assume that political parties that espouse this idea will gradually deepen their popular support, and that institutions reflecting traditional values will tend to be seen as more legitimate than those that do not. Unfortunately, Russian political culture is most often viewed not as an asset to establishing Russian democracy but as something that needs to be overcome.

This excessively narrow view of Russian political culture is one of the most serious stumbling blocks that now remain to improved relations with Russia. Policy-makers generally choose among policy alternatives based on their sense of what is possible, as well as what is desirable. Simply broadening the conceptual framework, therefore, opens up new possibilities in Russian domestic, economic, political, and foreign policy development. If Russian domestic developments are viewed as popular democratic aspirations reasserting themselves, then the sense of inevitable conflict between Russia and the West wanes. To be sure there would still be ample room for disagreements, but these would become manageable incidents within the broader context of shared values, much like our current disputes with Germany or Japan.

Greater pluralism in our perspectives on Russian political culture would thus allow us to break the spell that containment has cast upon U.S. foreign policy. Containment rested upon a consensus among U.S. foreign policymakers regarding the nature of the Soviet threat. The remarkable longevity of this consensus rested on three assumptions: first, that communist political values had been accepted as legitimate by the majority of the peoples within the Soviet Union, beginning with the Russians; second, that the populace attributed any improvement in their standard of living to the present regime; and third, that there was no functional memory of alternative values that could undermine the present value system, much less pose any threat to Soviet rule.[88]

The durability of containment is a tribute to the strategic and historical insights of George F. Kennan in his famous "X" article, "The Sources of Soviet Conduct."[89] Despite the fact that the substantive issues over which the two sides disagreed were continually changing, our underlying assumptions about the Soviet Union changed very little. The reason for this lies in Kennan's view of Russian history, which proved to be the most enduring component of his policy. By offering both a strategic response to Soviet expansion and a historical explanation of Soviet/Russian motives for expansion, Kennan offered the first *total* explanation for Soviet behavior, and in so doing he linked containment inextricably to a rather dismal view of Russian political culture.

For Kennan, Russian history was an unmitigated succession of failed opportunities, of rulers distant and unresponsive to the needs of their population, and of a populace that, though worthy of our compassion and sympathy, was incapable of effecting any political changes on its own. By emphasizing Russia's "Asiatic" and "oriental" world view, he defined its political tradition as alien to the West. Kennan emphasized the passivity and sterility of Russian political traditions, and by using the terms "Russian" and "Soviet" interchangeably, conveyed a sense of fundamental continuity between the Russian political traditions and the current Soviet system. The people, he concluded, are rather pitiable spectators to the political process, lacking both the civic and the spiritual resources with which to challenge the regime. Later, when Kennan speaks of containment's ultimately eroding the communist regime, he sees its final demise as the result of external pressures upon the Soviet leaders, having little to do with popular discontent.

Kennan's "X" article has justly been called the single most influential foreign policy article of the twentieth century. It fused together what were then two distinct elements of America's postwar attitude toward the Soviet Union: the sense that Soviet expansion was somehow a threat to American interests; and the perceived lack of democratic alternatives to communist rule due to Russia's "unwestern" political tradition. The argument that Russians lacked the ability to resist the expansion of their government either at home or abroad thus provided a much-needed continuity of theme and purpose for the new containment policy. Even after serious disagreements erupted in the United States over the size and scope of Soviet expansion, this historiosophic consensus provided such intellectual cohesiveness to American foreign policy toward the Soviet Union that the diplomatic historian John Lewis Gaddis would refer to all postwar policies as merely variations of containment.[90]

With the collapse of communism the essential preconditions for containment would seem to have disappeared. Not so, argue influential analysts such as Richard Pipes, Henry Kissinger, and Zbigniew Brzezinski. They point to resurgent Russian imperialism as the new threat and urge an approach to global security that links American interests to those of the border states surrounding Russia.[91] Now it is specifically Russia that is being contained, not communism.

Retaining the strategic cohesiveness of containment while shifting the focus away from communism to Russia, however, is no easy task. Russia has undeniable cultural and historical links with the West that lead even a staunch anticommunist like Jeane J. Kirkpatrick to wonder publicly: "What is Russia if not 'Western?' The East/West designation of the Cold War made sense in a European context, but in a global context Slavic/Orthodox people are Europeans who share in Western culture. Orthodox theology and liturgy, Leninism and Tolstoy are expressions of Western culture."[92]

Samuel Huntington has recently provided a solution to this dilemma by redefining our conflict with Russia as an enduring conflict of civilization values. In a widely discussed article in *Foreign Affairs,* Huntington identifies "civilization identity" as the major force shaping the next century. "The next world war, if there is one, will be a war between civilizations," and among the six or seven major civilizations that will be competing with the West, one will be "Slavic-Orthodox" civilization.[93] Like Kennan before him, Huntington argues that basic Western values ("individualism, liberalism, constitutionalism, human rights, equality, liberty, the rule of law, democracy, free markets, the separation of church and state") have little resonance in Orthodox culture.[94] Russia may yet have a chance to join the West, but only if it redefines its civilization identity along Western lines. Given the burden of

Russian history, however, the chances for success are slim. Indeed, Huntington sees the traditionalists now emerging in Russia as more alien than the former Soviet Marxists, with whom "a Western democrat could carry on an intellectual debate."[95]

To meet the new challenges of civilization identity Huntington proposes a mixture of containment and co-optation. First, he calls upon the West (North America and Western Europe) to unify and consolidate in preparation for the coming conflict. The West should then seek to "incorporate" related societies in Eastern Europe and Latin America, while actively supporting interest groups and values sympathetic to it in non-Western regions such as Japan and Russia. Finally, the West must contain the expansion of hostile civilizations, primarily Confucian and Islamic.[96] Thus, with the end of communism, containment has faltered but not fallen. While Brzezinski and others seek to redefine Russia's threat to the West, Huntington reaffirms its fundamental cultural alienation from the West. This combination, which proved so successful for Kennan, may yet succeed in revitalizing containment for the foreseeable future.

Huntington's analysis is certainly not new. It has much in common with Lucian W. Pye's notion that there will be a coming global clash between national cultures and the "world culture" of modernization.[97] Moreover, his view that conflicts between civilizations are inevitable rests on the premise that fundamental political choices are driven by certain immutable characteristics of political culture. Huntington's piece, therefore, reveals the importance of theories of political culture to American foreign policy thinking.

What the modern-day advocates of containment seem to fear even more than communism is the disintegration of a common Western purpose. As long as the Soviet Union threatened, containment served to bind together the many centrifugal interests among and within Western states. The benefits of a common purpose to international stability are obvious, but how can that stability best be achieved after the collapse of communism? Might not a common Western purpose based upon the search for values that we share with different cultures, rather than those that separate us, be more durable?

This brings us back to the importance of broadening our conceptual framework. Coming up with a new and comprehensive foreign policy vision is hard enough. It is impossible to imagine without a redefinition of Russian political culture. This redefinition is unlikely to proceed very far, however, without the inclusion of opinion leaders from Russia itself. The notion that the West is the universal standard for political and economic development has become so thoroughly entrenched in American political science that it is difficult to imagine a critical self-evaluation, particularly one inspired by the "losing side" in the Cold War.[98]

Yet it is precisely such a critical, spirited, and equal exchange of views that offers the best hope for rediscovering our common political and cultural heritage. And there is much in this heritage, as the historian Benedict Sumner points out, that is already familiar to Russians:

> Russian nineteenth-century literature is Russian through and through, but it is also European. Nearly all Russian writers were deeply versed in French, German, and English literature; most in the originals, partly in translation; and probably in no country was the range or quality of translations wider or higher. Greek and Latin were a mainstay of the upper-class schools of the first forty years of the century, and again of its last quarter. Similarly, Russian social thought and philosophy developed from European thinkers and were subject to the influence of the same trends as were dominant in the West.[99]

Speaking in Moscow in early 1990, Assistant Secretary of State for Human Rights and Humanitarian Affairs Richard Schifter gave a thoughtful example of how Western values can be asserted within a thoroughly Russian context, thereby strengthening the bonds of both:

> There was a time when it was argued that we have differing ideas about the human dimension, that we have differing notions as to what the words "human rights" mean. What many have come to recognize and acknowledge is that we are all part of the same civilization, that our notions about the ideal relationship between governments and the people are quite similar, even though [they] may not be identical.
> We should not be surprised by this similarity . . . We draw our ethical values from the same religious tradition. We read each other's literature. We benefit from each other's contributions to science and technology. And we have also exchanged political ideas . . .
> To be sure, there were those who contended that the ideas of freedom propagated by the Enlightenment of the 18th Century were inappropriate for what was called the Soviet social system. These defenders of the old order, I submit, were betraying the heritage of this country's great exponents of freedom, such as Pushkin and Tolstoy . . .
> I have mentioned Pushkin and Tolstoy because not only their names but also their writings are part of the heritage of the civilization to which we belong. But they did not stand alone in their affirmation of a belief in a free and open society. There are many others who kept the spark of a belief in liberty alive even under the most adverse circumstances.[100]

Schifter's sensitivity to the aspirations of Russia's alternative political culture stands in sharp contrast to the didactic and overbearing approach of many Western advisers — that it is Russia that must learn from the West how to be civilized: the former can build understanding and open doors, whereas the latter can only breed hostility and resentment.

Contemplating Russia as an integral and necessary part of the West is certainly no easy task. What makes this challenge particularly poignant for both sides is that the ideals of the October Revolution were shared by an influential portion of the Western intellectual elite.[101] If, as Sir Michael Howard suggests, Marxism is a quintessentially Western ideology, then its durability in the USSR is at least partly attributable to the fact that Russia in the early twentieth century was already an integral part of the West. Conversely, only by destroying what was universal in Russian culture could the Bolsheviks hope to triumph. Yet destroying those universal values deprived the Bolsheviks of the tempering influences of the nineteenth-century Russian intelligentsia, and transformed the Party into a radically antiwestern movement. Only by restoring this universalism can the resurrection of totalitarianism be prevented. For Russia, therefore, reintegration with the West will be an intellectual and psychological process of reaffirming its past, not of overcoming it.

Perhaps, just as important, if envisioned as a joint endeavor this reintegration will have a salutary impact upon social developments in both Russia and the West. The values advocated by Russia's neo-Slavophiles — nationality, fairness, patriotism, statehood, spirituality, morality — are in great demand throughout the world.[102] Modern societies yearn for the community of traditional societies (the integration of *Gemeinschaft* and *Gesellschaft,* as German sociologists put it), and increasingly blame themselves for its loss. For peculiar historical reasons, many of Russia's leading neo-Slavophile intellectuals found themselves in the West, at the crossroads of modernity and tradition in the twentieth century. How ironic — yet how rich with significance — that it is precisely here in the West that they labored to establish the historically rooted sense of community, tempered by a respect for the individual, that postindustrial societies now yearn for. By viewing Russia's experience as part of our common discourse of values, perhaps we in the West can gain new insights to apply to ourselves.

Tradition, therefore, need not be feared by those who cherish modernity and the West. True, to the extent that cultures preserve their distinctive traditions, differences will persist, but similarities will also be reinforced. Here, too, an interpretive approach to political culture may help in viewing the West as a richer and more varied tapestry of traditions than we had heretofore imagined.

Although this book has focused attention on the persistence of democratic aspirations within Russian political culture, the struggle between statist and nonstatist traditions is far from over. There is evidence to suggest, however, that for the first time historical circumstances and popular sentiment are both conspiring against the return of state absolutism. One sees it in the skepticism regarding the state's ability to provide for basic needs. One sees it in the "weariness of empire" exhibited at all levels of society.[103] Finally, one sees it in the widespread disenchantment with "revolutions" of any kind. Once held out as the great promise of mankind, it is now recognized as nothing more than an acute symptom of social illness.

This results in a fascinating paradox, noted by many visitors to Russia: beneath the vociferous pessimism about the immediate future, one often finds a strong undercurrent of optimism about Russia's long-term future. As one Russian economist put it, "In twenty years, we will be a normal country. In fifty years, we will be a very affluent country. In a hundred years, Europe will join us."[104]

A few reasons for optimism can be discerned even in today's Russia. For the first time in generations, Russia can now pursue its vision of good government without the threat of war. The pains of economic transition are generally perceived as temporary. Even the demise of Russia as an imperial power, perhaps the most traumatic consequence of the end of communism, seems to be tempered by a recognition that Russia has little choice but to become both a democratic and a multiethnic state. This recognition, by the way, distinguishes Russia from many of its neighbors, where the status of minorities continues to be a source of domestic friction. Finally, the centrifugal forces within the USSR that exploded in 1991 are already giving way to the centripetal forces of history, language, and culture, particularly in Russia, Ukraine, and Belarus.[105]

What many Russians seem to recognize, perhaps only intuitively, is that the longevity of Russia's alternative political culture and its slow but steady progress toward the institutionalization of civil society offer good reason to view the twenty-first century with optimism. As we in the West learn to appreciate the diversity of strands in Russian political culture, perhaps that future will begin to appear more promising to us as well.

Notes / Index

Notes

1. Political Culture and the Failure of Sovietology

1. "Demokratiya ne terpit demagogii," *Pravda* (February 10, 1989), p. 1.
2. Raymond M. Duch, "Tolerating Economic Reform: Popular Support for Transition to a Free Market in the Former Soviet Union," *American Political Science Review,* vol. 87, no. 3 (September 1993), pp. 590–608; James L. Gibson, Raymond M. Duch, and Kent L. Tedin, "Democratic Values and the Transformation of the Soviet Union," *Journal of Politics,* vol. 54, no. 2 (May 1992), pp. 329–371; James L. Gibson and Raymond M. Duch, "Political Intolerance in the USSR," *Comparative Political Studies,* vol. 26, no. 3 (October 1993), pp. 286–329; William Reisinger et al., "Political Values in Russia, Ukraine and Lithuania: Sources and Implications for Democracy," *British Journal of Political Science,* vol. 24 (April 1994), pp. 183–224; Arthur H. Miller et al., "Reassessing Mass Support for Political and Economic Changes in the Former USSR," *American Political Science Review,* vol. 88, no. 2 (June 1994), pp. 399–411. In his article "Continuity and Change in Russian Political Culture," *British Journal of Political Science,* vol. 21 (October 1991), pp. 393–422, Jeffrey Hahn speculates about what implications this evidence might have for our traditional view of Russian political culture.
3. Cited in Gabriel Almond, *A Discipline Divided: Schools and Sects in Political Science* (London: Sage Publications, 1990), p. 163.
4. Cited in William Adams, "Politics and the Archeology of Meaning," *Western Political Quarterly,* vol. 39 (September 1986), p. 559.
5. Gabriel Almond and Sidney Verba, *The Civic Culture: Political Attitudes and Democracy in Five Nations* (Princeton: Princeton University Press, 1963).
6. On the popularity of pre–1917 symbols, see S. Vasiltsov, "O nashikh simvolakh," *Rossiya* (December 18, 1991), p. 3. Vasiltsov notes that "only every fifth or sixth Russian" now identifies with symbols of the Soviet era.
7. Stephen White, *Political Culture and Soviet Politics* (New York: St. Martin's Press, 1979), p. 5.

8. Stephen Welch, "Issues in the Study of Political Culture: The Example of Communist Party States," *British Journal of Political Science*, vol. 17, part 4 (October 1987), p. 480.

9. Howard J. Wiarda, "Political Culture and National Development," *The Fletcher Forum*, vol. 13, no. 2 (Summer 1989), p. 193.

10. Gabriel Almond, "Comparative Political Systems," *Journal of Politics*, vol. 18 (1956), pp. 391–409.

11. Ibid., p. 391.

12. Ibid., p. 393.

13. Lucian W. Pye, "Culture and Political Science: Problems in the Evaluation of the Concept of Political Culture," *Social Science Quarterly*, vol. 53, no. 2 (September 1972), pp. 289–290.

14. Lucian W. Pye, "Political Culture," in David L. Sills, ed., *International Encyclopedia of the Social Sciences*, vol. 12 (New York: Macmillan Co. and Free Press, 1968), p. 218.

15. Almond and Verba, *The Civic Culture*, p. 17.

16. Ibid., p. 12.

17. Ibid., p. 8.

18. Frederick C. Barghoorn, "Soviet Russia: Orthodoxy and Adaptiveness," in Lucian W. Pye and Sidney Verba, eds., *Political Culture and Political Development* (Princeton: Princeton University Press, 1965), pp. 450–511.

19. Robert C. Tucker, "Culture, Political Culture, and Communist Society," *Political Science Quarterly*, vol. 88, no. 2 (June 1973), p. 175.

20. Pye, "Political Culture," p. 218.

21. Almond and Verba, *The Civic Culture*, p. 12.

22. Lowell Dittmer, "Political Culture and Political Symbolism: Toward a Theoretical Synthesis," *World Politics* (1977), p. 554.

23. William T. Bluhm, *Ideologies and Attitudes: Modern Political Culture* (Englewood Cliffs, N.J.: Prentice-Hall, 1974), p. 11.

24. Walter A. Rosenbaum, *Political Culture* (New York: Praeger, 1975), p. 51.

25. Tucker, "Culture, Political Culture, and Communist Society," p. 181.

26. William Adams, "Politics and the Archeology of Meaning," *Western Political Quarterly*, vol. 39 (September 1986), p. 550.

27. Ibid., p. 562.

28. Cited in Tucker, "Culture, Political Culture, and Communist Society," p. 177.

29. Frederick C. Barghoorn and Thomas F. Remington, *Politics in the USSR*, third ed. (Boston: Little, Brown & Co, 1986), p. 36.

30. Roger Kanet, *The Behavioral Revolution and Communist Studies* (New York: Free Press, 1971), p. 18.

31. Archie Brown, "Ideology and Political Culture," in Seweryn Bialer, ed., *Politics, Society, and Nationality inside Gorbachev's Russia* (Boulder, Col.: Westview Press, 1989), pp. 17–18; Stephen White, "Continuity and Change in Soviet Political Culture: An Emigre Study," *Comparative Political Studies*, vol. 11 (1978), pp. 381–395.

32. Alex Inkeles and Raymond A. Bauer, *The Soviet Citizen: Daily Life in Totalitarian Society* (Cambridge, Mass.: Harvard University Press, 1961), pp. 392–393.

33. Ibid., p. 242.
34. Ibid., p. 235.
35. Ibid., p. 392.
36. Ibid., pp. 233–246.
37. Ivan D. London and Miriam B. London, "A Research-Examination of the Harvard Project on the Soviet Social System: I. The Basic Written Questionnaire," *Psychological Reports*, vol. 19 (1966), pp. 1011–1109.
38. See "Making a Living," especially pp. 124–128, in Inkeles and Bauer, *The Soviet Citizen*, section V. London and London, "A Research-Examination of the Harvard Project," pp. 1019–1020.
39. Inkeles and Bauer, *The Soviet Citizen*, p. 54.
40. The word "career," for example, is translated simply as *karyera*, without any appreciation of the negative and unethical connotations that "making a career" (*sdelat sebe karyeru*) has in Russian. London and London, "A Research-Examination of the Harvard Project," pp. 1024, 1029.
41. Inkeles and Bauer, *The Soviet Citizen*, p. 12.
42. Several articles are conveniently excerpted in the Appendix to London and London, "A Research-Examination of the Harvard Project." One might also note that a previous survey conducted among émigrés by Dallin did not run into such problems and controversies.
43. See Tatyana Zaslavskaya, "The Novosibirsk Report," *Survey*, vol. 28, no. 1 (Spring 1984); and "The Secret Dream of a Soviet Tomorrow," *Samizdat Bulletin*, no. 160 (August 1986), pp. 1–12.
44. James Millar, ed., *Politics, Work, and Daily Life in the USSR: A Survey of Former Soviet Citizens* (Cambridge, England: Cambridge University Press, 1987). See especially the articles by Donna Barry, Brian D. Silver, and William Zimmerman.
45. Zbigniew Brzezinski and Samuel P. Huntington, *Political Power: USA/USSR* (New York: The Viking Press), pp. 9–14.
46. Inkeles and Bauer, *The Soviet Citizen*, pp. 246–247.
47. Margaret Mead, *Soviet Attitudes toward Authority* (New York: William Morrow, 1955), p. 26.
48. Ibid., p. 9. See also Geoffrey Gorer and John Rickman, *The People of Great Russia: A Psychological Study* (New York: Norton, 1962); and Geoffrey Gorer, "Some Aspects of the Psychology of the People of Great Russia," *The American Slavic and East European Review*, vol. 8 (October 1949).
49. Mead, *Soviet Attitudes*, p. 14.
50. See Gabriel Almond, "The Intellectual History of the Civic Culture Concept," in Gabriel Almond and Sidney Verba, *The Civic Culture Revisited: An Analytic Study* (New York: Sage Publications, 1989), p. 14; and Lucian W. Pye, "Political Culture Revisited," *Political Psychology*, no. 3 (1991), p. 489.
51. Barghoorn and Remington, *Politics in the USSR*, p. 36.
52. Brown, *Soviet Politics and Political Science*, pp. 89–104.
53. Ibid., p. 97.
54. White, *Political Culture*, p. 22.
55. Mary McAuley, "Political Culture and Communist Politics: One Step Forward,

Two Steps Back," in Archie Brown, ed., *Political Culture and Communist Studies* (Armonk, N.Y.: M. E. Sharpe, 1985), p. 23.

56. Stephen White, "Soviet Political Culture Reassessed," in Brown, ed., *Political Culture and Communist Studies* p. 66.

57. Gabriel Almond, *Schools and Sects in Political Science* (London: Sage Publications, 1990), p. 157.

58. Almond, *A Discipline Divided,* p. 150.

59. Ibid., pp. 150–152. Almond cites the examples of the United States and Great Britain. In *The Civic Culture,* Almond had rated both these nations as "high" in civic culture because of the high degree of popular trust in their political leadership. Survey evidence in the 1970s and 1980s has reversed this assessment, which Almond later attributed to political moods that do not affect "the basic legitimacy of American and British political and social institutions." *A Discipline Divided,* pp. 149–150.

60. Archie Brown and Jack Gray, eds., *Political Culture and Political Change in Communist States* (New York: Holmes & Meier, 1977), p. 13.

61. The one exception I could find was a chapter by Archie Brown in which he tries to portray Gorbachev's reforms as evidence of a political-cultural shift in society promoted by a political subculture within the elite radicalized by the Twentieth Party Congress. The relationship of this subculture to the dominant authoritarian political culture is unclear, however; hence the reader is still left wondering, why Gorbachev and why now? See Archie Brown, "Ideology and Political Culture," in Bialer, ed., *Politics, Society, and Nationality,* pp. 1–40.

62. This appears to be the consensus today, as well. See the discussion in the special edition "The Strange Death of Communism: An Autopsy," *The National Interest,* no. 31 (Spring 1993).

63. Even after the coup, there were some who continued to speak of how he was merely biding his time, in anticipation of orchestrating yet another political comeback. One of the strangest episodes was Jerry Hough's keynote speech to the AAASS in Miami, where he laid out a scenario in which Yeltsin was Gorbachev's puppet, and the attempted coup — yet another masterly episode in Gorbachev's grand strategy for transforming the Soviet Union.

64. Moshe Lewin, *The Gorbachev Phenomenon* (Berkeley: University of California Press, 1988), p. 4.

65. The "reforms will survive only as long as Gorbachev does" school included such notables as Stephen White, Robert V. Daniels, and Jerry Hough, yet even skeptics like Marshall Goldmann and Peter Reddaway seemed to concede the point, arguing that reforms were unlikely precisely because Gorbachev himself could not last.

66. McAuley, "Political Culture and Communist Politics," p. 17.

67. Almond, *A Discipline Divided,* pp. 143–148.

68. Ibid., p. 150.

69. This definition is adapted from William M. Reisinger, "Political Culture as Concept and Theory: Remaining Tasks for the Renaissance," unpublished manuscript (1993), pp. 9–10.

70. Tucker, "Culture, Political Culture, and Communist Society," p. 182.
71. Cited by Michael Brint, *A Genealogy of Political Culture* (Boulder, Col.: Westview Press, 1991), p. 88.
72. Tucker, "Culture, Political Culture, and Communist Society," pp. 173–190; Richard Fagen, *The Transformation of Political Culture in Cuba* (Stanford: Stanford University Press, 1969), p. 6.
73. Tucker, "Culture, Political Culture, and Communist Society," p. 176.
74. Lowell Dittmer, "Comparative Communist Political Culture," *Studies in Comparative Communism* (Spring–Summer 1983), p. 11.
75. Dittmer, "Political Culture and Political Symbolism," p. 555.
76. Almond, "Communism and Political Culture Theory," in *A Discipline Divided*, pp. 157–169.
77. White, *Political Culture*, p. 20.
78. Cited by Dittmer, "Political Culture and Political Symbolism," p. 559.
79. Dittmer, "Comparative Communist Political Culture," p. 12.
80. Dittmer, "Political Culture and Political Symbolism," p. 557.
81. Brint, *A Genealogy of Political Culture*, pp. 89–90.
82. Dittmer, "Political Culture and Political Symbolism," p. 568.
83. On the historic preservation movement, see John Dunlop, *The Faces of Russian Nationalism* (Princeton: Princeton University Press, 1983), pp. 263–264. On the village prose writers, see Nicolai N. Petro, "'The Project of the Century': A Case Study of Russian Nationalist Opposition," *Studies in Comparative Communism* (Winter–Fall 1987), pp. 235–252; and Wolfgang Kasack, *Entsiklopedicheskiy slovar Russkoy literatury s 1917 goda* (London: Overseas Publications Interchange Ltd., 1988), p. 255.
84. Dittmer, "Political Culture and Political Symbolism," pp. 578–579.
85. Because of the innate tendency of the human mind to think in binary oppositions, such myths, Claude Levi-Strauss argues, usually come bundled in pairs. Dittmer, "Political Culture and Political Symbolism," p. 580.
86. Tucker, "Culture, Political Culture, and Communist Society."
87. Geoffrey Hosking, "The Beginnings of Independent Political Activity," in Geoffrey Hosking et al., *The Road to Post-Communism* (London: Pinter Publishers, 1992), p. 1.
88. See Dittmer, "Comparative Communist Political Culture," p. 12; Grzegorz Ekiert, "Democratic Processes in East Central Europe: A Theoretical Reconsideration," *British Journal of Political Science*, vol. 21, no. 3 (July 1, 1991), pp. 285–313; and Giuseppe Di Palma, "Legitimation from the Top to Civil Society: Politico-cultural Change in Eastern Europe," in Nancy Bermeo, ed., *Liberalization and Democratization* (Baltimore: Johns Hopkins University Press, 1992), p. 67.
89. Di Palma, "Legitimation from the Top to Civil Society," p. 70.
90. Vaclav Havel et al., *Power of the Powerless: Citizens against the State in Central-Eastern Europe* (London: Hutchinson, 1985), p. 43.
91. Ibid., p. 40.
92. Vladimir Tismaneanu, *Reinventing Politics: Eastern Europe from Stalin to Havel* (New York: Free Press, 1992), p. 146.

93. John Keane, ed., *Civil Society and the State: New European Perspectives* (London: Verso, 1988).

94. Vaclav Benda et al., "Parallel Polis, or an Independent Society in Central and Eastern Europe: An Inquiry," *Social Research*, vol. 55, no. 1–2 (Spring–Summer 1988), pp. 211–246.

95. Howard L. Biddulph, "Soviet Intellectual Dissent as a Political Counter-Culture," *Western Political Quarterly*, vol. 25 (September 1972), pp. 531–532.

96. Di Palma, "Legitimation from the Top to Civil Society," p. 68.

97. The most ambitious effort in this regard is the four-volume series *The Soviet Union and the Challenge of the Future* (New York: Paragon House, 1987–1989), ed. Morton A. Kaplan and Alexander Shtromas. For a useful contrast of the émigré and Western debates over the viability of the USSR, see the essays by Terry McNeil and Vladislav Krasnov in vol. 1, pp. 315–397.

98. Peter Rutland, "Sovietology: Notes for a Post-Mortem," *The National Interest*, no. 31 (Spring 1993), p. 122.

2. Constrained Autocracy in Russian History

1. Gabriel Almond, *A Discipline Divided: Schools and Sects in Political Science* (London: Sage Publications, 1990), p. 150.

2. Stephen White, *Political Culture and Soviet Politics* (New York: St. Martin's, 1979), p. 40.

3. Ibid., p. 64.

4. Stephen White, "The USSR: Patterns of Autocracy and Industrialism," in Archie Brown and Jack Gray, eds., *Political Culture and Political Change in Communist States* (New York: Homes and Meier, 1977), p. 34.

5. Richard Pipes, "The USSR or Russia?: The Historical Perspective," in Uri Ra'anan and Charles M. Perry, eds., *The USSR Today and Tomorrow: Problems and Choices* (Lexington, Mass.: D. C. Heath and Co., 1987), p. 28.

6. Richard Pipes, *Russia under the Old Regime* (New York: Charles Scribner's, 1974).

7. Pipes, "USSR or Russia?" p. 30.

8. One of the articles of Peter's Military Charter of 1716 reads: "His Majesty is an absolute monarch who need not answer to anyone in the world for his actions, but has the power and authority, as a Christian sovereign, to rule his domain and his lands according to his own will and discretion." Sergei Pushkarev, *Self-Government and Freedom in Russia* (Boulder, Colo.: Westview Press, 1988), p. 19.

   Feofan Prokopich attempted to do the same for Ivan IV, but failed because Ivan was a typical Muscovite ruler, constrained by boyars. The Fundamental Laws of 1832 proclaimed: "The Russian Empire is ruled on the firm basis of positive laws and statutes which emanate from the Autocratic Power." The First Article of the Code of Laws of the Empire set forth the unlimited authority of the autocrat, and until 1906 an imperial decree as well as imperial commands and verbal instructions had the force of law.

9. James H. Billington, "Looking to the Past," *Washington Post* (January 22, 1990), p. A11; S. Frederick Starr, "Prospects for Stable Democracy in Russia,"

Occasional Paper, The Mershon Center at Ohio State University (November 1991). See also his chapter "Local Initiative in Russia before the Zemstvo," in Terrence Emmons and Wayne S. Vucinich, eds., *The Zemstvo in Russia: An Experiment in Local Self-Government* (Cambridge, England: Cambridge University Press, 1982).

10. Ivan IV (the "Terrible"), Russia's most autocratic tsar, for example, complained bitterly that he was bound "hand and foot" by the nobility's *mestnichestvo* system, which obliged him to respect hereditary ranks when rewarding service to the state. Sergei G. Pushkarev, *Obzor russkoy istorii* (New York: Chekhov Publishing House, 1953), pp. 188–189.

11. Nikolai Kostomarov, "Nachalo edinoderzhaviye v drevnei Rusi," in V. N. Storozhev, ed., *Russkaya istoriya* (Moscow: izd. I. D. Sytin, 1898), p. 209.

12. Cited by Pushkarev, *Self-Government and Freedom,* pp. 7–9.

13. Ibid., p. 11.

14. White, *Political Culture and Soviet Politics,* pp. 25–26.

15. Pushkarev, *Obzor,* pp. 203–210.

16. Ibid., pp. 196–197.

17. Pushkarev, *Self-Government and Freedom,* p. 11.

18. Ibid., pp. 10–11.

19. Maxime Kovalevsky, *Russian Political Institutions* (Chicago: University of Chicago Press, 1902), pp. 57–62. The Russian phrase for ascension to the throne, *venchanie na tsarstvo,* actually implies a marital contract.

20. Paul Dukes, *The Making of Russian Absolutism, 1613–1801* (London and New York: Longman, 1986), p. 6.

21. Pushkarev, *Obzor,* p. 315.

22. Marc Raeff, *Understanding Imperial Russia* (New York: Columbia University Press, 1984), p. 47.

23. Cited by Pushkarev, *Obzor,* p. 310.

24. Sergei Utechin, *Russian Political Thought: A Concise History* (New York: Frederick A. Praeger, 1963), p. 41.

25. Raeff, *Understanding Imperial Russia,* p. 39.

26. Ibid., p. 76.

27. Astonishingly, in the 1980s the Soviet journalist Vasiliy Peskov found a small clan of Old Believers surviving in a remote region of Siberia, completely isolated from the rest of society. His account of their flight from both tsarist and Soviet religious persecution has appeared in English as *Lost in the Taiga* (New York: Doubleday, 1992).

28. Pushkarev, *Obzor,* pp. 338–339.

29. Raeff, *Understanding Imperial Russia,* p. 91.

30. Ibid., p. 100.

31. S. Frederick Starr describes how the gentry would try to reallocate government funds to servicing the needs of their estate, and concludes that "the preform gentry was quite capable of identifying and acting on its real corporate interest" but saw no such interest in the institutions that had been established. "Local Initiative in Russia before the Zemstvo," in Emmons and Vucinich, *The Zemstvo in Russia,* p. 14.

32. Dukes, *The Making of Russian Absolutism,* pp. 158–159.

33. Ibid., p. 158.
34. Utechin, *Russian Political Thought,* pp. 47–48.
35. Ibid., pp. 49–51.
36. Pushkarev, *Obzor,* p. 382.
37. Ibid., pp. 382–384.
38. Ibid., p. 385.
39. Michael Karpovich, *Imperial Russia, 1801–1917* (New York: Holt, Rinehart, Winston, 1960), p. 32.
40. Fyodor M. Dostoyevsky, "Obyasnitelnoe slovo po povodu pechataemoy nizhe rechi o Pushkine," *Polnoe Sobranie Sochinenii v tridtsati tomakh,* vol. 26 (Leningrad: Nauka, 1984), pp. 129–136.
41. Pushkarev, *Self-Government and Freedom,* pp. 51–52.
42. Jacob Walkin, *The Rise of Democracy in Pre-Revolutionary Russia* (New York: Praeger, 1962), p. 167.
43. Sergei Pushkarev, *The Emergence of Modern Russia, 1801–1917* (Edmonton, Alberta, Canada: Pica Pica Press, 1985), pp. 272–273.
44. Vladimir Zhelyagin and Nikolai Rutych, *Rossiya v epokhu reform* (Frankfurt a. Main: Possev-Verlag, 1981), pp. 31–33. In 1916 the All-Russian Union of Zemstvo's budget was six hundred million rubles, only a fraction of it provided by the state treasury. Walkin, *The Rise of Democracy,* p. 170.
45. S. Svatikov, *Obshchestvennoe dvizhenie v Rossii: 1700–1895* (Rostov na Donu: izd. N. Paramonova "Donskaya Rech," 1905), chaps. 22–26.
46. Pushkarev, *Self-Government and Freedom,* p. 65.
47. Walkin, *The Rise of Democracy,* p. 205.
48. Pushkarev, *Self-Government and Freedom,* pp. 66, 99.
49. Ibid., pp. 197–198.
50. Walkin, *The Rise of Democracy,* p. 208.
51. Terence Emmons, "The Zemstvo in Historical Perspective," in Emmons and Vucinich, *The Zemstvo in Russia,* p. 433.
52. Cited in Zhelyagin and Rutych, *Rossiya v epokhu reform,* p. 92.
53. M. Polivanov, "Zemstvo i demokratiya," *Novyi zhurnal,* no. 67 (1962), pp. 253–268.
54. Cited in Pushkarev, *Self-Government and Freedom,* p. 53.
55. Emmons, "The Zemstvo in Historical Perspective," p. 427.
56. Walkin, *The Rise of Democracy,* p. 207.
57. Marc Ferro, "The Aspirations of Russian Society," in Richard Pipes, ed., *Revolutionary Russia: A Symposium* (New York: Doubleday, 1969), pp. 198–199.
58. Cited in Pushkarev, *Self-Government and Freedom,* p. 49.
59. The procedure for electing representatives to the new representative body, the Duma, involved electors from four categories: landowners, peasants, city residents, and factory or mine workers. In addition, polling rights were weighted in favor of propertied landowners, similar to restrictions in Europe and America. For all these difficulties, however, with the exception of students, soldiers, migrant workers, and nomadic peoples, nearly the entire male population above the age of 25 was eligible to vote.
60. Stephen White et al., *Communist and Post-Communist Political Systems* (New York: St. Martin's, 1990), pp. 38–39.

61. Full religious freedom was extended to all faiths, though limitations on place of residence and entrance into universities were not lifted for "persons of Judaic faith." Zhelyagin and Rutych, *Rossiya v epokhu reform,* pp. 122–124.

62. Pushkarev, *Self-Government and Freedom,* pp. 97–100.

63. On the crucial role of the zemstvos in Russian economic progress, see Otto Hoetzsch, *The Evolution of Russia* (New York: Harcourt, Brace, and World, 1966). For a general discussion of economic trends during this period, see Alexander Gerschenkron, "Problems of Russian Economic Development," in Cyril E. Black, *The Transformation of Russian Society* (Cambridge, Mass.: Harvard University Press, 1960), pp. 42–71; Edmond Thiery, *La Transformation economique de la Russia* (Paris, 1914); Peter I. Lyashchenko, *History of the National Economy of Russia to the 1917 Revolution* (New York: Macmillan, 1949), especially pp. 669–696; and Peter A. Khromov, *Ekonomicheskoe razvitie Rossiy v XIX-XX vekakh,* 1800–1917 (Moscow: izd-vo. polit. lit-ry, 1950).

64. Pushkarev, *Modern Russia,* pp. 267–268; Zhelyagin and Rutych, *Rossiya v epokhu reform,* p. 252.

65. D. B. Pavlov and V. V. Shelokhaev, "Oktybristy, 'partiya propavshei gramoty,' " *Polis,* no. 2 (1993), p. 150.

66. Zhelyagin and Rutych, *Rossiya v epokhu reform,* p. 186.

67. Hans Rogger, *Russia in the Age of Modernisation and Revolution, 1881–1917* (London and New York: Longman, 1987), p. 14.

68. Dukes, *The Making of Russian Absolutism,* p. 86. For more on popular opposition to Peter's reforms see Michael Chernyavksy, *Tsar and People: Studies in Russian Myths* (New Haven: Yale University Press, 1961); N. B. Golikova, *Politicheskie protsessy pri Petre I* (Moscow: izd. Moskovskogo universiteta, 1957); and James Cracraft, "Opposition to Peter the Great," in Marshall Shatz et al., eds, *Imperial Russia, 1700–1917: State, Society, Opposition* (DeKalb, Ill.: Northern Illinois University Press, 1988).

69. This debate over Peter the Great encapsulates a broader, ongoing debate between the "state school" of Russian history, beginning with the historian Nikolai Karamzin, and the "society school" advanced by Nikolai Polevoy and Nikolai Kostomarov. The latter would not be at all surprised by the spontaneous emergence of social forces opposing the state, whereas the former would expect the state to be the prime instigator of social change.

70. Hans Rogger, *Russia in the Age of Modernisation,* p. 12.

71. Cited by Zhelyagin and Rutych, *Rossiya v epokhu reform,* p. 247.

72. For a discussion of the ideological debates within the zemstvo movement, see Polivanov, "Zemstvo i demokratiya," pp. 253–268.

73. One of the first Western authors to note this phenomenon was John Dunlop; see his chapter "The Rise of Monarchist and Restorationist Sentiment in the Contemporary Soviet Union," in his book *The New Russian Nationalism* (Washington, D.C.: CSIS, 1985), pp. 49–59. For a modern neo-Slavophile perspective, see V. Karpets, "Rossiyskoe samoderzhavie i Russkoe budushchee," *Veche,* no. 35 (1989), pp. 15–42; and an interview with the noted sculptor Vyacheslav Klykov, "'My zhivem v epokhu istoricheskogo vozmezdiya . . .,'" *Nash sovremennik,* no. 5 (1994), pp. 40–46.

74. Mikhail Agursky, *Ideologiya natsional-bolshevizma* (Paris: YMCA Press, 1980), pp. 51–52.
75. Cited by Hans Kohn, *The Mind of Modern Russia* (New Brunswick, N.J.: Rutgers), pp. 253, 255.
76. Agursky, *Ideologiya natsional-bolshevizma*, p. 74.
77. Ibid., p. 76.
78. For the traditional interpretation, see Adam Ulam, "Russian Nationalism," in Seweryn Bialer, ed., *The Domestic Context of Soviet Foreign Policy* (Boulder, Colo.: Westview Press, 1981), pp. 3–18; and Cyril Black, *Understanding Soviet Politics*, (Boulder, Colo.: Westview Press, 1986), pp. 180–210.
79. For a bibliography of Soviet sources on Pamyat, see Nicolai N. Petro, "Perestroika from Below," in Alfred J. Rieber and Alvin Z. Rubinstein, eds., *Perestroika at the Crossroads* (Armonk, N.Y.: M. E. Sharpe, 1991), pp. 132–133.
80. Julia Wishnevsky, "The Emergence of 'Pamyat' and 'Otechestvo,'" *Radio Liberty Research Bulletin* (RL 342/87).
81. Boris P. Kurashvili, "Aspekty perestroiki," *Sovetskoe gosudarstvo i pravo* (December 1987), p. 8.
82. The editorial staff of the Latvian literary journal *Daugava* (February 1989, p. 91) claims that Pamyat was given a square to speak in after a phone call from the regional Party committee *(obkom)*.
83. G. Baklanov, *Znamya* (October 1988), p. 234; "U menya ostalos oshchushchenie uzhasa," *Moskovskie novosti* (August 7, 1988), p. 2.
84. Nina Andreyeva, "Ne mogu postupatsya," *Sovetskaya Rossiya* (March 13, 1988), p. 3.
85. Georgiy Pryakhin on *Vremya* (September 18, 1987). *FBIS Daily Report — Soviet Union* (September 21, 1987), p. 34.
86. "Nechistaya igra na nechistykh chuvstvakh," *Izvestiya* (August 14, 1988), p. 6.
87. Vladimir Tismaneanu, "Friends and Foes of Glasnost," *Orbis* (Fall 1987), p. 374. Other sources, however, place the number of participants as low as one hundred: "Pamyat: Gorbachev's Strange Friends," *Soviet Analyst* (June 3, 1987), p. 7. The results of the 1990 elections to the Congress of People's Deputies in Leningrad confirm this. Despite running well-organized campaigns in Leningrad, a city where they have established their most visible presence, Pamyat candidates received only 6–7 percent of the popular vote. Akselrod Frumkin, "Sem protsentov za 'Pamyat,'" *Vestnik evreyskoy sovetskoy kultury* (April 26, 1989), p. 4.
88. Frederick Barghoorn, "Russian Nationalism and Soviet Politics," in Robert Conquest, ed., *The Last Empire* (Stanford: Hoover Institution Press, 1986), p. 34.
89. Sergey Kuginyan et al., *Postperestroika* (Moscow, 1990), cited by Aleksandr Shtamm, "Totalitarnoe myshlenie v posttotalitarnuyu epokhu," *Za Rossiyu*, no. 6 (293), 1993, p. 2.
90. Darrell P. Hammer, "The 'Traditionalist' Opposition in Soviet Politics," Final Report on Contract No. 804–802, the National Council for Soviet and East European Studies.

3. Orthodoxy's Symphonic Ideal

1. For Huntington, the West's next great challenge will come from the non-Western world views which are trying to "unsecularize" the world. See "The Coming Clash of Civilizations, or, the West against the Rest," *New York Times* (June 6, 1993), p. E19. In Almond's ranking of social systems, secularism plays an equally important role. See Gabriel Almond, "Comparative Political Systems," *Journal of Politics*, vol. 18 (1956), pp. 391–409.

2. Cited by James W. Warhola, "The Role of Russian Orthodoxy in Russian Political-Cultural Transformation," unpublished paper delivered at 1992 New England Political Science Association annual meeting (April 1993), p. 5.

3. Robert C. Tucker, *Political Culture and Leadership in Soviet Russia* (New York: W. W. Norton, 1987), pp. 116–117. The same point is made by Zernov: "From the first day of his life until his last breath a Russian Orthodox was a participant in his Christian community. Belonging to it was more important to him than his nationality or state allegiance: the common people of Russia often described themselves by the single word Pravoslavny (Orthodox) and called one another by the same name." Nicolas Zernov, *The Russian Religious Renaissance of the Twentieth Century* (New York: Harper & Row, 1963), p. 54.

4. Timothy Ware, *The Orthodox Church* (New York: Penguin Books, 1983), p. 125.

5. Sergei Pushkarev, *Self-Government and Freedom in Russia* (Boulder, Colo.: Westview Press, 1988), pp. 1–7.

6. Sergei Pushkarev et al., *Christianity and Government in Russia and the Soviet Union* (Boulder, Colo.: Westview Press, 1989), pp. 1–8; Vasiliy Klyuchevsky, *Tserkov i Rossiya: Tri lektsii* (Paris: YMCA Press, 1969), pp. 7–60.

7. Fr. John Meyendorff, *Byzantine Theology* (New York: Fordham University Press, 1979), p. 213.

8. Anton Kartashev, "Tserkov i gosudarstvo," in Serge Verkhovsky, ed., *Pravoslavie v zhizni* (New York: Chekhov Publishing House, 1953), pp. 155–156.

9. Ibid., p. 156.

10. Meyendorff, *Byzantine Theology*, p. 214.

11. Pushkarev, *Christianity and Government*, p. 5.

12. Yu. K. Begunova, ed., *Za zemlyu russkuyu* (Moscow: Sovetskaya Rossiya, 1981), p. 14.

13. According to S. W. Baron, while under Tatar domination "Russian metropolitans . . . became the mainstay of Russian national feeling . . . Even more than in the medieval West these institutions [monasteries] had become focal centers of trade and industry . . . thus furnishing both economic and intellectual leadership to their respective districts." S. W. Baron, *Modern Nationalism and Religion* (New York: Harper and Bros., 1947), p. 167. I am indebted to Peter Quimby of the University of Wisconsin (Madison) for this citation.

14. Pushkarev, *Christianity and Government*, pp. 10–13.

15. Some one hundred were established near cities and one hundred and fifty in the wilderness. Sergei Pushkarev, *Obzor Russkoy istorii* (New York: Chekhov Publishing House, 1953), p. 149.

16. Pushkarev, *Christianity and Government*, pp. 17–18.
17. Ibid., p. 22.
18. R. G. Skrynnikov, *Tsarstvo terrora* (St. Petersburg: Nauka, 1992), pp. 289–292; Daniel Rowland, "Did Muscovite Ideology Place Limits on the Power of the Tsar (1540s–1660s)?" *The Russian Review*, vol. 49 (1990), pp. 143–151.
19. Pushkarev, *Christianity and Government*, p. 38.
20. Georgiy Fedotov, *Imperiya i svoboda* (New York: Possev-S.Sh.A., 1989), pp. 71–72, 77.
21. One seventeenth-century Arabian traveler to Russia marveled at how the tsar, "whilst bringing in person the gifts to the patriarch, address[ed] the latter in the following words: 'Thy son, the Czar Alexis, bows before thy holiness, and brings thee this and that.'" Maxime Kovalevsky, *Russian Political Institutions* (Chicago: University of Chicago Press, 1902), p. 63.
22. Kartashev, "Tserkov i gosudarstvo," pp. 199–200. See also his little-known essay "Russkaya tserkov perioda Imperii," *Russkoe vozrozhdenie*, no. 4 (1978), pp. 184–207.
23. Donald W. Treadgold, "Russian Orthodoxy and Society," in Robert L. Nichols and Theofanis Stavrou, eds., *Russian Orthodoxy under the Old Regime* (Minneapolis: University of Minnesota Press, 1978), p. 23.
24. Marc Szeftel, "Church and State in Imperial Russia," in Nichols and Stavrou, *Russian Orthodoxy under the Old Regime*, p. 130.
25. Ibid.
26. Zernov, *The Russian Religious Renaissance*, p. 67.
27. Fr. John Meyendorff, "Russian Bishops and Church Reform in 1905," in Nichols and Stavrou, *Russian Orthodoxy under the Old Regime*, pp. 170–182.
28. Frederick C. Barghoorn and Thomas F. Remington, *Politics in the USSR*, third edition (Boston: Little, Brown & Co, 1986), p. 7.
29. Catherine Evtuhov, "The Church in the Russian Revolution: Arguments for and against Restoring the Patriarchate at the Church Council of 1917–18," *Slavic Review*, 50 (Fall 1991), p. 503.
30. Leonard Schapiro, *Russian Studies* (New York: Penguin Books, 1986), pp. 68–92. Zernov, *The Russian Religious Renaissance*, pp. 55–60; and George Putnam, *Russian Alternatives to Marxism: Christian Socialism and Idealistic Liberalism in Twentieth-Century Russia* (Knoxville: University of Tennessee Press, 1977).
31. James H. Billington, "The Case for Orthodoxy," *The New Republic* (May 30, 1994), p. 25.
32. Nikita Struve, *Christians in Contemporary Russia* (New York: Scribners, 1967), p. 33.
33. Tikhon's letter, printed in *Izvestiya* on June 28, 1923, is excerpted in Struve, *Christians in Contemporary Russia*, pp. 350–351.
34. Mikhail Heller and Aleksandr Nekrich, *Utopia in Power* (New York: Summit Books, 1986), pp. 222–277.
35. Nikita Struve, *Les Chretiens en URSS* (Paris: Editions du Seuil, 1963), pp. 362–366.
36. Pushkarev, *Christianity and Government*, pp. 56–65.
37. Rusak received a sentence of seven years hard labor and five subsequent years

of "internal exile" in 1986 for smuggling this work out to the West. Pushkarev, *Christianity and Government,* p. 67.

38. Robert Conquest, *Religion in the USSR* (New York: Praeger, 1968), p. 34.
39. Pushkarev, *Christianity and Government,* p. 67.
40. Ibid.
41. Cited by Zernov, *The Russian Religious Renaissance,* p. 204. For a detailed study refer to Wassilij Alexeev and Theofanis G. Stavrou, *The Great Revival: The Russian Orthodox Church under German Occupation* (Minneapolis: Burgess Publishing Co., 1976).
42. Michael Bourdeaux, *Patriarch and Prophets: Persecution of the Russian Orthodox Church* (New York: Praeger, 1970), p. 30.
43. Archpriest Viktor Potapov, "'. . . molchaniem predaetsya Bog,'" *Grani,* no. 166 (1992), p. 212.
44. For a listing see I. M. Andreev, *Kratkiy obzor istoriy Russkoy Tserkvi ot revolyutsii do nashikh dnei* (Jordanville, N.Y.: Holy Trinity Monastery Press, 1952), p. 51.
45. Potapov, "'. . . molchaniem predaetsya Bog,'" p. 217.
46. For more on the evolution of Russian religious philosophy see Zernov, *The Russian Religious Renaissance;* Georgy Fedotov, *A Treasury of Russian Spirituality* (New York: Harper Torchbooks, 1961); and Simeon Frank, *Iz istorii Russkoy filosofskoy mysli kontsa 19-ogo i nachala 20-ogo veka* (Washington, D.C.: Inter-Language Literary Associates, 1965), pp. 5–17.
47. Cited by Zernov, *The Russian Religious Renaissance,* p. 128.
48. Ibid., p. 125.
49. David Joravsky, "Cultural Revolution and the Fortress Mentality," in Abbott Gleason et al., eds., *Bolshevik Culture* (Bloomington: Indiana University Press, 1985), p. 99. Joravsky notes that "the exiles were, and still are, pictured as the last agents of enemy ideology doomed to extinction by the revolution, yet they are also pictured as dangerous people since many Soviet people would respond favorably to the ideology of these enemy agents, if they had not been exiled" (p. 110).
50. Zernov, *The Russian Religious Renaissance,* p. 229.
51. For a history of this remarkable school, see Donald A. Lowrie, *St. Sergey in Paris: The Orthodox Theological Institute* (London: S.P.C.K., 1954).
52. See the conclusion of Zernov, *The Russian Religious Renaissance,* for a detailed biographical listing.
53. Anton V. Kartashev, *Vozsozdanie Sv. Rusi* (published by the special committee under Silvester, bishop of Messina and vicar of the metropole of Russian Orthodox churches in Western Europe: Paris, 1956), p. 19.
54. Ibid., p. 49.
55. Ibid., pp. 91–93.
56. Georgy Fedotov, *Khristianin v revolyutsii: sbornik statey* (Paris: YMCA Press, 1957), p. 142.
57. Ibid., p. 24.
58. Ibid., p. 135.
59. Ibid., pp. 134–135.
60. Ibid., pp. 74–75.

61. Ibid., p. 17.
62. In a review of my book *Christianity and Russian Culture in Soviet Society* (Boulder, Colo.: Westview Press, 1990), for example, William Fletcher dismisses Kartashev, Fedotov, "and someone else" (Ilyin) as "lesser lights of the first emigration." *Russian Review*, vol. 51, no. 1 (January 1992), pp. 136–137.
63. Igor Vinogradov, "Bezumanaya 'russkaya ideya,'" *Moskovskie novosti* (June 11, 1989), p. 11.
64. Cited in Zernov, *The Russian Religious Renaissance*, p. 124.
65. Ellis, *The Russian Orthodox Church*, p. 288.
66. David Lane, *Politics and Society in the USSR* (New York: New York University Press, 1978), p. 468.
67. Struve, *Les Chretiens en URSS*, pp. 200–218.
68. Ibid., pp. 212–213.
69. "Rossya i tserkov segodnya" and "Tserkov i vlast," *Volnoe slovo*, no. 6 (Frankfurt a. Main: Possev, 1972), p. 86.
70. Ibid., pp. 69–75.
71. Struve, *Les Chretiens en URSS*, pp. 265–268.
72. Nikolai Eshliman and Gleb Yakunin, "Otkrytoe pis'mo Patriarkhu Alekseyu," *Grani*, no. 61 (October 1966), pp. 122–167.
73. Ellis, *The Russian Orthodox Church*, pp. 327–329.
74. Ibid., pp. 328–330. See also Barbara Wolfe Jancar, "Religious Dissent in the Soviet Union," in Rudolf L. Tokes, ed., *Dissent in the USSR: Politics, Ideology, and People* (Baltimore: Johns Hopkins University Press, 1975), pp. 191–232.
75. Cronid Lyubarsky, "Soziale Basis und Umfang des Sowjetischen Dissidententums," *Osteuropa*, vol. 29, no. 11 (November 1979), p. 928.
76. Ellis, *The Russian Orthodox Church*, p. 376.
77. Aleksandr Solzhenitsyn, "Pismo patryarkhu," *Sobraniye Sochinenii* (Vermont and Paris: YMCA Press, 1981), vol. 9, pp. 120–125.
78. Cited by Ellis, *The Russian Orthodox Church*, p. 305.
79. Lev Regelson, *Tragediya Russkoy Tserkvi* (Paris: YMCA Press, 1977), pp. 417–428, 436.
80. Cited by Ellis, *The Russian Orthodox Church*, p. 275.
81. "O seminare A. Ogorodnikova," *Possev* (February 1979), p. 7.
82. Ibid., p. 6.
83. Cited in Ellis, *The Russian Orthodox Church*, p. 351.
84. Kent R. Hill, *The Puzzle of the Soviet Church: An Inside Look at Christianity and Glasnost* (Portland, Oregon: Multnomah Press, 1989), section V, "The Gorbachev Era and Beyond," pp. 217–348.
85. "Predvaritelnye itogi tysyachiletnego opyta," *Ogonyok*, no. 10 (March 5–12, 1988). Reprinted in Dmitrii S. Likhachev, *Reflections on Russia* (Boulder, Colo.: Westview Press, 1991), p. 131.
86. One anthology on the independent press noted the existence of more than twenty-five religious and philosophical samizdat journals in 1988. Roman Redlikh, comp., *Svoimi silami: antologiya nezavisimoy zhurnalistiki, 1987–1988 gg.* (Frankfurt a. Main: Possev, 1989).
87. Articles by Aleksandr Nezhnyi during this period include: "Zakon i sovest,"

Ogonyok, no. 50 (December 10–17, 1988); "Razrushennyi khram," *Izvestiya* (September 21, 1988), p. 3; "O chem nam govoryat stoletiya," *Druzhba narodov* (June 1988), pp. 200–209; and "Vozmozhnosti dialoga," *Moskovskie novosti* (March 20, 1988), p. 13.
88. V. Ya. Kurbatov, V. G. Rasputin, and I. Seliverstov, "Ne ocherednoe, a samoe neobkhodimoe," *Moskovskiy literator* (February 3, 1989), p. 3.
89. Mark Zakharov, "Bez programmy," *Ogonyok,* no. 16 (April 15–22, 1989).
90. Stanislav Dzhimbinov, "The Return of Russian Philosophy," *Russian Social Science Review,* vol. 35, no. 2 (March 1994), pp. 15–28; Nicolai N. Petro, "Challenge of the 'Russian Idea,'" in Nicolai N. Petro, ed., *Christianity and Russian Culture in Soviet Society* (Boulder, Colo.: Westview Press, 1990), pp. 223–227.
91. Grigory Nekhoroshev, "Moleben po novomuchenikam," *Sovetskaya molodezh* (Latvia), July 25, 1989, p. 2.

4. The "Russian Idea"

1. Lucian W. Pye and Sidney Verba, *Political Culture and Political Development* (Princeton: Princeton University Press, 1965), p. 529.
2. Adam Ulam, "Russian Nationalism," in Seweryn Bialer, *The Domestic Context of Soviet Foreign Policy* (Boulder, Colo.: Westview Press, 1981), p. 14.
3. Timothy Colton, *The Dilemma of Reform in the Soviet Union,* second edition (New York: Council on Foreign Relations, 1986), pp. 118–119.
4. Nicholas Berdyaev, *The Russian Idea* (Westport, Conn.: Greenwood Press, 1948), p. 252.
5. William Adams, "Politics and the Archeology of Meaning," *Western Political Quarterly,* vol. 39 (September 1986), pp. 553.
6. Hans Kohn, *The Idea of Nationalism* (New York: Collier Books, 1967), pp. 13–16.
7. Leonard Schapiro, *Rationalism and Nationalism in Russian Nineteenth-Century Political Thought* (New Haven: Yale University Press), p. 5; and Hans Kohn, ed., *The Mind of Modern Russia: Historical and Political Thought of Russia's Great Age* (New Brunswick, N.J.: Rutgers University Press, 1955), p. 16.
8. Schapiro, *Rationalism and Nationalism,* p. 69.
9. Ibid., pp. 70–71.
10. Ibid., pp. 163, 161.
11. Ibid., p. 83.
12. Leonard Schapiro, *Russian Studies* (New York: Penguin, 1988), p. 79.
13. Nicholas Zernov, *The Russian Religious Renaissance of the Twentieth Century* (New York: Harper & Row, 1963), pp. 136–137.
14. *Iz glubiny,* second ed., introductory essays by N. Poltoratzkyj and N. Struve (Paris: YMCA Press, 1967), p. xix. The same terminology is also used by Leonard Schapiro; see "The *Vekhi* Group and the Mystique of the Revolution," Ellen Dahrendorf, ed., *Russian Studies* (New York: Penguin, 1988).
15. Ivan A. Ilyin, *Nashi zadachi:* staty, 1948–54 gg. (Paris: Obschche-voinskiy soyuz, 1956), p. 207.
16. Ibid., p. 209.

17. Ivan A. Ilyin, *Osnovy borby za natsionalnaya Rossiya* (NTSNP General Representation in Germany, 1938).

18. Ibid., p. 40.

19. Ibid., p. 31.

20. Ibid., p. 36.

21. Ilyin, *Nashi zadachi,* p. 672.

22. Ibid., p. 402.

23. The late Mikhail Agursky believed that for neo-Slavophiles the reduction of government power over the lives of individuals was as central to their mission as the restoration of Russian cultural and spiritual values. Mikhail Agursky, "Natsionalnyi vopros v SSSR," *Kontinent,* no. 10 (1976), p. 163.

24. On Lenin's view of Russia see Sergei Pushkarev, *Lenin i Rossiya* (Frankfurt a. Main: Possev, 1978), and Nikolai Ulyanov, *Zamolchannyi Marx* (Frankfurt a. Main: Possev, 1969).

25. Nikolai D. Deker and Andrei Lebed, eds, *Genocide in the USSR: Studies in Group Destruction* (published by the Institute for the Study of the USSR. New York: Scarecrow Press, 1958), pp. 118, 132.

26. Mikhail Heller and Aleksandr Nekrich, *Utopia in Power* (New York: Summit Books, 1986), p. 224.

27. Hugh Seton-Watson, "Russian Nationalism in Historical Perspective," in Robert Conquest, ed., *The Last Empire* (Stanford: Hoover Institution Press, 1986), p. 26.

28. Vladlen Sirotkin, "Ni khrama, ni dorogi k khramu," *Nedelya,* no. 6 (1988), p. 11.

29. Galina Litvinova, "Starshyi ili ravnyi?" *Nash sovremennik,* no. 6 (June 1989), p. 17.

30. Maurice Friedberg, George Gibian, Geoffrey Hosking, Frederick Barghoorn, and Wolfgang Kasack, among others, have pointed to the tension between Russian and Soviet literary values and noted the former's potential popularity as an alternative world view.

31. Alain Besançon, "Nationalism and Bolshevism," in Robert Conquest, *Last Empire,* p. 9.

32. Aleksandr Zaichenko, "Imushchestvennoe neraventsvo," *Argumenty i fakty,* no. 27 (1989), p. 5. It is interesting to note that in a critical reply, the economist A. Popov comes up with figures that are not much different after adjusting for inflation: upper class (more than 250 rubles per person per month), 7.1 percent; middle class (150 rubles per person per month), 31.3 percent; and lower class, 61.6 percent. A. Popov, "Bogatye i bednye," *Argumenty i fakty,* no. 42 (1989).

33. A. Zaichenko, "S.Sh.A.-S.S.S.R: Lichnoe potreblenie," *Sovetskaya molodezh* (December 28, 1988), p. 2.

34. Françoise Thom, *Le Moment Gorbatchev* (Paris: Hachette / Pluriel), pp. 18–19.

35. Ibid., pp. 28–30.

36. Bruce B. Auster, "When High Hopes Meet Harsh Realities," *US News and World Report* (April 3, 1989), p. 43.

37. L. Khakhalin, "Vot fakty!" *Semya,* no. 66 (1989), p. 15.

38. "The Truth about Alcoholism in the USSR: Brief Results of the 1983 Sociological Study Done by a Laboratory of the Novosibirsk Department of the USSR Academy of Sciences," *Samizdat Bulletin,* no. 143 (March 1985), p. 2.
39. Litvinova, "Starshyi ili ravnyi?" pp. 10–20. Some of these findings were foreshadowed somewhat by Murray Feshbach's "The Soviet Union: Population Trends and Dilemmas," *Population Bulletin,* vol. 37, no. 3 (August 1982), pp. 1–44; and subsequently confirmed in a number of post-Soviet articles; see Aleksandr Anichkin et al., "Govoryat, Rossiya vymiraet . . .," *Moskovskie novosti,* no. 20 (1992).
40. Litvinova, "Starshyi ili ravnyi?" p. 16.
41. Ibid., p. 12.
42. The systematic nature of this policy is corroborated by the fact that already by the late 1950s the RSFSR was only sixth in per capita national income among the fifteen republics, and only tenth in average annual growth rate. Erich Goldhagen, ed., *The Ethnic Scene in the Soviet Union* (New York: Praeger, 1968), p. 69.
43. Litvinova, "Starshyi ili ravnyi?" pp. 11–12.
44. The largest recipients of funds were Georgia, with a 16 percent subsidy per capita, then Turmenistan, Kirghizia, and Uzbekistan, each receiving 13 percent per capita subsidies. Andrei Illarionov, "Kazhdoy respublike po trudu" (June 1–15, 1989), *Tartusskiy kuryer.*
45. Ron Popeski, "Russian Premier Calls for Better Deal for His People," *Reuters* (May 18, 1990).
46. Alexander Rahr, *RFE/RL Daily Report* (May 15, 1990), p. 6.
47. Donald D. Barry and Carol Barner-Barry, *Contemporary Soviet Politics,* third edition (Englewood Cliffs, N.J.: Prentice-Hall, 1987), p. 247.
48. From 1939 to 1955 the republics receiving the largest influx of immigrants from other republics were Russia (4,770,000 arrivals) and Kazakhstan (1,530,000 arrivals). The republics suffering the largest emigrations were the Ukraine and Belorussia for the same period. Deker and Lebed, *Genocide in the USSR,* p. 6.
49. Litvinova, "Starshyi ili ravnyi?" p. 15.
50. Ibid., p. 18.
51. Ibid., p. 15. For 1993, deaths in the Russian federation continued to outpace births by a factor of 1.57. Although the inward migration of Russians from the "near abroad" has limited the net decline in Russia's population to half a million, Russia's fertility index remains well below the 2.11 necessary to maintain the population. Keith Bush, "Population Decline Continues," *RFE/RL Daily Report* (February 17, 1994).
52. Vladimir Soloukhin, "Chitaya Lenina," *Rodina,* no. 10 (1989), p. 71.
53. A. R., "Bum poshel na spad," *Moskovskie novosti,* no. 47 (November 19, 1989), p. 4.
54. A. Arefyev, "Molodezh i perestroika," *Argumenty i fakty,* no. 20 (1989), p. 3.
55. Adherents to this movement are commonly referred to as "Russites," *vozrozhdentsy,* "Russophiles," or "the Russian Party." See Barghoorn, "Russian Nationalism and Soviet Politics"; John Dunlop, *The Faces of Contemporary Russian Na-*

tionalism (Princeton: Princeton University Press, 1983); and Susan Massie, "Is There a New Russian Spirit?" Speech delivered to the Senator John Heinz Seminar, Council on Foreign Relations (December 3, 1986).

56. This group includes Valentin Rasputin, Boris Mozhaev, Viktor Astafyev, Vladimir Soloukhin, Sergei Zalygin, Fedor Abramov, Vasiliy Belov, Gavriil Troepolskiy, the late Vasiliy Shukshin, Vladimir Tendryakov, and Valentin Ovechkin. Their views have also been adopted by writers of other nationalities and literary genres, among them the Moldavian Ion Drutse, the Belorussian Vasil Bykov, the Abkazian writer Chingiz Aitmatov, and the Ukrainian Boris Oleynik.

57. Wolfgang Kasack, *Entsiklopedicheskiy slovar Russkoy literatury s 1917 goda* (London: Overseas Publications Interchange Ltd., 1988), p. 255; Friedberg, "Authentic Russian Values and Aspirations," pp. 217–233.

58. Cited by Boris Rumer, "Soviet Writers Decry Loss of Spiritual Values in Society," *Christian Science Monitor* (October 7, 1986), p. 1.

59. This despite persecution in 1982 that culminated in the purging of the editorial board of *Nash sovremennik* after a Central Committee decree of July 1982 that castigated authors who "display a confused world outlook and an incapacity to examine social phenomena historically, from clearly defined class positions." On the Party actions against noted village writers see Geoffrey Hosking, "The Paradoxes of Soviet Fiction in the 1980s," pp. 134–135; and the postscript in John Dunlop, *The Faces of Contemporary Russian Nationalism,* pp. 291–294.

60. Nicolai N. Petro, "'The Project of the Century': A Case Study of Russian Nationalist Opposition," *Studies in Comparative Communism* (Winter–Fall 1987), pp. 235–252.

61. Dmitriy Likhachev, *Zametki o Russkom,* second, revised edition (Moscow: Sovetskaya Rossiya, 1984), pp. 54–55.

62. The organizers of this singular conference included the Philosophical Society of the USSR, the Znanie Society of the RSFSR, the Scientific Council of the USSR Academy of Science on the Problems of Russian culture, the All-Russian Cultural Fund, the Moscow section of the Philosophical Society of the USSR, local chapters of the Philosophical Society of the USSR and the Institute of Marxism-Leninism of the Central Committee of the CPSU.

63. Natalya Ivina, "Russkaya entsiklopediya," Lidya Ermakova, "Nachinaya s praslavyan," *Sovetskaya Rossiya,* no. 110 (May 13, 1989); Oleg Trubachev, "Tysyacheletnyaya zhizn naroda," *Sovetskaya Rossiya* (January 4, 1989).

64. V. Surkova, "Russkiy tsentr nachinayet deistvovat," *Vechernyaya Moskva* (December 12, 1988).

65. "Vserossiyskaya akademiya," *Pravda* (February 2, 1989).

66. Ibid.,

67. Nicolai N. Petro, "Perestroika from Below: Voluntary Socio-Political Associations in the RSFSR," in Alfred J. Rieber and Alvin Z. Rubinstein, eds., *Perestroika at the Crossroads* (New York: M. E. Sharpe, 1991), pp. 110–116.

68. Aleksandr Lavrin, "Pristupaya k Solzhenitsinu," *Literaturnaya gazeta* (August 2, 1989), p. 2.

69. M. F. Antonov et al., "Pismo v sekretaryat pravleniya soyuza pisateley RSFSR," *Literaturnaya Rossiya* (August 4, 1989), p. 4.

70. Stanislav Lesnevskiy, "'O slavyanofilakh, rusfobakh, i lyubvi k Rossii . . .,'" *Knizhnoe obozrenie,* no. 35 (September 1, 1989), p. 1.

71. "Podmeny," *Literaturnaya Rossiya,* no. 45 (1989), p. 2.

72. Petr Krasnov, "Svoboda i 'iskhodnyi proekt,' " *Literaturnaya Rossiya,* no. 40 (October 6, 1989), p. 6.

73. Lesnevskiy, " 'O slavyanofilakh,' " p. 1.

74. For an extensive discussion of these literary debates from 1988 to 1991, see Vladislav Krasnov, *Russia beyond Communism* (Boulder, Colo.: Westview Press, 1991). A more recent polemic can be found in Viktor Matizen's interview with the leader of the Christian Democratic movement, Viktor Aksyuchits, "Khristyanskie demokraty demokratichnee prochikh," *Novoye Russkoye Slovo* (June 1, 1993), p. 8.

75. Georgy Vladimov, "O sostoyanii vlasti i o 'Russkoi partii,' " no. 7, 8, *Possev* (July and August 1983); Fyodor M. Dostoyevsky, "Obyasnitelnoe slovo po povodu pechataemoy nizhe rechi o Pushkine," *Polnoe Sobranie Sochinenii v tridtsati tomakh,* vol. 26 (Leningrad: Nauka, 1984), p. 133.

76. Likhachev, *Zametki o russkom,* p. 43. The noted social psychologist Leonard W. Doobs makes a similar distinction in *Patriotism and Nationalism* (New Haven, Conn.: Yale University Press, 1964), p. 6. On the contemporary Russian usage of the term "patriotic" and "nationalist," see Lev Gudkov, "Natsionalnoe soznanie: versiya zapada i Rossii," *Rodina,* no. 2 (1994), pp. 14–18.

77. Françoise Lesourd, "Une expression nouvelle de l'idee nationale russe: Dmitri Lihachev," *Cahiers du Monde Russe et Sovietique,* vol. XXVIII, no. 3–4 (December 1987), pp. 323–346.

78. Anthony Smith, *Theories of Nationalism* (London: Duckworth, 1971), p. 9.

79. Nikolai Karamzin, *Memoir of Ancient and Modern Russia,* ed. and trans. Richard Pipes (Cambridge, Mass.: Harvard University Press, 1955); on Vladimir Solovyov's views, see *A Solovyov Anthology,* arranged by S. L. Frank (London: SCM Press, 1950).

80. Ksenya Myalo, "Oborvannaya nit," *Novyi mir* (August 1988), pp. 245–257.

81. Barghoorn, "Russian Nationalism," p. 34.

82. Dunlop, *Faces of Contemporary Russian Nationalism,* p. 277.

5. Russia's Alternative Political Organizations

1. John B. Dunlop, *The New Russian Nationalism* (Washington, D.C.: CSIS, 1985), p. 56.

2. Ibid., p. 58. For the Russian text see Vasiliy Matasov, *Beloe dvizhenie na Yuge Rossii, 1917–1920* (Montreal: Monastery Press, 1990), pp. 181–183.

3. Vladimir Brovkin, "Identity, Allegiance and Participation in the Russian Civil War," *European History Quarterly,* vol. 22, no. 4 (October 1992), pp. 541–568.

4. Vladimir I. Shishkin, "The October Revolution and Perestroika," *European History Quarterly,* vol. 22, no. 4 (October 1992), p. 545; Oliver H. Radkey, *The Unknown Civil War in Soviet Russia* (Stanford, Calif.: The Hoover Institution Press, 1976).

5. Donald W. Treadgold, *Twentieth-Century Russia,* fourth edition (Chicago: Rand McNally, 1976), p. 272.

6. These include the "Provisional Statute for the Administration of the Regions Occupied by the Volunteer Army"; the "Proclamation of the Committee of Members of the Constituent Assembly" of July 24, 1918; "Proclamation" of the Supreme Administration of the North in Archangelsk of August 2, 1918; the "Resolution of the [Ufa] State Conference" of September 23, 1918, entitled the "Constitution of the Ufa Directorate" by Bunyan; General Krasnov's proc-lamation of May 17, 1918; and the Constitution adopted by the Circle to Save the Don. All these documents are excerpted in James Bunyan, *Intervention, Civil War, and Communism in Russia, April–December 1918: Documents and Materials* (New York: Octagon Books, 1976), pp. 283–285; 46–50; 304–306; 339–356, 34–36. On Siberia specifically see Paul Dotsenko, *The Struggle for Democracy in Siberia, 1917–1920* (Stanford, Calif.: The Hoover Institution Press, 1983).

7. Bunyan, *Intervention, Civil War, and Communism,* p. 305.

8. Ibid., p. 35.

9. Ibid., p. 49.

10. Ibid., pp. 355, 284, 49. In an attempt to appear "progressive," Denikin and Wrangel subsequently issued reformist land decrees. Nikolai Ross, *Vrangel v krymu* (Frankfurt a. Main: Possev, 1982).

11. Brovkin, "Identity, Allegiance and Participation in the Russian Civil War," p. 549.

12. Shishkin, "The October Revolution and Perestroika," p. 528.

13. Ibid., p. 531; Oliver H. Radkey, *The Election to the Russian Constituent Assembly of 1917* (Cambridge, Mass.: Harvard University Press, 1950), pp. 16–17.

14. Shishkin, "The October Revolution and Perestroika," p. 532.

15. Catherine Andreyev, *Vlasov and the Russian Liberation Movement: Soviet Reality and Emigre Theories* (Cambridge, England: Cambridge University Press, 1987), p. 12.

16. Boris G. Sergeyev et al., "Toward a Revolution in the USSR: The Thought and Action of NTS," unpublished manuscript, second revision (June 1958), p. 95.

17. *NTS: Union of Russian Solidarists* (Frankfurst a. Main: Possev, 1961), p. 12.

18. Sergeyev, "Toward a Revolution in the USSR," p. 75.

19. Igor Evlampiev, "Filosofskie i pravovye vzglyady I. A. Ilyina," *Pravovedenie,* no. 3 (1992), p. 88.

20. Ilyin spoke at many NTS gatherings and inspired aspects of their 1938 six-point platform. Sergeyev, "Toward a Revolution in the USSR," p. 95. See also Roman Redlikh's eulogy in Ilyin, *Nashi zadachi: staty, 1948–54 gg.* (Paris: Obshche-voinskiy soyuz, 1956), vol. 2, Appendix.

21. Sergeyev, "Toward a Revolution in the USSR," pp. 57–60, 73–78.

22. Ibid., p. 77. The only form of fascism that had any persistent appeal within the NTS was the Portuguese variety. Ibid., p. 188.

23. An NTS document from 1935 had stated that it was heir to the ideas of General Kornilov. Sergeyev, "Toward a Revolution in the USSR," p. 190. Struve agreed to devote regular sections of his newspaper to the NTSNP (pp. 183–184). On Shulgin see V. Zhelyagin, "Svyaz vremen," in V. Zhelyagin and N. Rutych, *Ros-siya v epokhu reform* (Frankfurt a. M.: Possev, 1981), pp. 325–326.

24. A young Russian historian, Kirill Aleksandrov, has recently unearthed new information regarding antiregime attitudes among Soviet troops fighting during the Soviet-Finnish war (November 30, 1939, to March 13, 1940). In many ways this skirmish serves as a prelude to the mass defections seen during World War II. Aleksandrov puts the number of Soviet prisoners falling into Finnish hands at an astounding 64,118. Kirill Aleksandrov, "Vyzov rezhimu," *Posev*, vol. XLIX, no. 6 (November–December 1993), pp. 104–112.

25. Andreyev, *Vlasov*, pp. 34–35, 93; Alexander Dallin, *German Rule in Russia, 1941–45* (London: Macmillan, 1957), p. 424. See also George Fischer, ed., *Soviet Opposition to Stalin: A Case Study of World War II* (Cambridge, Mass.: Harvard University Press, 1952).

26. Andreyev, *Vlasov*, p. 7. Dallin places this number considerably lower, at perhaps 900,000 military personnel and 750,000 laborers at its peak. Dallin, *German Rule in Russia*, p. 424.

27. Joachim Hoffmann, *Die Geschichte der Wlassow-Armee* (Freiburg: Verlag Rombach, 1984), p. 12.

28. Such ideas seem to have been fairly common among senior officers. Major General Krupennikov, commander of the Third Guard Army, captured just outside of Stalingrad, estimated that 70 percent of the officers in German hands would be willing to fight against the Soviet system, but again only as equal allies, not as mercenaries. Hoffmann, *Die Geschichte der Wlassow-Armee*, pp. 148–153. On the opposing side, Baron Kaulbars places the figure at closer to 80 percent when including all prisoners of war (p. 12).

29. Andreyev, *Vlasov*, pp. 91–93. Strik-Strikfeldt gives the following account of Vlasov's response to his invitation to join the fight against Stalin: "Against Stalin, yes. But for whom and what? And how? . . . Would the German officers of whom you spoke allow us to raise an army against Stalin? Not an army of mercenaries. It must take its orders from a National Russian Government. It is only an ideal that can justify the taking up of arms against one's own regime." Wilfried Strik-Strikfeldt, *Against Stalin and Hitler* (New York: The John Day Company, 1973), p. 75.

30. Kazantsev writes that the NTS had been discussing the possibility of a "Russian Napoleon" for at least ten years: "We had even given him an abstract name: 'komkor [corps commander] Sidorshuk.' In the hope that our group could offer valuable help to this Sidorshuk, for more than ten years we prepared ourselves to meet him." Juergen Thorwald, *The Illusion* (New York: Harcourt, Brace and Jovanovich, 1974), p. 61.

31. Andreyev, *Vlasov*, pp. 155–156. On Zaitsev's contribution to the *Skhema*, see p. 125. Kazantsev was apparently responsible for the social welfare aspects in the Smolensk declaration. Thorwald, *The Illusion*, pp. 100–101.

32. Aleksandr I. Solzhenitsyn, *The Gulag Archipelago, 1918–1956*, vols. I–II (New York: Harper & Row, 1973), pp. 268–269.

33. The text can be found in Andreyev, *Vlasov*, pp. 207–208.

34. Ibid., pp. 45–46. Hoffman also cites several examples of mass requests among captured military personnel still in the Soviet Union to join ROA. Hoffmann, *Die Geschichte der Wlassow-Armee*, pp. 153–154.

35. Andreyev, p. 100.

36. Ibid., pp. 49–50.
37. Sven Steenberg, *Vlasov* (New York: Knopf, 1970), p. 92.
38. Andreyev, *Vlasov*, p. 54.
39. Ibid., pp. 219–220.
40. In January 1945 he is given command of two poorly equipped divisions, which include a small tank corp, a reserve brigade, an officers school, and a small air force. At its height the Russian Army of Liberation was thus composed of no more than 50,000 men. Hoffmann, *Die Geschichte der Wlassow-Armee*, pp. 156–157, 80.
41. Ibid., p. 156.
42. Ibid., p. 12.
43. Since the fall of communism, several articles have appeared in the Russian press challenging the traditional Soviet view of Vlasov as nothing more than a traitor. See Vitaly Svintsov, "Kto zhe takoy A. Vlasov?" *Nezavisimaya gazeta* (December 25, 1993), p. 4; "General Vlasov byl klyuchevoy figuroy v oborone Moskvy?" *Rossiyskie vesti* (May 4, 1994), p. 7; D. Pospielovskiy, "Vlasov protiv naroda ne voeval . . .," *Novoe vremya*, no. 37 (1991), p. 2.
44. Oleh R. Martovych, *The Ukrainian Liberation Movement in Modern Times* (Edinburgh: Scottish League for European Freedom, n.d.), p. 131. L. Shankovsky et al., *The Ukrainian Insurgent Army in the Fight for Freedom* (New York: Dnipro, 1954).
45. There have been a number of postcommunist articles on Novocherkassk in the Russian press, including Oleg Bondarenko, "Iz nedavnego proshlogo," *Golos*, no. 36–37 (1992), p. 5; Evgeniy Lel, "Poslednyaya zhertva novocherkasskoy boyni," *Kazachya volya*, no. 1 (1992), p. 1; Oleg Bondarenko, "Novocherkassk zovet k pokayaniyu," *Kuranty* (April 10, 1992), p. 5. On other incidents of popular opposition, see John P. Hardt, ed., *The Soviet Economy in the 1980s* (Washington, D.C.: Joint Economic Committee of Congress, December 31, 1982), pp. 349–366. The most complete discussion of worker unrest is in Mikhail Nazarov, comp., *Solidarnost, 1980–82: o rabochem dvizhenii v Polshe i o rabochem dvizhenii v Rossii*, second edition (Frankfurt a. Main: Possev, 1982), pp. 210–297.
46. Cited by Peter Reddaway, "Soviet Policies on Dissent and Emigration: The Radical Change of Course since 1979," *Occasional Paper*, no. 192 (1984), presented at the Kennan Institute for Advanced Russian Studies, Washington, D.C.
47. For an interesting sociological study of the period and its impact on future Soviet reformers, see Viktor Voronkov, "Die Protestbewegung der 'Sechziger' Generation: Der Widerstand gegen das sowjetische Regime, 1956–1985," *Osteuropa*, vol. 43, no. 10 (October 1993), pp. 939–948.
48. Vladimir Gedilaghine, *Les Contestataires en U.R.S.S.* (Paris: Casterman, 1974), p. 38.
49. See George Bruderer, comp., *Protsess tsepnoy reaktsii* (Frankfurt a. Main: Possev, 1971).
50. Albert Boiter, ed., *Sobranie dokumentov samizdata* (Munich: Samizdat Archive Association), vol. 30, no. AS 2542.

51. "Printsipy komiteta prav cheloveka," *Posev,* no. 12 (December 1970), p. 13.
52. *Posev,* no. 11 (November 1975), p. 5.
53. *Posev,* no. 3 (March 1971), p. 4.
54. Boiter, *Sobranie dokumentov samizdata,* nos. AS 1264 and AS 1270.
55. Ibid., no. AS 2651.
56. " 'Levaya oppositsiya' v Leningrade," *Posev,* no. 3 (March 1979), p. 8.
57. Nazarov, *Solidarnost, 1980–82;* Jonathan Aves, "The Russian Labour Movement, 1989–91," in Geoffrey Hosking et al., *The Road to Post-Communism* (London: Pinter Publishers, 1992), pp. 138–156.
58. V. Tretyakov, "Strategiya i taktika," *Posev,* no. 3 (March 1971), p. 2.
59. "Peresmotr osnov oppositsionnogo dvizheniya," *Posev,* no. 7 (July 1982), pp. 30–39.
60. A. L., "Stroit novyi samizdat," *Posev* (quarterly), vol. 1 (1984), pp. 57–59.
61. Nicolai N. Petro, "Perestroika from Below: Voluntary Socio-Political Associations in the RSFSR," in Alfred J. Rieber and Alvin Z. Rubinstein, eds., *Perestroika at the Crossroads* (Armonk, N.Y.: M. E. Sharpe, 1991), pp. 102–135.
62. Aves, "The Russian Labour Movement," pp. 138–156.
63. Stephen Carter, *Russian Nationalism: Yesterday, Today, Tomorrow* (New York: St. Martin's, 1990), p. 82. See also John Dunlop, *The New Russian Nationalism,* and Vladislav Krasnov, "Russian National Feeling: An Informal Poll," in Robert Conquest, ed., *The Last Empire* (Stanford, Calif.: The Hoover Institution Press, 1986), pp. 109–130.
64. "VSKhSON," *Volnoe Slovo,* documental series, no. 22 (Frankfurt a. Main: Possev, 1972), p. 95.
65. Ibid., pp. 88–89, 116.
66. *Russia Cristiana* (Milan, Italy), no. 118, pp. 32–37.
67. Evgeniy Vagin, "Istoricheskaya preemstvennost v sovetskoy oppositsii," *Golos Zarubezhya,* no. 5 (1977), p. 9.
68. Ibid., pp. 8–9.
69. Vladimir Osipov, "Berdyaevskiy kruzhok v Leningrade," *Posev,* no. 1 (January 1972), p. 3.
70. Nikolai Berdyaev, *Istoki i smysl russkoy revolyutsii* (Paris: YMCA Press, 1975), p. 146.
71. "VSKhSON," *Volnoe Slovo,* p. 89.
72. Ibid., pp. 43–45, 50.
73. Ibid., pp. 90–91.
74. Vagin, "Istoricheskaya preemstvennost," p. 10.
75. Osipov, "Berdyaevskiy kruzhok," p. 4.
76. Sergeyev, "Toward a Revolution in the USSR," pp. 115–116.
77. *NTS: Union of Russian Solidarists,* p. 31.
78. *The Trial of Gerald Brooke and the NTS* (Frankfurt a. Main: Possev, n.d.), p. 26.
79. *Na sluzhbe Rossii* (Frankfurt a. M.: Possev, n.d.), pp. 19, 71.
80. L. Kulayeva, "'Za svobodnuyu Rossiyu,' " *Za Rossiyu,* no. 5 (304), 1994, p. 6. On the current NTS Structure in Russia, see "O materialnoy baze," *Vstrechi* insert in *Za Rossiyu,* no. 8–9 (307–308), 1994, p 1.
81. *Neue Zürcher Zeitung* (December 22, 1967), p. 1.

82. *Posev,* no. 8 (August 1973), p. 23.
83. See Nazarov, *Solidarnost, 1980–82,* pp. 210–297.
84. "Vlast dolzhna opravdat: doverie naroda," a statement of the NTS Council, April 1993, *Vstrechi,* vol. XLII, no. 316 (April 1993), pp. 1–2.
85. The NTS member George Miller also served as an adviser to Anatoly Chubais's committee on state privatization. "Chto takoe NTS," *Posev,* no. 1 (January–February 1994), p. 124.
86. "Soyuz i vybory," "Vstrechi" insert in *Za Rossiyu,* no. 1 (300), 1994, p. 1; Mark Feigin, "O pravovom edinstve," *Russkaya mysl,* no. 4018 (February 24–March 2, 1994), p. 8.
87. Its regional campaign platform was published in the January–February issue of *Posev* (now published in Russia) for 1994, pp. 5–7.
88. Borys Lewytzkyj, *L'Opposizione Politica nel Uniona Sovietica* (Milan: Rusconi Editore, 1974), p. 76.
89. "Levaya oppositsya," pp. 8–9.
90. Zbigniew Brzezinski, ed., *Dilemmas of Change in Soviet Politics* (New York: Columbia University Press, 1969); Stephen Cohen, *Rethinking the Soviet Experience* (New York: Oxford University Press, 1985); Moshe Lewin, *Political Undercurrents in the Soviet Economic Debates* (Princeton: Princeton University Press, 1974); H. Gordon Skilling and Franklyn Griffiths, *Interest Groups in Soviet Politics* (Princeton: Princeton University Press, 1971).
91. Alexander Shtromas, "How the End of the Soviet System May Come About," in Alexander Shtromas and Morton Kaplan, eds., *The Soviet Union and the Challenge of the Future, vol. 1: Stasis and Change* (New York: Paragon House, 1988), pp. 201–300.
92. Roy Medvedev, *Kniga o sotsyalisticheskoy demokratii* (Amsterdam: Alexander Herzen Foundation, 1972), p. 25.
93. *Seyatel,* nos. 1 and 2; *Volnoe Slovo: samizdat izbrannoe,* no. 5 (Frankfurt a. Main: Possev, 1971), p. 55.
94. *Seyatel,* pp. 57–58.
95. Ibid., p. 113.
96. Ibid., pp. 65–66.
97. Ibid., p. 65.
98. Tatyana Zaslavskaya, "The Novosibirsk Report," *Survey,* vol. 28, no. 1 (Spring 1984), p. 88.
99. "The Secret Dream of a Soviet Tomorrow," *Samizdat Bulletin,* no. 160 (August 1986), pp. 1–12.
100. Bill Keller, "Gorbachev Aide Urges an Alternative to the Party," *New York Times* (May 24, 1988), p. A12.
101. Robert C. Tucker, *Political Culture and Leadership in Soviet Russia: From Lenin to Gorbachev* (New York: W. W. Norton, 1987), p. 132.
102. For a detailed discussion, see Jeffrey C. Goldfarb, *Beyond Glasnost: The Post-Totalitarian Mind* (Chicago: University of Chicago Press, 1989), section two.
103. Described in Petro, "Perestroika from Below," pp. 116–117.
104. "Demokratiya i initsyativa," *Pravda* (December 27, 1987), p. 1; "Demokratiya ne terpit demagogii," *Pravda* (February 10, 1989), p. 1.

105. Mikhail Malyutin, "Neformaly v perestroike," in Yuri Afanasyev, ed., *Inogo ne dano* (Moscow: Progress, 1988), p. 223. For an interesting discussion of the impact of samizdat on society, see Vlad Tupikin, "Samizdat: Emu ne strashna ni KGB, ni svoboda slova," *Novaya ezhednevnaya gazeta* (June 10, 1994), p. 4.

106. Dimitrii Rogozin, former co-chairman of the Russian Constitutional Democratic Party, told me that the search for values led him and his young companions to the pre–1917 Constitutional Democrats. A poll of members of the People's Party of Free Russia, then headed by Aleksandr Rutskoi, showed that 30 percent saw themselves as the natural successors of the pre–1917 Constitutional Democrats, while 28 percent identified intellectually with the Social Democrats (evenly split between Bolsheviks and Mensheviks). Among members of Nikolai Travkin's Democratic Party of Russia, 37 percent saw themselves as kindred to either the Constitutional Democrats or the Octobrists, while only 15 percent identified with the Social Revolutionaries (a peasant-based party), and almost no one with the Social Democrats. Anna Poretskaya, "Grazhdanskiy soyuz," *Nezavisimaya gazeta* (July 22, 1992), p. 2.

6. Back to the Future of Russian Politics

1. Andrei Kozyrev, "And Now: Partnership with Russia's Democrats," *Washington Post* (October 10, 1993), p. C7.

2. It is interesting to note that many Russian neo-Slavophiles, and even some neo-Bolsheviks, cite with approval Japan's success in modernizing the economy while preserving a traditional culture distinct from the West. See Aleksandr Solzhenitsyn, "Three Key Moments in Modern Japanese History," *National Review,* vol. 35 (December 9, 1983), pp. 1536–1538; Mikhail Antonov, "Na uzkoy doroge sektanstva," *Literaturnaya Rossiya,* no. 20 (1992), pp. 3–4; and "Nuzhna patrioticheskaya ekonomika, ili na puti k svyatoy Rusi," *Vek XX i Mir,* no. 3 (1992), pp. 10–12.

3. Ambassador Pickering interviewed on *The Macneil-Lehrer Newshour,* February 9, 1994.

4. Robert D. Blackwill, former national security adviser to President George Bush, cited by David S. Broder, "A 'Success Story' Gone Sour," *Washington Post* (December 19, 1993), p. C8.

5. Samuel Huntington, "The Clash of Civilizations?" *Foreign Affairs,* vol. 72, no. 3 (Summer 1993), pp. 22–49.

6. "Sociological Data about Parties," in *Political Parties and Movements: A Quarterly of the Interlegal Centre for Political and Legal Studies,* no. 1 (1993), p. 16. Even a survey of the Soviet elite taken in June 1991 showed only 10 percent fully in agreement with the statement, "The Congress of People's Deputies and the Supreme Soviet have contributed to the process of democratization." Judith Kullberg, "The End of New Thinking," An Occasional Paper from the Mershon Center (July 1993), p. 12.

7. "Russians Pine for a Firm (Socialist) Hand," *Current Digest of the Post-Soviet Press,* vol. XLV, no. 45 (December 8, 1993), p. 19. Similar findings are cited by Richard Sakwa, *Russian Politics and Society* (London and New York: Routledge),

pp. 33, 283; and Aleksandr Rubtsov, "Legendy i mify novogo sovka," *Moskov-skie novosti*, no. 4 (1992).

8. Basil Dmytryshyn, *USSR: A Concise History*, fourth edition (New York: Charles Scribner's Sons, 1984), p. 613.

9. "The Text of the Draft Constitution," *Current Digest of the Post-Soviet Press*, vol. 45, no. 45 (1993), p. 4.

10. Carl Linden, "Can Russia Be Founded Anew?" *Eurasian Reports*, vol. 3, no. 2 (Winter 1993), p. 10.

11. Aleksandr Solzhenitsyn, *Rebuilding Russia* (New York: Farrar, Straus, and Giroux, 1991).

12. Sergey Peregudov, Aleksey Zudin, and Irina Semenenko, "Sotsyal'noe soglas-iye," *Svobodnaya mysl*, no. 18 (1992), pp. 25–43; Evgeny Kozhokin, "Gosudars-tvennaya Duma i Zemsky sobor," *Segodnya* (April 15, 1994), p. 9. A fascinating manifestation of this trend on the local level has been the emergence of the zemstvo union in Saratov, described in "Programmnye printsipy Saratov-skogo zemskogo soyuza," *Saratovskie vesti* (May 14, 1994), p. 2; and "Saratov-skiy zemskiy soyuz: vmeste—k pobede," *Saratovskie vesti* (May 27, 1994), p. 2.

13. Citing a poll in July 1992 and the pro-Yeltsin outcome of the April 1993 refer-endum, Richard Sakwa likewise concludes that, although reforms were not popular, most people appreciated the need for them. Sakwa, *Russian Politics*, p. 282. Exit polls conducted by the International Republican Institute immedi-ately after the December 1993 elections among 167 respondents in ten Russian cities show that, though there is great dissatisfaction with current policies and political leadership, only 25.5 percent described the speed of reforms as "too quick," 10.9 percent as "about the right speed," while 53.3 percent deemed it "not fast enough." "Russia: Election Observation Report, December 12, 1993" (Washington, D.C.: International Republican Institute), Appendix I, p. iii.

14. Andrew Greeley, "God Is Alive and Well and Living in Moscow," a study of the International Social Survey Program, first draft (released for publication December 9, 1993), p. 8.

15. Ibid., p. 10. Interestingly, among "communist-leaning voters," 70 percent say they have a great deal of confidence in the Church, and only 13 percent feel it has too much power (pp. 21–22).

16. Ibid., pp. 10–11, 22.

17. "In their sexual attitudes Russians are tolerant of premarital and extramarital sex . . . [but] they are strongly opposed to homosexual sex—68%—only some-what lower than the 75% rate in the United States. . . ." Greeley, "God Is Alive," pp. 10–11. This contrasts sharply with surveys conducted in the USSR in 1990 and 1991 in which more than 30 percent reportedly supported execut-ing homosexuals. See Stephen White, "Toward a Post-Soviet Politics?" in Ste-phen White et al., eds., *Developments in Soviet and Post-Soviet Politics* (Durham, N.C.: Duke University Press, 1992), p. 20.

18. James H. Billington, "Rediscovering Russia's Religious Heritage," *Trinity News*, vol. 41, no. 2 (Spring 1994), p. 9; Walter Laquer, *Black Hundred: The Rise of the Extreme Right in Russia* (New York: Harper Collins, 1993).

19. The high of 18 percent was reported in a poll published by *Literaturnaya gazeta*

(February 20, 1991) in which the RCDM tied for second place among all parties. Dunlop, "Christian Democracy: Antidote to Extreme Russian Nationalism?" Working Paper Series in International Studies (I–91–2), The Hoover Institution, Stanford University.

20. "Party Slates for Duma Election Pared to 13," *Current Digest of the Post-Soviet Press,* vol. XLV, no. 45 (1993), p. 19. Despite their own inability to register, twelve deputies in the First State Duma have joined together to form a Christian Democratic electoral group.

21. Fr. Vyacheslav Polosin, "Razmyshlenie o teokratii v Rossii," *Grani,* vol. 44, nos. 156 and 157, pp. 232–255, pp. 229–257. The first half of the essay was published under the pseudonym Sergei Ventsel.

22. Ibid., no. 157, p. 257.

23. Ibid.

24. Ibid., p. 249.

25. Ibid., p. 245.

26. Vigen Guroian, "Church and Nationhood: A Reflection on the 'National Church,'" *Union Seminary Quarterly Review,* vol. 46, no. 1/4 (1992), p. 173.

27. Stanley S. Harakas, "Orthodox Church-State Theory and American Democracy," *Greek Orthodox Theological Review,* vol. 21 (1976), pp. 399–421, and "The Church and the Secular World," *Greek Orthodox Theological Review,* vol. 17 (1972), pp. 167–199.

28. Cited by Archpriest Victor Potapov, "'. . . molchaniem predaetsya Bog,'" *Grani,* no. 166 (1992), p. 205. For a discussion of the relationship between the clergy and the faithful in Orthodoxy, see Nicolas Zernov, *The Russian Religious Renaissance of the Twentieth Century* (New York: Harper & Row, 1963), pp. 281–282. For Kartashev's views, refer to his *Vozsozdanie Sv. Rusi* (published by the special committee under Silvester, bishop of Messina and vicar of the metropole of Russian Orthodox churches in Western Europe: Paris, 1956), p. 123.

29. Anton Kartashev, "Tserkov i gosudarstvo," in S. Verkhovskiyed, *Pravoslavie v zhizni* (New York: Chekhov Publishing House, 1953), pp. 174–175.

30. "Parlamentarii molyatsya," *Rossiyskaya gazeta* (June 8, 1994), p. 1.

31. One recent example is the agreement signed between the Moscow patriarchate and the Russian Army on March 2, 1994. According to press reports, priests will be encouraged to visit garrisons and organize educational religious conferences. As Russian Defense Minister Paul Grachev remarked on the occasion, "The younger generation's spiritual education has never been so important." Stephen Foye, "Russian Army, Church Sign Joint Statement," *RFE/RL Daily Report,* no. 43 (March 3, 1994).

32. Timothy Garton Ash, *The Magic Lantern* (New York: Random House, 1990).

33. One of his harshest critics was Valentin Rasputin, who, though later appointed to Gorbachev's presidential advisory council, had earlier suggested, half in jest, that Russia might withdraw unilaterally from the USSR. Also, throughout Gorbachev's tenure, Aleksandr Yakovlev remained a close adviser. Early in his career Yakovlev had been a vociferous opponent of Russian nationalist themes in literature. Alexander G. Rahr, *A Biographic Directory of One Hundred Leading*

Soviet Officials, fourth edition (Munich: Radio Liberty Research, October 1988), p. 225.

34. Nicolai N. Petro, "Rediscovering Russia," *Orbis* (Winter 1990), pp. 42–45. Yeltsin's remarks about Lenin and Solzhenitsyn were all the more noteworthy because they came just days after the chief Party ideologist Vadim Medvedev declared Solzhenitsyn's views to be in fundamental conflict with the Soviet system. Yeltsin's remarks were censored by the central press, but were reprinted in a few regional papers and later distributed in samizdat. For a more recent discussion of Yeltsin's use of nationalist themes see Steven Sestanovich, "Russia Turns the Corner," *Foreign Affairs* (January–February 1994), pp. 93–94.

35. Upon Zhirinovsky's release in February 1994, *Izvestiya* wrote that he had more to fear from Rutskoi than did Yeltsin, because of the general's ability to draw on the support of moderate conservatives. Alexander Rahr, "Zhirinovsky and Rutskoy," *RFE/RL Daily Report,* no. 40 (February 28, 1994). Tension between the two has been reported in the press. Alexander Rahr, "Zhirinovsky Attacks Rutskoy," *RFE/RL Daily Report,* no. 59 (March 25, 1994).

36. "Party Slates for Duma Election," *Current Digest of the Post-Soviet Press,* pp. 18–19.

37. Igor Klyamkin, "Postkommunisticheskaya demokratiya i ee istoricheskie osobennosti v Rossii," *Polis,* vol. 14, no. 2 (1993), p. 22.

38. Ustina Markus, "Belarusian Majority Favors Restoration of USSR," *RFE/RL Daily Report,* no. 59 (March 25, 1994).

39. Wendy Sloane, "Russian Privatization Races Ahead," *Christian Science Monitor* (June 29, 1994), p. 3.

40. "Predvybornyi blok 'Vybor Rossii': Ekonomicheskaya programma v deistvii," *Volga-Ural,* no. 44 (December 1993), p. 8. James A. Duran, Jr., "Russia and Ukraine: Political and Economic Update," *Atlantic Council Bulletin,* vol. V, no. 5 (June 15, 1994), p. 2.

41. Valery Martyanov, "Banki nachali okhotu ne melkogo vkladchika," *Delovye lyudi,* no. 3 (1994), pp. 22–25.

42. "Predvybornyi blok 'Vybor Rossii,' " p. 8. Elena Tokareva, "Propustite vpered zemel'nye zakony," *Rossiyskaya gazeta* (April 23, 1994), p. 2.

43. Louisa Vinton, "Chubais: Voucher Privatization a Success," *RFE/RL Daily Report,* no. 124 (July 1, 1994).

44. "After the Fall," *Economist* (September 24, 1994), p. 78; Adi Ignatius, "The Russian Market Takes on New Luster," *Wall Street Journal* (July 11, 1994), p. 1.

45. Duran, "Russia and Ukraine," p. 2.

46. Fyodor Sizyi, "Nashi bogatye tozhe zaplachut," *Komsomol'skaya pravda* (May 17, 1994), p. 3; Ann Sheehy, "Central Bank Report on Unemployment," *RFE/RL Daily Report,* no. 119 (June 24, 1994).

47. One of the most thorough surveys of public attitudes toward economic reforms for 1992 and 1993 is Aleksandr Komozin's, "Shokovaya ekonomika: tendentsii obshchestvennogo mneniya naseleniya Rossii," *Sotsis,* no. 11 (1993), pp. 10–17. A poll of Muscovites in March 1994 yielded similar results. See the ITAR-TASS report of March 30, 1994, "Bolshinstvo moskvichei schitaet, chto pravitelstvo Rossii dolzhno dovesti reformy do kontsa."

48. Peter Grier, "Chaos in Russia Gives U.S. Pause in Sending Aid," *Christian Science Monitor* (January 25, 1994), p. 18. Jeffrey Sachs, "Betrayal," *The New Republic*, vol. 210, no. 5 (January 31, 1994), p. 14.

49. Daniel Schneider, "'Economic Coup' Chokes Russian Reform," *Christian Science Monitor* (January 27, 1994), p. 4.

50. Sobyanin's results and the ensuing debate were reported in Valery Vyzhutovich, "Tsentrizbirkom prevrashchaetsya v politicheskoe vedomstvo," *Izvestiya* (May 4, 1994), p. 4; Larisa Aidinova, "Falshivye vybory, mertvye dushi?" *Vek*, no. 18 (May 13–19, 1994), p. 3; Evgeniy Popov, "Utechka ili provokatsiya?" *Sovetskaya Rossiya* (May 7, 1994), p. 2; and Oleg Zhirnov, "Demokrat Sobyanin dal kommunistam shans," *Obshchaya gazeta*, no. 22 (June 3–9, 1994), p. 7.

51. "Dogovor ob obshchestvennom soglasii," *Rossiyskaya gazeta* (April 29, 1994), pp. 1–2. For commentary on the obligations of the parties see "Obyazatelstva storon v sootvetsvii s dogovorom," *Kommersant-Daily* (May 6, 1994), p. 3.

52. "Shans na obshchestvennoe primirenie," *Rossiyskaya gazeta* (April 28, 1994), p. 1; Aleksandr Batygin, "Vchera v Kremle govorili o mire," *Rossiyskaya gazeta* (June 29, 1994), p. 1.

53. Among the most recent are the "Accord in the Name of Russia," initiated in March 1994 by the former chief justice of the Constitutional Court Valery Zorkin, the former vice-president Aleksandr Rutskoi, the Communist Party leader Gennady Zyuganov, and others, and the "All-Russian National Patriotic Center," organized by the head of the Constitutional-Democratic Party, Mikhail Astafyev, the former political prisoners Vladimir Osipov and Leonid Borodin, the demographer Ksenya Myalo, and the mathematician Igor Shafarevich. See Evgeny Popov, "Otechestvo. Nravstennost. Professionalizm," *Sovetskaya Rossiya* (May 31, 1994), p. 2; and "Preemstvennost i sozidaniye," *Patriot*, no. 21 (May 1994), pp. 2–3. A third group, "Toward a New Accord," was organized by the leaders of the Russian Movement for Democratic Reforms, and seeks to include other political leaders in the CIS. Dimitriy Orlov, "Tsentristy za konfederatsiyu," *Rossiyskie vesti* (July 1, 1994), p. 2.

54. Daniel Schneider, "Russia Parliament Head Pushes Perestroika," *Christian Science Monitor* (February 18, 1994), p. 7.

55. Although little mention was made of it in the press, this amnesty was accompanied by a sweeping pardon of all those accused of economic crimes (for example, profiteering) during the Soviet period. This highly charged issue was no doubt added as a compromise to attract moderates to vote for the measure. Daniel Schneider, "Release of Parliament Foes Shows Yeltsin's Weakness," *Christian Science Monitor* (February 28, 1994), p. 2.

56. Vera Tolz, "Speaker of State Duma on Rutskoi's Speech," *RFE/RL Daily Report*, no. 90 (May 11, 1994).

57. Notable exceptions include Jeffrey W. Hahn, *Soviet Grassroots: Citizen Participation in Local Soviet Government* (Princeton, N.J.: Princeton University Press, 1988); Stephen Kotkin, *Steeltown USSR: Soviet Society in the Gorbachev Era* (Berkeley, Calif.: University of California Press, 1991); and A. Magomedov, "Politicheskie elity rossiyskoy provintsii," *MEMO*, no. 4 (1994), p. 72.

58. Supreme Soviet of the Russian Federation, Preamble, para. 3, *Dogovor, Konsti-*

tutsiya (Moscow: Izvestiya, 1992), p. 81. For a discussion of the evolution of Russian nationalities policy under Yeltsin, see Nicolai N. Petro, "Can Decentralization Solve Russia's Ethnic Problems?" in Ian M. Cuthbertson and Jane Liebowitz eds., *Minorities: The New Europe's Old Issue* (New York: Institute for East-West Studies, 1993), pp. 185–208.

59. "Tatarstan, Russia Sign Treaty — Who Gave in?" *Current Digest of the Post-Soviet Press,* vol. 47, no. 7 (March 16, 1994), pp. 11–12.

60. Tamara Zamyatina, "Klyuch k politicheskoy stabilizatsii," *Rossiyskaya gazeta* (June 3, 1994), p. 2.

61. Magomedov, "Politicheskie elity," p. 72.

62. For a good overview of these trends, see Yu. Oleshchuk, "Novaya Rossiya i integratsionnye tendentsii v SNG," *MEMO,* no. 4 (1984), pp. 83–92.

63. A. B. Zubov and V. A. Kolosov, "Chto ishchet Rossiya?" *Polis,* no. 1 (1994), pp. 93–112.

64. Dimitriy Kamyshev, "Lidery regionov berut ne chislom, a umeniem," *Kommersant-Daily* (May 17, 1994), p. 3.

65. A. B Zubov, V. A. Kolosov, Vladimir Petukhov, and Andrei Ryabov, "Ne meshaite nam zhit, pomogite vyzhit," *Rossiya,* no. 19 (May 18–24, 1994), p. 3.

66. V. Sukhovolskiy and A. Sobyanin, "Dozhivet li kommunisticheskaya partiya do 2000 goda?" *Vek,* no. 14 (April 15–21, 1994), p. 3.

67. The term "nationalist" in contemporary Russian political usage nearly always describes attributes of state or governmental authority, rather than ethnic or regional identity. In this respect it is akin to the Western usage of the term "patriotic," implying allegiance to the government or the state. For a discussion of current usage of these and related terms see Lev Gudkov, "Natsionalnoe soznanie: versiya zapada i Rossii," *Rodina,* no. 2 (1994), pp. 14–18.

68. Petukhov and Ryabov, "Ne meshaite nam zhyt," p. 3. Russia's premier pollster, Boris Grushin, also confirms this shift in public opinion toward entrepreneurship. Whereas in 1990 the majority polled categorically disagreed with the statement, "Should people be allowed to get rich?" by 1992, 88 percent agreed with it. Amy Smith, "Public Opinion Polls not the Full Story," Meeting Report of the Kennan Institute for Advanced Russian Study, vol. X, no. 2 (1992).

69. Zubov and Kolosov, "Chto ishchet Rossiya?" p. 104.

70. Petukhov and Ryabov, "Ne meshaite nam zhit," p. 3.

71. Yuri Levada, "Obshchestvennoe menenie v god krizisnogo pereloma: Smena paradigmy," *Segodnya* (May 17, 1994), p. 10.

72. Yuri Oleshchuk, "Sdvig malozametnyi, no vazhnyi," *MEMO,* no. 3 (1994), pp. 71–82; B. G. Kapustin and I. M. Klyamkin, "Liberalnye tsennosti v soznanii Rossiyan," *Polis,* no. 1 (1994), pp. 68–92.

73. Linden, "Can Russia Be Founded Anew?" p. 12; Janine Ludlum, "Reform and the Redefinition of the Social Contract under Gorbachev," *World Politics,* vol. 43 (January 1991), pp. 284–312.

74. Barrington Moore, *Social Origins of Dictatorship and Democracy* (Boston: Beacon Press, 1966), p. 414.

75. Sestanovich, "Russia Turns the Corner," pp. 93–97; and Dimitry Simes, "The Return of Russian History," *Foreign Affairs* (January–February 1994), pp. 78–82.

76. Stephen White, "Towards a Post-Soviet Politics," in Stephen White et al., eds., *Developments in Soviet and Post-Soviet Politics* (Durham, N.C.: Duke University Press, 1992), p. 15.

77. Sakwa, *Russian Politics and Society,* p. 134.

78. White, "Towards a Post-Soviet Politics," p. 15.

79. Kullberg, "The End of New Thinking," pp. 9, 12.

80. "Sociological Data about Parties (May–August 1992)," pp. 15–16.

81. G. Zyuganov, "Put Rossii k narodovlastiyu i sotsyalizmu," *Al-kods,* no. 9 (April 1994), p. 2.

82. Cited by Ivan Boltovskiy, "Zyuganov prodolshaet delo g. Yakovleva," *Vechernyi Leningrad,* no. 11 (1994), p. 2.

83. K. Strel'tsov, "Ne maskiruites' pod kommunistov," *Mysl,* no. 6 (1994), pp. 2–3; Boris Slavin, "Otkaz ot marksizma pogubit kompartiyu," *Golos kommunista,* no. 6 (May 1994), p. 3.

84. Lyudmila Aleksandrova, "Pochemu kommunisty ne khotyat podpisyvat Dogovor," *Rossisskaya gazeta* (April 27, 1994), p. 1.

85. Valery Vyzhutovich, "Krasnye derutsya do poslednego," *Novoye russkoye slovo* (December 3, 1993), p. 40. The Party's dependence on political compromise with the regions was emphasized in the April 1994 report of the deputy head of the Communist Party bloc in the State Duma, Viktor Zorkaltsev. "Kommunisty v Dume," *Al-Kods,* no. 13 (May 1994), p. 7; and "Zavtra nastupit bez ukaza," *Pravda* (May 7, 1994), pp. 1–2.

86. Daniel Schneider, "Russia's Parliament Finally Buckles Down," *Christian Science Monitor* (January 21, 1994), p. 7; Julia Wishnevsky, "Militant Communist Calls for Removal of President and Government," *RFE/RL Daily Report,* no. 59 (March 25, 1994).

87. N. Belyavea et al., "Politicheskie sily Rossii — 1993," Interlegal Research Fund, 1993, pp. 10–11.

88. James H. Billington, "Looking to the Past," *Washington Post* (January 22, 1990), p. A11.

89. George F. Kennan, "The Sources of Soviet Conduct," *Foreign Affairs* (July 1947), pp. 566–582.

90. John Lewis Gaddis, *Strategies of Containment* (New York: Oxford University Press, 1982).

91. Henry Kissinger, "Be Realistic about Russia," *Los Angeles Times* syndicate (January 25, 1994); Richard Pipes, "Russia Heats Up the New Cold War," *Sunday Telegraph* (February 27, 1994); Zbigniew Brzezinski, "The Premature Partnership," *Foreign Affairs* (March–April 1994), pp. 67–82.

92. Jeanne J. Kirkpatrick, "The Modernizing Imperative," *Foreign Affairs* (September–October 1993), pp. 22–23.

93. Huntington, "The Coming Clash of Civilizations?" p. 22.

94. Ibid., p. 40.

95. Ibid., p. 44.

96. Ibid.

97. Lucian W. Pye, "Political Science and the Crisis of Authoritarianism," *American Political Science Review,* no. 84 (1990), pp. 3–19.

98. Howard J. Wiarda, a specialist on Latin America, first made this point in his

article "The Ethnocentrism of the Social Sciences: Implications for Research and Policy," *Review of Politics* (April 1981), pp. 163–197. One need only refer to the furor over Frank Fukuyama's piece "The End of History" (*The National Interest,* Summer 1989, pp. 3–18) for confirmation of this ethnocentrism. Hardly any of Fukuyama's critics challenged his assumption that the steady advance of Western rationalism and consumerism would benefit mankind; rather, they quibbled with his choice of timing.

99. B. H. Sumner, *A Short History of Russia* (New York: Harcourt, Brace and Co., 1949), p. 308.

100. "Human Rights and Perestroika," Remarks by Assistant Secretary of State for Human Rights and Humanitarian Affairs Richard Schifter at a seminar sponsored by the Helsinki Commission for the Soviet Friendship Societies in Moscow, USSR, on February 1, 1990.

101. Paul Hollander, *Political Pilgrims* (New York: Oxford University Press, 1981).

102. Sakwa, *Russian Politics and Society,* p. 162.

103. According to the presidential nationalities adviser Emil Pain, 70 percent of Russians oppose the idea of empire *(imperskaya ideya)*. Teimuraz Mamaladze, "Blesk i nishcheta konfliktologii," *Izvestiya* (May 18, 1994), pp. 1–4.

104. Daniel Yergin and Thane Gustafson, *Russia 2010* (New York: Random House, 1993), p. 177.

105. Strong trends toward integration with Russia have been manifest in the eastern Ukraine and Belarus since the 1994 summer elections there. Similar sentiments have also been reported in Moldova. "Party Favoring Ties with Russia Builds Lead in Moldova Elections," *New York Times* (March 1, 1994), p. A8.

Index

Absolutism, 29, 30–31, 42, 181; opposition to tsarist, 31, 34–42, 61; vs. autocracy, 34, 54, 67, 89–90; end of, 48; defenders of, 52. *See also* Autocracy
Action Group for the Defense of Human Rights, 81
Adams, William, 8
Afghanistan, 57. See also *Pamyat*
Aganbegyan, Abel, 145
Agrarian Party, 163, 164, 167
Aksakov, Konstantin, 41, 90
Aksyuchits, Viktor, 155, 173
Aleksey, Metropolitan, 63, 80
Alexander I, 40
Alexander II, 42, 43, 44
Alexander III, 43
All-Russian Academy of Painting, Sculpture, and Architecture, 106
All-Russian Society for the Preservation of Historical Monuments (VOOPIK), 134
All-Union Conference of Leftist Groups, 143
All-Union Social Christian Union for the Liberation of People (ASCULP), 134–136, 140
Almond, Gabriel, 13, 15, 16, 19, 20, 21, 28, 60; "Comparative Political Systems," 5; *The Civic Culture,* 6, 7, 24
American Revolution, 40
Amnesty International (Group-73), 129
Ananyev, Anatoly, 107, 108
Andreyev, Catherine, 120, 123
Andreyeva, Nina, 57

Andropov, Yuri, 140, 145
Anne, Empress, 38, 39
Antoniy, Metropolitan, 67
Antonov, Mikhail, 106
Armenia, 130. *See also* Human rights movement
ASCULP. *See* All-Union Social Christian Union for the Liberation of People
Ash, Timothy Garton: *The Magic Lantern,* 158
Association of Russian Artists, 106
Astafyev, Viktor, 103
Atheism, 70, 72, 73, 82, 84, 103, 154
Autocracy *(samoderzhavie),* 3, 18–19, 29, 32, 33, 34, 151, 156; constrained, 23, 28–59, 61, 69, 89, 93, 110, 151–158
Autonomy, regional, 165–166
Azerbaijan, 97, 130

Bagehot, Walter, 22
Balashov, Dimitriy, 105
Baltic states, 25, 101, 158, 172
Barghoorn, Frederick, 58, 110
Barry, Brian, 16–17
Basic State Laws (1906), 49, 50
Battle of Kulikovo, 63, 85
Bauer, Raymond, 10, 11, 12
Belarus, 160, 161, 182
Belinsky, Vissarion, 41
Bellyustin, Ioann Stepanovich, 67
Belov, Vasiliy, 58
Benda, Vaclav, 25
Bennet, Helju, 37

www.ingramcontent.com/pod-product-compliance
Lightning Source LLC
Chambersburg PA
CBHW072118020426
42334CB00018B/1633